9780836950229

DISCARDED

ETHAN ALLEN

AND THE

GREEN-MOUNTAIN HEROES.

KINNEY'S HEROIC STATUE OF
GEN. ETHAN ALLEN.

Engraved by J. C. Buttre from a Daguerreotype, taken under the direction of the artist.

ETHAN ALLEN

AND THE

GREEN-MOUNTAIN HEROES

OF '76.

Ethan Allen

WITH A SKETCH OF THE

EARLY HISTORY OF VERMONT.

BY HENRY W. DE PUY.

BOOKS FOR LIBRARIES PRESS
FREEPORT, NEW YORK

First Published 1853
Reprinted 1970

STANDARD BOOK NUMBER:
8369-5022-4

LIBRARY OF CONGRESS CATALOG CARD NUMBER:
70-114874

PRINTED IN THE UNITED STATES OF AMERICA

CONTENTS.

INTRODUCTION 11

CHAPTER I.

EARLY HISTORY OF VERMONT.

Early Discoveries—Cartier at Hotchelaga—Interview with the Natives—Return to France—Champlain—His Discoveries—Hudson—The Green Mountains—The Six Nations—The Adirondacks—Fire Arms—Torture of a Prisoner—War between the French and Indians—Corlear—French Expedition against the Mohawks—First English Prisoners in Canada—Montreal attacked by the Indians—Massacre at Schenectady—French Invasion of New Hampshire—Death of Major Waldron—English Expedition against Canada—Sir William Phipps—Captain John Schuyler—French Emulation of Indian Cruelty—Burning of Deerfield—REV. JOHN WILLIAMS—The March over the Green Mountains—Death of Mrs. Williams—The Forest Sermon—The Daring Boy—Sufferings of the Captives—Ransom of Rev. Mr. Williams—The Bell of St. Regis—Border Warfare—Colonial War with Canada—English Army on Lake Champlain—Fleet on the St. Lawrence—Peace—First Settlements in Vermont—Frontignac—Joliet—Exploration of the Mississippi—Lake Champlain—Crown Point—Progress of the English and French Colonies—Fort Dummer—Lovewell's War—The Jesuit Rolle—Siege of Louisbourg—Indian Depredations—Massacre at Fort Massachusetts—Heroic Defense of "Number Four"—Captain Hobbs—Saratoga—The Abbe Picquet—French War 1756—Sir William Johnson—Expedition against the French Johnson's Victory over Dieskau—Indian Depredations—Capt Johnson—Subjugation of Canada again undertaken — Gen Abercrombie—JOHN STARK—His Intrepidity—Montcalm's Advances toward Fort William Henry—Massacre at Fort Edward—ISRAEL PUTNAM—William Pitt—Putnam's Battle with Fire—

Abercrombie's Defeat at Ticonderoga—Capture of Putnam—Cruelties inflicted upon him—Attempt to burn him—Rescue—The Fair Captive—Amherst takes Ticonderoga and Crown Point—Destruction of the Village of St. Francis—General Wolfe—His Death and Victory at Quebec—Death of Montcalm—Vaudreuil defeated at Montreal—Canada surrendered to the English—Close of the French War, ...13 to 116

CHAPTER II.

THE NEW-HAMPSHIRE GRANTS.

The Peace of 1763—Advance of the English Settlements—The Delius Grant—Conflicting Grants by the British Crown—Controversies arising therefrom—New-York Charter—Correspondence between the Governors of New Hampshire and New York—Charter of Bennington—Grants of Lands by the Governor of New Hampshire—Proclamation of Governor Colden—Counter-Proclamation—Appeal to the King—An Ambiguous Decree—Excitement among the People—Agent sent to England—Determination to repel the New-York Claimants—ETHAN ALLEN—His early Life—He becomes interested in the New-Hampshire Grants—Journal of IRA ALLEN—Scheme of a Land Speculator—The Allens in New York—Ira Allen's Foresight—Adventure with a Ghost—SETH WARNER—Personal Appearance of Warner—His Favorite Pursuits—CAPT. REMEMBER BAKER—Is a Soldier in the French War—Removes to the New-Hampshire Grants—Samuel Robinson—Settlement of BENNINGTON—Establishment of a Church and a School—Jedediah Dewey—Oppressive Measures of New York—Indictments—Convention of the Settlers—Samuel Robinson—The King's Order—It is disregarded by Governor Tryon—Proclamation—Indictments—Ejectment Trials at Albany—Anecdote of Allen—New Attempts to deprive the People of their Property—Defensive Measures—"Hideous Groans"—The Green-Mountain Boys—Reward offered for the Arrest of Allen—Allen's Proclamation—His Courage—Attack upon Captain Baker's House—His Capture and Rescue—Attempt to arrest Warner—A Rumored Invasion—Conciliation—Allen's Protest—Joy in Bennington—Quarrel Renewed—Letter to Governor Tryon—The "Beech-Seal"—The Scotch Emigrants—Proceedings in Clarendon—"The

CONTENTS.

Bloody Law"—Allen's Opinion of it—Public Meetings—Doctor Samuel Adams—Benjamin Hough—Allen's Certificate—Trials of the Pioneers—Tyranny of the Government—Rescue of a Prisoner—Treason Trials—Murder of William French—Dawn of the Revolution,...116 to 196

CHAPTER III.

ETHAN ALLEN.

Character of the Patriots of '76—Ethan Allen—His Position—Review of the Causes which produced the Revolution—The Stamp Act—The Tea Tax—The First Congress—Measures of Resistance—Contemplated Enterprise against Ticonderoga—Ethan Allen chosen its Leader—His Plan—The Boy-Guide—Allen crosses the Lake—The Fortress attacked—Confusion of the Enemy—Allen and Delaplace—Surrender of the Garrison—Crown Point and Skenesborough Secured—Arnold's Naval Victory—Allen and Congress—Allen and Parson Dewey—Capture of Allen—NARRATIVE OF ALLEN'S CAPTIVITY—His Account of the Victory at Ticonderoga—He falls into the Hands of the Enemy—A Singular Shield—Barbarity of Colonel Prescott—Allen put in Irons—The Tenpenny Nail—Allen's Challenge of Doctor Dace—Magnanimity of Captain Littlejohn—The Duel—Reliance upon Allen's Honor—Cruel Treatment of Prisoners—The Petty Tyrant—Voyage to England—Allen's Sufferings—Landing at Falmouth—Expected Execution of Allen—His Letter to Congress—Reflections upon Death—Conversations with his Visitors—Captain Symonds—The Generous Irishmen—Allen sails from England—The Voyage—Arrival in America—From Bad to Worse—Meeting with old Enemies—Illness—Cruelty and Kindness—Mrs. Blacden—Removal to New York—A Humane Commander—Allen's Gratitude—The Prison Ship—Battle of Bennington—Allen on Parole—The American Prisoners in New York—Barbarity of the British—Incredible Sufferings—Starvation, Disease and Death—Washington—General Howe—The British Bribe—Allen's Reply—Allen and Rivington—Captain Vandyke—Mr. Miller—Majors Wells and Paine—Mr. Fell—Evacuation of Ticonderoga—Battle of Hubbardton—Triumph of Allen—Burgoyne's Surrender—Burgoyne's Proclamation—Allen and the British Officer—Allen's Liberation—His Return to Vermont,....................196 to 279

CHAPTER IV.

THE GREEN-MOUNTAIN HEROES.

Charter of the Early Settlers of this Country—Influence of their Example—The Puritans and the Followers of Penn—Indian Converts—Origin of the Revolution—Reflections on the Character and Services of Congress—DECLARATION OF INDEPENDENCE—Bunker Hill—Ticonderoga—Campaign of 1775—General Montgomery—General Schuyler—Montgomery enters Canada—Death of Captain Baker—ETHAN ALLEN—Siege of St. John's—Mutiny—James Livingston—Surrender of Fort Chambly—SETH WARNER—The Green-Mountain Rangers—Repulse of Carleton—Surrender of St. John's—Carleton's Retreat from Montreal—Extraordinary March of Arnold—The British retire to Quebec—The Assault Begun—Death of Montgomery—The Cowardly Commanders—Honors to Montgomery—His Character—His Widow—Arnold—Major Morgan—Retreat of the Americans—Reinforcements—Energy of Warner—General Gates—Naval Preparations—Battle on Lake Champlain—Plans of the British—Supplies for Ticonderoga—Close of the Campaign of 1776—General Carleton—The Green-Mountain Pledge—Burgoyne—The Campaign Opened—Evacuation of Ticonderoga—General St. Clair—Retreat of the Americans—Battle of Hubbardton—Advance of the British—Jane McCrea—Account of her Murder—A New-Hampshire Patriot—General Stark—Movements of Burgoyne—The Foray upon the Green Mountains—Battle at Cambridge—Skirmishing—Rain—The Bellicose Parson—Stark's Speech—Battle of Bennington—The British Reinforced—The Victory at Bennington—General Stark's Account—Colonels Warner and Herrick—Honor to General Stark's Genius—Important Consequences of this Victory—Censure of Stark in Congress changed to Thanks—General Burgoyne's Opinion of his Antagonist changed—Spoils and Trophies—Expenses of Stark's Brigade—Traveled Cannon—British, German and Tory Prisoners—Lions and Lambs—Curiosity to see Lord Napier—A Bereaved Mother—General Lincoln—Colonels Brown and Johnson at Lake George—Brown's Success—Generals Gates and Burgoyne—Engagement at Saratoga—British Testimony to American Patriotism—The Spirit of '76; Death rather than Dishonor—Burgoyne's Difficulties thicken—He Surrenders—Medal and Thanks to General

CONTENTS. ix

Gates—Feats of the Green-Mountain Boys—British Retreat from Ticonderoga, with loss—Difficulties of the Inhabitants of the New-Hampshire Grants—Their Need of a Government—Declare their Independence as a State—Congress refuses to receive them—They form a Constitution—Council of Safety—Its Officers and Powers—Ira Allen on Ways and Means—A Regiment raised and paid from Tory Property—Governor Chittenden—Incidents of his Life—Ira Allen Secretary of State—His Appearance and Services—Measures of Vermont opposed—ETHAN ALLEN'S Return—His Welcome—His Military Distinction—Is Agent from Vermont to Congress—Governor Clinton's Proclamation—General Allen's Counter-Proclamation—He advocates Law and Order—A Hanging Postponed—Excitement in consequence—General Allen's Speech—"Somebody shall be Hanged "—General Allen's Quarrel with his Brother Levi—The Tooth-drawing—COLONEL SETH WARNER—Dies in Poverty—Inscription on his Tomb—His Widow's Petition to Congress—Widow Storey—Her Secret Retreat—Destruction of Royalton—Pursuit of the Indians—Their Kindness to Female Prisoners—Anecdotes of the Indians—Daring of Mrs. Stone—Mrs. Barker and her Infants—Adverse Claims for Vermont Territory—Congress censures Vermont—Vermont extends its Territory—Poetry for the Green-Mountaineers—British Overtures to Ethan Allen—Allen's Letter to Congress—General Haldimand negotiates privately with Vermont Leaders—Allen and Fay mislead the English—Their Commission—General Haldimand's Instruction to his Agent—The Agent's Notes of Interviews—Ira Allen's Ingenious Delays—Notice of his Career—Washington reconciles Vermont and Congress—Feeling of the People—Difficulties with New York—Ethan Allen suppresses Insurrection—His Characteristic Proclamation—Vermont admitted an Independent State, 1789—Ethan Allen's Retirement—Becomes an Author—Character of his Book—A popular Anecdote of him Contradicted—His Integrity—Scene in Court—Changes his Residence—Characteristic Courtship of his Second Wife—Amusing Account of the Marriage—"The Church Militant and the Church Military "—Allen's Kindness—The Lost Children Found—Tribute to his Patriotism—His Death—Inscription on his Tomb............................279 to 428.

INTRODUCTION.

"Far be from me or my friends," says a distinguished writer, "such frigid philosophy, as may conduct us, indifferent and unmoved, over any ground that has been dignified by wisdom, bravery or virtue. The man is little to be envied whose patriotism would not gain force upon the plains of Marathon, or whose piety would not grow warm among the ruins of Iona." And thus, among the objects that attract the attention of people, in all countries, as they advance in civilization, few are sought with more avidity than the facts concerning their early history.

Our patriotism is warmed, and our virtue is strengthened, while gazing upon the fields where the blood of our ancestors was shed in defense of liberty, or while perusing the story of the perils, sufferings, and self-sacrificing heroism of those who won our national independence. Nothing, therefore, can tend more strongly to the preservation of the liberties of our own favored and happy country, than a familiarity with the deeds, and an admiration for the character, of our revolutionary ancestors. Our glorious institutions can be in no danger while there is a sentiment of patriotism among the people, which glows at the recital of our country's renown, and which cherishes the memory of its heroes. To foster this feeling, as well as to direct attention to a class of patriots whose claims to the grateful remembrance of those who enjoy the blessings of free institutions have been too much disregarded, is the design of the present volume.

No portion of our country has a history so replete with stirring events as that bordering upon Lake Champlain. Situated between the French province of Canada and the English colonies, and simultaneously claimed by each, it was, for one hundred and fifty years, the grand highway of their warlike expeditions against each other, and the scene upon which their bloodiest and most hotly contested battles were fought. Here many of the heroes of the American Revolution received their first experience in the art of war, and achieved that renown which afterward placed them at the head of armies whose noble purpose sanctified their resort to the awful arbitrament of battle. There, too, the most powerful and threatening army sent out to crush the freedom of this country, began its march in triumph, and there ended it in a most disastrous defeat. The history of the Green-Mountain state, which stretches along the east shore of Lake Champlain, is so closely interwoven with that of the armies which have trodden its soil, and of the wars in which they were engaged, that the one cannot be fairly written to the exclusion of the other.

In addition to the usual authorities on American history consulted in the preparation of this volume, especial indebtedness to the following is acknowledged — Slade's Vermont State

Papers—Williams' and Thompson's Histories of Vermont—and Chipman's Lives of Warner, Chittenden and Chipman. These are all Vermont authors. Rev. Samuel Williams, D. D., author of the first History of Vermont, was the grandson of Rev. John Williams, the "Deerfield Captive," and father of Charles K. Williams, for many years Chief Justice of Vermont, and recently the popular governor of that state. He was one of the founders and the principal benefactor of the University of Vermont, at Burlington. For several years he employed his talents, almost if not quite gratuitously, in delivering lectures in natural philosophy, and in forwarding the progress of the University. With only four hundred and eighty dollars raised by subscription, he purchased the first philosophical apparatus for the institution. That this apparatus might be as complete as possible, Dr. Williams expended the money in the most frugal manner, admitting nothing of foreign manufacture which could be made at home, and nothing of brass where it might be made of wood. Dr. Williams had removed to Vermont as early as 1777, and resided at Rutland. In 1793, he published his History of Vermont, in one volume. The narrative was then brought down to the Revolutionary war; but the work was afterward greatly enlarged, and, in 1809, was published in two volumes of about five hundred pages each. The history of the state was brought down to the period of the publication of the work. The few copies of it yet in existence are highly prized. The copy which the writer of this obtained, although much worn, printed on coarse paper, and roughly bound, cost as much as a dozen volumes of new works got up in the most faultless modern style. Rev. Zadock Thompson, of Burlington, has also published a large work of six hundred pages of small type, comprising the Natural and Civil History and a Gazetteer of the state. It is a work of great research and value, and as a large portion of it can be of especial interest to Vermonters only, it should hold a prominent place in the library of every citizen of that state.

The compiler is indebted to the courtesy of several gentlemen of Vermont for important assistance in the preparation of these pages. From the Hon. Charles K. Williams was received a file of the "State Banner," published at Bennington in 1841, and containing a series of "Historical Readings," by Hon. Hiland Hall, which have been freely used in the portion of this work relating to the difficulties between New York and the New-Hampshire Grants. From George F. Houghton, Esq., of St. Albans, many valuable suggestions were derived, as well as a most eloquent address on the Life of Seth Warner, delivered by him before the Vermont legislature. This and two other addresses, by Prof. James D. Butler, on the early history of Vermont, have supplied these pages with several important incidents not found elsewhere. Chauncey Goodrich, Esq., of Burlington, and Brigadier-general Ethan Allen Hitchcock, (grandson of the "Hero of Ticonderoga,") also communicated facts which have enriched the present work.

Hon. Henry Stevens, the distinguished antiquary of Vermont, courteously placed a considerable portion of his large and

INTRODUCTION.

invaluable collection of State Papers at the disposal of the compiler. For many years, Mr. Stevens has been indefatigable in collecting documents concerning the early history of Vermont. The papers of the early settlers of the state — the correspondence of Revolutionary officers — and the documents in the archives of the nation, or copies of them, have been treasured up by Mr. Stevens. Vermont is under great obligations to him for his services in searching for and arranging official papers and other testimony touching the origin, progress, and final consummation of the struggle which resulted in giving to the American Switzerland that proud individuality of which it so justly boasts. Vermont will only do justice to itself, its founders, and to Mr. Stevens, when these records of a state whose history is more remarkable than that of any other in the union, are placed before the public. When this is done, the world will be satisfied that these early settlers were men of no common mould, and their services will be better understood and more gratefully appreciated than at present.

For a mere handful of men to resist the combined efforts of New York on the one side and New Hampshire on the other, while repulsed if not rejected by the home government, and menaced by a foreign foe — involved the exercise of no ordinary sagacity, and an amount of nerve and energy with which, in this day, we are not familiar. But so it was. While maintaining an open war with the neighboring states, they protected the whole line of our frontier by keeping on terms with the common enemy, while at the same time they rendered more efficient aid to the government which discarded them, than either of the states alluded to. The official correspondence with Washington — comprised in the Papers of Mr. Stevens — goes to demonstrate this beyond a doubt.

The engraving of the Heroic Statue of Gen. Ethan Allen will be regarded as an attractive feature of the present volume. The Statue is the production of B. H. Kinney Esq., a young and self-taught Vermont artist; and, although his first great undertaking, is of promising excellence, and gives evidence of a high order of artistic ability. It is the length and breadth, the depth and power of Ethan Allen, morally and historically considered, and in his physical no less than in his intellectual characteristics,— an artistic realization of one of the most practical and common-sense characters that ever lived. Those who look upon it are at once convinced that it is an actual likeness of the Hero of Ticonderoga. This is the best evidence of the genius of the sculptor, that his work is invariably regarded as a truthful representation. The statue is of heroic size — one-third larger than life — and represents the subject in a bold, commanding attitude; his camp cloak thrown from his left and resting on his right shoulder; his hand grasping the sword at his side; and his whole expression resolute and full of energy — as if he had just uttered those memorable words at Ticonderoga, and intended to see his demands complied with at all hazards. The engraving is the more valuable as it is the only picture of the statue that the sculptor has permitted to be engraved. As the reader may be interested to know something more of Mr. Kinney, the following

INTRODUCTION. xvii

notice of his career, as furnished by himself in a private letter to a friend, will appropriately close this notice of his statue:

"I was bred, from infancy to manhood, in the town of Sunderland, Bennington county, Vermont — the town in which Ethan Allen first lived, and which for nearly twenty years was his residence. During my boyhood I listened to the tales respecting the great hero of the Green Mountains, with those thrilling emotions and the wild delight which is only known to mountaineers. Many were the acts of "desperate valor," performed by my schoolmates and myself, in sham fights emulating the daring deeds of the Green-Mountain Heroes of '76. And the impression which I received at that time of the noble spirit of patriotism which stimulated the fearless and true-hearted Hero of Ticonderoga, has grown brighter and brighter as I have grown to years of manhood, and witnessed the neglect of duty to their country, in the pursuit of selfish ends, so characteristic of a considerable portion of the prominent men of this age. This is the reason of my selecting ETHAN ALLEN as the first great subject of my labors in my favorite art."

ETHAN ALLEN,

AND

THE GREEN-MOUNTAIN HEROES OF '76.

CHAPTER I.

EARLY HISTORY OF VERMONT.

> "——— the savages, of murderous soul,
> In painted bands, dark to the combat roll,
> With midnight orgies, by the gloomy shade,
> On the pale victim point the reeking blade;
> Or cause the hamlet, lulled in deep repose,
> No more to wake, or wake to ceaseless woes."
> HUMPHREYS.

OF the adventurous band of navigators, who, early in the sixteenth century, sailed westward in the wake of those frail caravels, the Mina, Pinta, and Santa Maria, James Cartier, a Frenchman, was the first to explore the interior of the vast continent to which Columbus had led the way. While sailing along the Atlantic coast, in 1534, in search of a passage to China, he discovered the mouth of a great river, to which he subsequently gave the name of "St. Lawrence."* The following spring, in the belief that the St. Lawrence was the desired channel to the East Indies, a larger expedition was equipped, which Cartier conducted direct to this noble stream, and sailed two hundred leagues inland. There the navigation was obstructed by "a

---

* Thus named in honor of the Saint whose festival occurred on the day (10th August) of its discovery.

great and swift fall." At this point, Cartier found a large Indian village, bearing the name of Hochelaga. The population was more numerous, the wigwams were more substantially built, and the town was more strongly fortified than any other occupied by the aborigines, of which the early settlers of the country have given a description. Cartier conciliated the natives by presents of hatchets, beads and rings — articles more magnificent than any of which they had previously had a conception — and they regarded him and his associates as celestial beings. To Cartier all was so new and strange, that he almost deemed himself transported to some land of enchantment. He erected a fort where the city of Montreal now stands, calling it, in honor of his king, Mount Royal. There he passed the winter, formed alliances with the Indians, and took formal possession of the country, which he named New France. Ascending the hill which towered above his fortress, and overlooked the country for many miles around, he was enraptured with the scene upon which he gazed. Before him the mighty St. Lawrence, coming solemnly from an unknown land, rolled on majestically toward the ocean; the distant horizon was bounded by the lofty mountains of Vermont,* crowned with perpetual verdure; while illimitable forests, robed in the gorgeous hues of autumn, were spread out before him in every direction. Donnacona, the Indian king who conducted him to the summit of the hill, informed him that he might sail westward on the great river, for three moons — passing through several immense lakes —

---

* So called when the state was organized, from two French words, *verd*, green, and *mont*, mountain.

without reaching its source; that the river had its origin in a sea of fresh water to which no limits were known. Far to the south-west, he continued, there was another great river,* which ran through a country where there was no ice or snow; to the north, there was a large inland sea of salt water,† extending to a region of perpetual ice; while southward there were rivers and smaller lakes, penetrating a beautiful and fertile country, belonging to a powerful and warlike nation called the Iroquois.

The next spring, Cartier, taking with him Donnacona and several of the natives, returned to France, and represented to the king the advantages that would result from a settlement in this country, principally by means of the fur trade; but the fallacious opinion then prevalent among all the nations of Europe, that such countries only as produced gold and silver were worth the possession, had such influence on the monarch, that he slighted the judicious advice of Cartier, and deferred making any establishment in Canada. But, although this object was generally neglected, some individuals entertained just views of its importance; and among the most zealous for prosecuting discoveries and making a settlement there, was Roberval, a nobleman of Picardy. The king, at length convinced of the expediency of the measure, resolved to send Cartier, accompanied by this nobleman, again to Canada. The expedition was undertaken in 1540, and an attempt was made to found a colony; but in the course of a year or two, the enterprise was abandoned. The colony was broken up, and for upward of half a

* The Ohio. † Hudson's Bay.

century, the French made no further attempt to establish themselves on the St. Lawrence.

In 1600, one Chauvin, a commander in the French navy, made a voyage to Canada, from which he returned, with a profitable cargo of furs. The public now began to turn more attention to this country. An armament was equipped, and the command given to Pontgran. He sailed in 1603. Five years afterward, Samuel de Champlain, who had accompanied Pontgran's expedition, founded the city of Quebec.* In 1609, accompanied by several friendly Indians, he proceeded to the locality described by Cartier. He afterward sailed up the Richelieu or Sorel river, and entered a lake to which he gave his own name.† He also visited Lake George, which, from the extreme purity of its waters, he called St. Sacrament.‡ It is inferred from his own narrative, that he then proceeded across the country, and touched the Hudson river at Glen's Falls. During the same season, Henry Hudson sailed up the river to which his name is given, as far as Albany. Possibly, at the same time that Champlain was resting near the head waters of the Hudson, the English navigator was encamped scarcely forty miles below. Strange that two adventurers, in the service of different sovereigns, ruling three thousand miles

* This was the original Indian name, signifying *narrow*, because the St. Lawrence, which, from that point to the ocean, is from ten to fifteen miles wide, is there reduced to a width of about one mile.

† The Indian name of Lake Champlain was *Canaideri-Guarunte*, signifying the mouth or door of the country. Another Indian name was *Petawa-Bouque*, signifying alternate land and water.

‡ The original Indian name was *Horicon*, meaning *Silver Water*. It was also called *Canaideri-oit*, or *The Tail of the Lake*.

away, and approaching from different points of the compass, should so nearly meet in the vast forests of wild America — each exploring a part of the continent never before traversed by Europeans. Strange, too, that the vicinity where these adventurers so nearly met, should, for almost a hundred and fifty years, be the boundary between the nations respectively represented by them, and the scene of their frequent and bloody conflicts for supremacy.

Although that beautiful portion of Vermont bordering on Lake Champlain was thus early explored, and although settlements were made in its immediate vicinity, by the Dutch at Albany in 1613 — by the English at Springfield, on the Connecticut, in 1635 — and by the French at Montreal in 1640, the whites did not permanently occupy any portion of the territory comprised in the present boundaries of the State, until the year 1724. Situated between the settlements of the French on the one hand, and those of the English on the other, it was constantly exposed to the incursions and depredations of both, in the almost incessant warfare maintained between them. The dense forests of the Green Mountains became the favorite lurking places of the wielders of the tomahawk, and resounded with the war-whoop of those savages who were willing to be allies for either of the contending parties. They were traversed by the prisoners taken in the French wars, and were witnesses of their heroism and of their sufferings. For these reasons, actual settlements were perilous and impracticable. It was a disputed ground between the English and the French, on which many a guerilla battle was fought. And thus the history of Vermont is so closely interwoven with that of the regions adjacent, that it will be necessary, in the progress of this narrative, in order to exhibit a complete view of the transactions in which Vermont was interested, or in which its early heroes bore a distinguished part, often to carry forward an account of events which transpired beyond the geographical limits of the state.

In his expedition across the lake which bears his name, Champlain was accompanied by only two Frenchmen — the balance of the party, amounting to about sixty, were Huron and Algonquin warriors, who had determined on a hostile excursion into the territory of the Iroquois, or, as they were afterward designated by the English, the Five Nations.

This federal association is said to have derived its origin from the most remote antiquity; and, as the name imports, it comprehended five Indian nations, of which the Mohawks have obtained the most lasting renown, and which were confederated, on terms of the strictest equality, in a perpetual alliance, for united conquest and mutual defense. The members of this united body reckoned themselves superior to all the rest of mankind, and the distinctive appellation which they adopted* was expressive of this opinion. But the principles of their confederacy displayed far more policy and refinement than we might expect from the arrogance of their barbarous name. They had embraced the Roman practice, of increasing their strength by incorporating the people of other nations with themselves. After every conquest of an enemy, when they

* *Ongue-Honwe*,— that is, "Men surpassing all others."

had indulged their revenge by some cruel executions, they exercised their usual policy, in the adoption of the remaining captives; and frequently with so much advantage, that some of their most distinguished sachems and captains, were derived from defeated and adopted foes. Each nation had its own separate republican constitution, in which rank and office were claimed only by age, procured only by merit, and enjoyed but by the tenure of public esteem. In no community was age accorded more respect, or youth endowed with greater beauty.* The people of the several nations, and especially the Mohawks, were distinguished by the usual Indian qualities of attachment to liberty, fortitude in the endurance of pain, and preference of craft and stratagem to undisguised operations in war,† and by a more than usual degree of perseverance, resolution, and active intrepidity. Almost all the tribes around this people, and even many at a great distance, who were not included in their confederacy, acknowledged a subjection to it, paid a tribute which two aged sachems were annually deputed to collect, ‡ and were restrained from making war or peace without the consent of the Five Nations. It was the policy of all the

* Such was the efficacy of the Indian mode of life, in developing the finer proportions of which the human frame is susceptible, that, when the statue of the Apollo-Belvidere was beheld, for the first time, by Benjamin West, the distinguished American painter, he started at the unexpected likeness, and exclaimed, "How like it is to a young Mohawk warrior!"

† In this peculiarity most of the Indian tribes resembled the ancient Spartans; as they did also in the diligence with which they cultivated conciseness of speech.

‡ "I have often had opportunity to observe what anxiety the poor Indians were under, while these two old men remained in that part of the

chiefs to affect superior purity, and to distribute among the people their own share of tribute and plunder. All matters of common concernment were transacted in general meetings of the sachems of each nation; and the influence of time, aided by a long course of judicious policy and victorious enterprise, had completely succeeded in causing the federal character and sentiments to prevail over the peculiarities of their subordinate national associations. When, at a period subsequent to the first visit of the Europeans, the Tuscarora tribe was vanquished, they were permitted to revive their broken estate, by ingrafting it on this powerful confederacy, by being associated as a new member of the general union, instead of being diffused and losing their identity among the other tribes, and the confederacy thereafter obtained the name of the Six Nations. Both the French and English writers, who have treated of the character or affairs of this people, have concurred in describing them as at once the most judicious and politic of the native powers, and the most fierce and formidable of the native inhabitants of America.

When the French under Champlain settled in Canada, they found the Five Nations engaged in a bloody war with the powerful tribe of Adirondacks, by whom they had been driven from their original possessions around Montreal, and between the Connecticut river and Lake Champlain, now the state of Vermont, and forced to seek an asylum in the region bounding on

country where I was. An old Mohawk sachem, in a poor blanket, and dirty shirt, may be seen issuing his order with as arbitrary an authority as a Roman dictator."— *Colden.*

Lake Ontario and the Mohawk river. The Five Nations, however, were regaining their lost ground, and had compelled the Adirondacks to fly for safety behind the strait where Quebec is built. But the tide of success was suddenly turned by the arrival of Champlain, who naturally joined the Adirondacks, because he had settled on their lands. Near the place where the fortress of Ticonderoga was afterward erected, the Indians, with whom Champlain was exploring the country, encountered a body of two hundred Iroquois, who were on their way down the lake on a war expedition. Loud shouts at once arose from both parties, as they snatched up their weapons and prepared for action. Champlain and the two Frenchmen with him, each armed with an arquebuse,* participated in the conflict, and as the Iroquois had no previous knowledge of fire-arms, they soon fled in dismay, leaving fifty warriors dead on the field, while ten or twelve prisoners were captured by the Adirondacks.† All engaged in this expedition went to their homes highly

* "A sort of hand-gun; a species of fire-arms anciently used, which was cocked with a wheel. It carried a ball that weighed nearly two ounces. A larger kind, used in fortresses, carried a ball of three ounces and a half." — *Encyclopedia.*

† If, on this occasion, the Indians were for the first time witnesses of the deadly effect of fire-arms, the French were equally surprised by the fiendish cruelties inflicted by the Indian warriors upon their prisoners. "After proceeding about eight leagues down the lake," says Dr. Fitch in his admirable history of Washington county, "they landed after nightfall; and, taking one of the prisoners, made a speech to him, upbraiding him with the barbarities which he and his people had perpetrated in the war, without showing mercy in any instance, and informing him, that it would now devolve on him to submit to the same destiny. They then told him to sing if he had any courage: this he commenced

pleased with Champlain, and from this time onward, their several tribes were firmly attached to the French and their interests.*

doing, but in the most sad and dolorous tones. A fire had been previously kindled, and was now burning briskly. Each Indian took from it a brand, and commenced burning the skin of the poor creature, a little at a time, to make him suffer longer torment. Remitting this at times, they would then throw him on his back in the water. Afterward, pulling off his finger-nails, they put hot ashes on the ends of his fingers. Next, they tore the scalp from the top of his head, and then dropped melted pitch upon the naked skull. They then pierced holes through his arms near the wrists, and with sticks drew out therefrom the sinews and nerves, forcibly pulling upon them, until they were rent asunder. Strange cries at times were uttered by this miserable creature; yet, during the whole of the horrid performance, he was so firm and unshaken, that one would have said he did not feel any pain. The Indians urged Champlain to take a firebrand, and join them in their employment. But he remonstrated with them, telling them he was unused to such cruelties — that his people only shot at their enemies with their guns, and if they would only permit him to have one shot at the captive with his arquebuse, it was all he would ask. They would not consent to this; and, unable longer to endure the sight, he turned away with disgust. Perceiving his disquietude, they called him back, telling him to do as he had desired. He hereupon discharged his arquebuse at the sufferer with such effect, that, as Charlevoix intimates in describing this scene, he had no occasion for desiring a second shot. Even now that their victim was dead, they were not satisfied, but, ripping him open, they threw his entrails into the lake, and then cut off his head, arms and legs, preserving only his scalp, which they added to the number they had taken from those who had been killed in the battle. More atrocious still, they took his heart, and cutting it into a number of slices, gave a piece to one of his own brothers, and to each of the other prisoners, ordering them to eat it. These put it into their mouths, but were unable to swallow it; whereupon, some of the Algonquin Indians who guarded the prisoners, allowed them to spit out the whole and throw it into the water."

* Champlain died at Quebec, in December, 1634 — one hundred years after Cartier had discovered the St. Lawrence. He was governor of

From this period, an implacable war was carried on by the Iroquois against the Canadian settlements on the St. Lawrence. For a time, the conduct, the bravery, and especially the fire-arms of the French, proved an overmatch for the skill and intrepidity of the Five Nations, who were defeated in several battles, and reduced to great distress. It was at this critical juncture, that the first Dutch ship arrived in the Hudson river, with the colonists who established themselves at Albany. The Iroquois, easily procuring from these neighbors a supply of that species of arms to which alone their enemies had been indebted for their superiority, revived the war with so much impetuosity and success, that the nation of the Adirondacks was completely annihilated; and the French too late discovered, that they had espoused the fortunes of the weaker people.*

Canada from 1610 until the time of his death, with the exception of three years, during which period the English had possession of the country. By his arduous efforts, Quebec, as early as 1626, began to assume the appearance of a city. That year a stone fortress was built, and the colony was rapidly growing into power. Champlain died after having been more than thirty years a resident of Canada. He is represented by the writers of that time, as a man of much penetration, activity and intrepidity. He could not have succeeded in establishing a new city and colony in the midst of a populous, warlike, and savage nation, if he had lacked great ability, enterprise and courage. He was a man of eminent piety, and zealous in the propagation of the Catholic faith. He often said, "the salvation of one soul was of more value than the conquest of an empire."

* One of the stratagems of the Five Nations is worthy of mention. At one time they sent the French a proposal for a peace, to which the latter readily inclined, and requested the Indians to receive a deputation of Jesuits, whose exertions, it was expected, would conciliate their sincere friendship. The Five Nations willingly agreed, and desired to see the priests immediately; but the instant they got hold of them, they

Hence originated the mutual dread and enmity that so long subsisted between the French and confederated Indians, and entailed so many calamities upon both.

The French colony, being in extreme distress, solicited aid from the mother country. Two regiments were sent out by the king, and thus strengthened, Courcelles, governor of Canada, dispatched a party by the way of Lake Champlain, in the winter of 1665, to attack the Five Nations. The French, less accustomed to the climate, and less acquainted with the country than their savage enemies, attempted vainly to imitate their rapid and secret movements. They lost their way among the wastes of snow, and often enduring the greatest misery, arrived, without knowing where they were, at the village of Schenectady, which a Dutchman of consideration, named Corlear, had recently founded. The French, exhausted and stupefied with cold and hunger, resembled rather an army of beggars, than of hostile invaders, and would have fallen an easy prey to a body of Indians who were in the village, if Corlear, touched with compassion at their miserable appearance, had not employed both influence and artifice with the Indians, to persuade them to spare their unfortunate enemies, and depart to defend their own people, against a more formidable attack in a different quarter, which he led them to expect. When the Indians were gone, Corlear and his townsmen gave refreshments to the famishing Frenchmen, and supplied them with provisions and other necessaries to carry

marched to attack the Indian allies of the French, and taking the priests with them as hostages, to enforce the neutrality of their countrymen, gave the Adirondacks a signal defeat.

them home: having taught them, by a sensible lesson, that it is the mutual duty of men to mitigate by kindness and charity, instead of aggravating by ambition and ferocity, the ills that arise from the rigors of climate and the frailty of human nature. The French governor expressed much gratitude for Corlear's* kindness, and the Indians never resented his benevolent stratagem. The names of two of the officers of Courcelles in this expedition are perpetuated, the one by the Sorel river, the other by the town of Chambly.

To retrieve the misfortunes of their winter expedition, the French, in the spring of 1666, with all the militia of Canada, amounting to twenty companies of foot, marched into the Mohawk country. The expedition was attended with great expense and fatigue, being continued for more than seven hundred miles through an uncultivated and hostile country; and failed in materially harassing the Indians. At the approach of the French, the savages easily found places of safety by retiring into the woods and swamps, where the French armies could not follow them. The result, however, was favorable to the cause of peace.

* This man enjoyed great influence with the Indians, who, after his death, always addressed the governors of New York with the title of *Corlear*, an expression, in their view, significant of kindness, friendship, and confidence. Grateful for his unexpected, if not undeserved hospitality, Courcelles invited Corlear to visit him in Canada. The invitation was accepted, but on his journey thither, this noble man was unfortunately drowned in Lake Champlain. The lake in which he perished, the Indians afterward called Corlear's Lake, by which name it was commonly known among the English and Dutch, for many years. The erroneous idea, that Champlain perished in the lake which bears his name, was obviously derived from this incident.

The French, exhausted with the expense and fatigue of the campaign, and mortified by their want of success, did not wish to repeat the experiment of another expedition into the Indian territory. The Indians were not pleased to see the war brought into the heart of their own territory, and were not yet able to oppose a large body of men armed and disciplined in the European manner, with much prospect of success. And at length, after a long period of severe but indecisive hostilities, both parties, wearied of war, but not exhausted of animosity, agreed to a general peace, which was concluded in the year 1667. Thus, for the first time, the blessings of complete peace were realized by the French colonies.

During the partial cessation of hostilities between the French and Indians, for almost twenty years, the former, by insidious artifices, did much to influence the Indians against the English settlers in New England, and doubtless afforded them aid in their barbarous warfare upon the English settlements. The French, whose suppleness of character and demeanor* was always more acceptable to the Indians in their native condition, than the grave, unbending spirit of the English, found it easier to cultivate and employ, than to check or eradicate the treachery and cruelty

* A curious instance of the complaisance of the French, is related by Oldmixon in his account of the savages who were greatly charmed with the good breeding of the French, in always appearing perfectly naked in their mutual conferences. Charlevoix, a French author, boasted that the French were the only Europeans who had ever succeeded in rendering themselves agreeable to the Indians. Whatever reason he may have had for this boast, he had no reason to glory in the means by which they courted popularity

of their Indian neighbors. The encouragement of the French allies prevailed with the Indians to reject all friendly overtures from the English, which, at first, they seemed willing to accept, and their native ferocity prompted them to signalize their enmity by a series of unprovoked and unexpected massacres. So openly did the French afford aid to the Indians toward the close of King Philip's war, that Frenchmen were known to accompany their war-parties, and several prisoners, taken in battle, were carried to Canada and sold to the French. Hatfield, a settlement on the Connecticut river, furnished the first of that long procession of prisoners who, during the succeeding seventy years, were transported from New England across the Green Mountains and over Lake Champlain to Canada. Toward the close of 1677, fifty Indians from Canada surprised the settlement, and captured about twenty prisoners, among whom were several women and children. On their march to Canada, the prisoners endured great hardships, and were often threatened with death. One man was actually burned at the stake, with the usual Indian barbarity. The remainder were sold to the French. Two of the women were wives of men named Wait and Jennings. On hearing that they had been conveyed to Canada, the husbands made application to the governor of Massachusetts for commissions, authorizing them to proceed to Canada, and ransom them. Starting in the winter, they pursued their perilous journey across Lake Champlain, and finally arrived at Chambly. There they found the captives, some of whom had been pawned by the savages for liquor. Paying two hundred pounds for the ransom of the prisoners, these noble men started in the spring of 1678 on their return home. Their progress was slow, for they were compelled to procure their provisions by hunting. Early in the summer they reached home, without accident. This was the first tour performed by New-England men across the country so often traversed for similar purposes in the subsequent wars, and which became the grand theater of military operations between the French and English in later times. After this event, tranquillity prevailed along the New-England frontiers for about ten years.

The peace which, for nearly twenty years, had been maintained between the French and the Five Nations, was broken in 1687, and hostilities were carried on between them with a mutual fury and ferocity, that seemed totally to obliterate the distinctions between civilized and savage men. Although unaided, the Five Nations maintained the struggle with an energy that promised the preservation of their independence, and finally, with a success that threatened even the subjugation of their civilized adversaries. Undertaking an expedition with twelve hundred of their warriors against Montreal, they conducted their march with such rapidity and secrecy, as to surprise the French in almost unguarded security. The suddenness and fury of their attack proved irresistible. They burned the town, sacked the plantations, put a thousand of the French to the sword, and carried away a number of prisoners whom they burned alive; returning to their friends with only a loss of three of their own number. They strained every nerve to follow up their advantage, and shortly after their attack on Montreal, possessed themselves of several fortresses which the garrisons abandoned in the panic. They reduced every station that the French possessed in Canada, to a state of the utmost terror and distress. Nothing could have saved the French from utter destruction, but the ignorance which disabled the Indians from attacking fortified places; and it was evident that a single vigorous act of interposition by the English colonists — compelled by treaty to remain inactive spectators of the contest — would have sufficed to terminate forever the rivalry of France and England in this quarter of the world.

The condition of the French in Canada, was suddenly raised from the brink of ruin, by the arrival of a strong reinforcement from the parent state, under the command of a skillful and enterprising officer, the old Count de Frontignac, who now assumed the government of the French settlements, and quickly gave a different complexion to their affairs. He set on foot a treaty with the Five Nations, and succeeded, meanwhile, in obtaining a suspension of their hostilities. About this time war was declared between France and England; and he boldly determined to revive the drooping spirits of the colony, by making an attack upon New York.

A considerable body of French and Indians was accordingly collected and dispatched in the depth of winter against New York. By a strange coincidence, which must ever stain the name of the French colonists with the blackest ingratitude and dishonor, this party, like their predecessors in 1665, after wandering for twenty-two days through deserts rendered trackless by snow, approached the village of Schenectady in so exhausted a condition that they had determined to surrender themselves to the inhabitants as prisoners of war. But, arriving at a late hour on an inclement night, (February 8, 1690,) and hearing from the messengers that they had sent forward, that the inhabitants were all in bed, without even the precaution of a public watch, they exchanged their intention of imploring mercy to themselves, for a plan of nocturnal attack and massacre of the defenseless people, to whose charity their own countrymen had once been so deeply indebted. This detestable requital of good with evil, was executed with a barbarity which of itself must be acknowledged to form one of the most revolting and terrific pictures that has ever been exhibited of human cruelty and ferocity. Dividing themselves into a number of parties, they set fire to the village in various places, and attacked the inhabitants with fatal advantage, when, alarmed by the conflagration, they endeavored to escape from the burning houses. The exhausted strength of the Frenchmen seemed to revive with the work of destruction, and to gather energy from the animated horror of the scene. Not only were all the male inhabitants they could reach put to death, but women and children were barbarously murdered. But either the delay occasioned by their elaborate cruelty, or the more merciful haste of the flames to announce the calamity to those who might still fly from the assassins, enabled many of the inhabitants to escape. The efforts of the assailants were also somewhat impeded by a sagacious discrimination which they thought it expedient to exercise. Though unmindful of benefits, they were not regardless of policy, and of a number of Mohawk Indians who were in the village, not one sustained an injury. Sixty persons perished in the massacre, and twenty-seven were taken prisoners. Of the fugitives who escaped half naked, and made their way through a storm to Albany, twenty-five lost their limbs from the intensity of the frost. The French having totally destroyed the village, retired across Lake Champlain loaded with plunder. They were pursued by a party of young men, who killed or captured twenty-five.

In concert with the expedition against New York under D'Aillebout, Frontignac sent a party of French and Indians, under the command of Sieur Hertel, to lay waste the frontier settlements of Massachusetts and New Hampshire.* This expedition was also

* At Salmon Falls, in New Hampshire, thirty persons were killed, and fifty-four, chiefly women and children, were carried into captivity. Among the prisoners was a Mr. Rodgers, who, being quite corpulent, was unable to carry the burden imposed upon him, and attempted to escape in the woods. The Indians caught him, stripped, beat and pricked him with their knives; then tied him to a tree and danced around him until they had kindled a fire. They gave him time to pray and take leave of his fellow-prisoners, who were compelled to witness his death. They pushed the fire toward him, and when he was almost stifled, took it away to give him time to breathe, and thus prolong his misery; they drowned his dying groans with their hideous singing and yelling; all the while dancing around the fire, and cutting off pieces of his flesh and throwing them in his face. When he was dead they left his body broiling on the coals, in which state it was found by his friends, and buried.

An anecdote of a different character is told of this expedition. While an Indian was preparing strings to bind a prisoner named Toogood, the latter seized his gun and went backward, keeping the gun pointed at the Indian, and threatened to shoot him if he alarmed the others, who had passed over the brow of a hill. By compelling the Indian to follow him some distance, he was enabled to make his escape, his adversary calling him *Nogood, Nogood.* When the Indian returned to his companions without gun or prisoner, they ridiculed him heartily.

successful, and marked with cruelties scarcely less monstrous than those committed at Schenectady. The success that attended these expeditions served to revive the spirits of the French colony, and at the same time occasioned great alarm in every part of the English plantations. Aided by Frontignac, the Indians made frequent incursions into the English settlements, and wherever they went committed the most horrid acts of savage cruelty.* The French, by giving premiums for scalps, and by purchasing the English prisoners, animated the Indians to exert all their activity and

* In 1689, the Indians, having resolved upon attacking Dover in New Hampshire, employed their usual art to lull the suspicions of the inhabitants. So civil and respectful was their behavior, that they occasionally obtained permission to sleep in the fortified houses in the town. On the evening of the fatal night, they assembled in the neighborhood, and sent their women to apply for lodgings at the houses devoted to destruction. When all was quiet, the doors were opened and the signal given. Against Major Waldron, one of the principal inhabitants, their animosity was particularly excited by his former harsh dealings with the Indians. They rushed into his house, and hastened to his apartment. Awakened by the noise, he seized his sword and drove them back; but when returning for his other arms, was stunned with a hatchet and fell. They then dragged him into his hall, seated him in an elbow-chair upon a long table, and insultingly asked, "Who shall judge Indians now?" After feasting upon provisions which they compelled the rest of the family to procure, each one, with a knife, cut gashes in Waldron's breast, saying, "I cross out my account!" They then cut off his nose and ears, and forced them into his mouth; and when, weakened from the loss of blood, he was about to fall from the table, his own sword was held under him, which put an end to his tortures. At other houses, similar acts of cruelty were perpetrated, and in the whole, twenty-three persons were killed, and twenty-nine carried prisoners to Canada, who were shortly sold to the French. Many houses were burned and much property was plundered; but so expeditious were the Indians, that they had fled beyond reach before the neighboring people could be collected.

EXPEDITION AGAINST QUEBEC.

address, and the frontier inhabitants endured the most aggravated sufferings.

To avenge these barbarities, a combined invasion of Canada was projected. An expedition commanded by Sir William Phipps,* sailed from Boston against Quebec; and the united forces of Connecticut and New York, under the command of General Winthrop, were to march against Montreal, by the way of Lake Champlain. The first, commanded by Phipps, consisted of forty vessels, and the number of troops on board amounted to over two thousand. These were furnished by Massachusetts and New Hampshire. Phipps arrived before Quebec so late in the season, that there was but little opportunity for accomplishing his purpose. The English were arrested in various

* Sir William Phipps was a native of Massachusetts, and notwithstanding a mean education, and the depression of the humblest circumstances, had raised himself by the mere vigor of his mind to a conspicuous rank, and gained a high reputation for spirit, skill and success. He kept sheep in his native province until he was eighteen years of age, and was afterward apprenticed to a ship-carpenter. When he was freed from his indentures, he pursued a seafaring life, and attained the station of captain of a merchant vessel. Having met with an account of the wreck of a Spanish ship, loaded with great treasures, near the Bahama Islands, about fifty years before, he conceived a plan of extricating the buried treasures from the bowels of the deep; and, transporting himself to England, he stated his scheme so plausibly, that the king was struck with it, and in 1683 sent him out with a vessel to make the attempt. It proved unsuccessful; and all his urgency could not induce the king to engage in a repetition of it. But the Duke of Albemarle, resuming the design, equipped a vessel for the purpose, and gave the command of it to Phipps, who now realizing the expectations he had formed, succeeded in raising specie to the value of $1,500,000, from the bottom of the ocean. Of this treasure he obtained a portion sufficient to make his fortune, with a still larger meed of general consideration and applause.

severe encounters, and compelled at length to make a precipitate retreat; and the fleet, after having sustained considerable loss in the voyage homeward, returned to Boston.

General Winthrop, with a thousand men, marched from Albany into the northern wilderness, with the design of passing through Lake Champlain and capturing Montreal. But this army, the forerunner of the many marshaled hosts that for almost a century afterward, made Lake Champlain and the country bordering on it their highway, was retarded by defective arrangements, and disappointed by the friendly Indians who had engaged to furnish them with canoes for crossing rivers. After marching some distance toward Montreal, the commander deemed it expedient to retreat without doing any injury to the enemy.

Vexed at having the expedition thus abandoned, and knowing that the friendly Indians were losing confidence in the energy and power of their English allies, Captain John Schuyler, (grandfather of General Philip Schuyler of our revolutionary history,) enlisted a force of thirty whites and one hundred and twenty Indians, the same fall, and made an excursion to the St. Lawrence, destroyed the village of La Prairie, took nineteen prisoners, devastated the country in the vicinity of Montreal, and returned in triumph to Albany.*

The following year, (1691,) Major Peter Schuyler, (brother to John Schuyler,) having acquired extraordinary influence with the Five Nations by his courage,

---

* Fitch's History of Washington County.

good sense, and friendly attention to their interests, undertook an expedition against Montreal, at the head of a considerable body of colonial and Indian forces. Though the invaders were finally compelled to retreat, the French sustained great loss in several encounters; and such was the spirit and animosity of the Five Nations, that they continued, during the winter, to' wage incessant and harassing hostilities against the French, although the colonial troops had returned to their homes. Count Frontignac was so exasperated by their continued assaults, that he condemned to a death accompanied by all the torments French ingenuity could devise, two Mohawk captives, whom the fate of war had thrown into his power.* The peace of Ryswick, in 1697, put an end to hostilities for a brief period, between the rival colonies of the French and English.

In a few years war again broke out in Europe, and hostilities speedily recommenced in America. The

* Shortly before the execution, some Frenchman, less inhuman than his governor, threw a knife into the prison, and one of the Mohawks immediately dispatched himself with it; the other, expressing contempt at his companion's mean evasion of glory, walked to the stake, singing in his death-chant, that he was a Mohawk warrior; that all the power of man could not extort an expression of suffering from his lips; and that it was ample consolation to him to reflect that he had made many Frenchmen suffer the same pangs that he must now himself undergo. When attached to the stake, he looked round on his executioners, their instruments of torture, and the assembled multitude of spectators, with all the complacency of heroic fortitude, and, after enduring for some hours, with composed mien and triumphant language, a series of barbarities too atrocious to be narrated, his sufferings were terminated by the interposition of a French lady, who prevailed with the governor to order that mortal blow, to which human cruelty has given the name of *coup de grace,* or stroke of *favor.*

first blow fell upon Deerfield, which was at that time the most northerly settlement on the Connecticut river, a few families at Northfield excepted. Against this place a party of two hundred French, and one hundred and fifty Indians was sent. They were under the command of Hertel de Rouville, assisted by four of his brothers, all of whom had become distinguished in the wars. They passed up Lake Champlain until they reached the Winooski (at that time called French) river. There they crossed over to Connecticut river, and traveled on the ice until they arrived in the vicinity of Deerfield. Early on the morning of March 12, 1704, Rouville attacked the village. The snow around the fort was in many places drifted nearly to the top of the palisades, and the enemy found no difficulty in surmounting these defenses. The occupants were buried in profound sleep. A simultaneous assault was made upon all the houses, the doors were broken open, and the people seized in their beds. When resistance was attempted, the tomahawk or musket ended the strife. A few were so fortunate as to escape by flight to the adjacent woods; but the greater part were either killed or made prisoners.

Early in the assault, about thirty Indians attacked the house of the Rev. John Williams, who, awaking from a sound sleep, instantly leaped from his bed, ran toward the door, and found a party entering. Calling to awaken a couple of soldiers in his chamber, he seized a pistol, presented it at the breast of the foremost Indian, and attempted to shoot him; but the pistol missed fire. He was instantly overpowered, bound, and kept for an hour without his clothes. Two

MASSACRE AT DEERFIELD.

of his young children were dragged to the door and murdered, and his negro-woman shared the same fate. Mrs. Williams and five children, the youngest of whom was but a few weeks old, were also captured.

Another dwelling-house was successfully defended by seven armed men and a few women, by whom it was occupied. While the brave defenders were pouring their fire upon the assailants from the windows and loop-holes, the no less brave women were busily employed in casting balls for future supply. Unable to carry the house, or intimidate the defenders to a surrender by all their threats and stratagems, the enemy gave up their efforts, and cautiously endeavored to keep out of the range of the shot. But notwithstanding their precautions, several were singled out and shot down by the marksmen in the house.

Having collected the prisoners, plundered and set fire to the buildings, Rouville began to retrace his march to Canada. But a party of the inhabitants who had escaped, returned to the village, and, joined by the men who had defended their house, and a few people who had hurried on from Hatfield, pursued the enemy, and a sharp skirmish ensued; but, being at length nearly encircled by a superior force, they were compelled to retire, with the loss of nine of their number. The pursuit, though highly honorable to the bravery of the pursuers, exposed the captives to imminent danger. During the fight, the English maintained their ground with great resolution, and at one crisis, Rouville, apprehending a defeat, sent orders for the captives to be tomahawked; but fortunately the messenger was killed before he delivered his orders.

Preparations were however made by the Indians who guarded the prisoners, to put them to death in case of the defeat of their party. On the retreat of the English, Rouville countermanded his order, and saved the captives.

The whole number of prisoners amounted to one hundred and twelve. Forty-seven were slain, and the loss of the enemy was about the same. The entire village was reduced to ashes with the exception of one house, which is still standing, and the traces of the tomahawks and bullets are still to be seen.

Soon after the action, Rouville commenced his march for Canada. Most gloomy were the prospects of the captives. Many were women then in a condition requiring the most tender treatment; some were young children whose feeble frames could not sustain the fatigues of a day; others were infants, carried in the arms of their parents. Several of the men were suffering from severe wounds. The distance to Canada was nearly three hundred miles, through a country wild and waste. It was in the midst of winter, and the ground was deeply covered with snow. The whole party was unsupplied with provisions, and dependent solely for food upon the game that should be killed on their route. The first day's march was necessarily slow and difficult. The Indians, probably from a desire to save the young to dispose of in Canada, or to retain for their own service, rather than from tenderness, assisted the parents by carrying the children upon their backs. At night, they encamped by clearing away the snow, spreading boughs, and constructing slight cabins of brush. The prisoners were as comfortably lodged as circumstances would admit. To prevent escapes, the most athletic were bound, and secured according to the Indian mode, and this was practiced at the subsequent night camps. Notwithstanding this precaution, Joseph Alexander, one of the prisoners, had the good fortune to escape. To deter others from similar attempts, Mr. Williams, who was considered as the head of the captives, was informed, that in case of another escape, the remainder should suffer death by fire. In the course of the night, some of the Indians became intoxicated with spirits which they had found at Deerfield, and fell upon Mr. Williams' negro and murdered him.

The second day's march was equally slow, and Mr. Williams was permitted, for a short time, to assist his distressed wife in traveling, who now began to be exhausted; but he was soon torn from her and placed at the head of the column, leaving her to struggle along unassisted. At the upper part of Greenfield meadow, it became necessary to pass Green river, a small stream then open, in performing which, Mrs. Williams fell into the water; but recovering herself, she with difficulty reached the shore and continued her route. An abrupt hill was now to be surmounted, and Mr. Williams, who had gained the summit, entreated his master (for so the Indian who captured him was called,) for leave to return and help forward his distressed wife, but was barbarously refused, and she was left to struggle with difficulties beyond her power. Her ferocious master finding her a burthen, sunk his hatchet in her head, and left her dead at the foot of the hill. Her body was soon after taken up by a party from field, and interred in the public burial-ground in that town, where her grave-stones, with those of her husband, Mr. Williams, are still to be seen.

Rouville encamped the second night in the northerly part of the present town of Bernardston. A young woman and an infant were dispatched in the course of this day's march. At this camp a consultation was held by the Indians in regard to killing and scalping Mr. Williams; but his master, unwilling to part with so valuable a prize, interfered and saved him from the hatchet. The next day the captives were more equally distributed for convenience of marching, and several exchanged masters. The fourth day brought the army to Connecticut river, about thirty miles above Deerfield, probably in the upper part of Brattleborough, Vermont. Here slight sledges were constructed, for the conveyance of the children, wounded and baggage, and the march, which was now on the ice, became more rapid. One female was this day relieved from her sufferings by a stroke of the hatchet.

The march on Connecticut river continued several days without any extraordinary incident, excepting now and then the murder of an exhausted captive. On the first Sunday, the prisoners were permitted to halt and rest themselves, and Mr. Williams delivered a discourse from these words : * " *The Lord is righteous, for I have rebelled against his commandments: Hear I pray you, all people, and behold my sorrow: My*

---

* This sermon is said to have been delivered at the mouth of Williams' river, in Rockingham, Vermont: from which circumstance the river received its name.

virgins and young men are gone into captivity." Lamentations, i. 18.

At the mouth of White river, Rouville divided his force into several parties, and they took different routes to the St. Lawrence. The one which Mr. Williams accompanied, ascended the former river, and passing the highlands to the Winooski, proceeded down that stream to Lake Champlain, and continued the march on the lake to Missisco bay, near which they joined a party of Indians on a hunting excursion. On reaching the Sorel, they built canoes and passed down to Chambly, where they found a French fort and a small garrison. Their route was then continued to the village of Sorel, where some of the captives had already arrived. Mr. Williams was thence conveyed down the St. Lawrence to the Indian village of St. Francis, and some time after, to Quebec; and after a short residence at that place, was sent to Montreal, where he was humanely treated by Governor Vaudreuil. Some of Mr. Williams' children accompanied another party, and after much delay and great suffering, arrived at various Indian lodges on the St. Lawrence. In a few instances, the captives were purchased of the Indians; but the greatest proportion were retained by them, at their lodges in various parts of the country. Of the one hundred and twelve taken at Deerfield, about seventeen were killed, or died on the march, and the sufferings of all were severe in the extreme. An anecdote is told of a boy among the prisoners who, having nothing given him to eat, ran up to an old Indian, and snatched a bone from his hands. Contrary to the expectation of the other captives, the Indian was not displeased, but laughed heartily at the courage of the lad. He was afterward treated with much kindness, and became a favorite with the Indians.

During his captivity, Mr. Williams was permitted to visit various places on the St. Lawrence, and in his interviews with the French jesuits, he found them zealously attached to the Roman Catholic religion, to which they spared no pains to convert him, as well as the other captives; and in some instances they inflicted punishments for non-compliance with their ceremonies. But they found him as zealously attached to his own faith, and through his influence, most of the captives continued firm in the protestant persuasion. In 1706, a flag-ship was sent to Quebec by Governor Dudley, by which fifty-seven of the captives were obtained and conveyed to Boston, among whom was Mr. Williams * and his children, with the exception of his daughter Eunice, who, notwithstanding all the exertions of her father to obtain her redemption, was left among the Indians, and, adopting their manners and customs, married a savage, by whom she had several children. Some time after the war, she with her husband, visited her relations at Deerfield, dressed in the Indian costume; and though every persuasion was tried to induce her to abandon the Indians, and to remain among her connections, all proved ineffectual; she returned to

* This worthy man was born at Roxbury, Massachusetts, in the year 1664. In 1683, after graduating at Hartford college, he became the pastor of the church at Deerfield, and was the first settled minister in the western part of Massachusetts. His people found in him an able, conscientious, and judicious friend, capable both of directing their devotions, and of assisting them in the difficulties and hardships of frontier life. After his return to Boston, several of the wealthiest parishes in

Canada, and there ended her days, a true savage. Twenty-eight of the captives remained in Canada, and, mixing with the French and Indians, and adopting their manners and customs, forgot their native country, and were lost to their friends.

New York having agreed with the French and western Indians to remain neutral, the enemy were enabled to pour their whole force upon Massachusetts and New Hampshire, the inhabitants of which, for ten

that vicinity, urged him to settle with them. He declined any offer of this kind, and, in accordance with a vow made in his captivity, he returned to Deerfield, collected his scattered flock, and began again with them the labors, and endured with them the privations and perils of a new settlement. His salary was at first forty pounds, but was raised in 1711 to sixty. He married a second wife, by whom he had several children. He remained at Deerfield until his death, in 1728. His grandson, Dr. Samuel Williams, was the first historian of Vermont. Charles K. Williams, the son of the latter, was for thirty years a judge of the supreme court of Vermont, and recently governor of that state.

One of the motives for the expedition against Deerfield, was to recover a bell which had been purchased in France for a Roman Catholic church at St. Regis, on the St. Lawrence. The French and English being then at war, the vessel in which the bell was shipped fell into the hands of the latter. It was taken to Salem, and in 1703, purchased for the church of Mr. Williams, at Deerfield. After the massacre at the latter place, " the bell was conveyed in triumph through the forest to Lake Champlain, at the spot where Burlington now stands, where the Indians buried it with the benedictions of father Nicolas, the priest of St. Regis, who accompanied them. Thus far they had carried it by means of timber upon their shoulders. They hastened home and returned in early spring, with oxen and sled, to convey the sacred bell, now doubly hallowed in their minds, to its destination. The Indians of the village had never heard the sound of a bell, and powerful was the impression upon their minds, when its deep tones, louder and louder, broke the silence of the forest, as it approached their village at evening, suspended upon a cross-piece of timber, and rung continually by the delighted carriers. It was hung in the steeple with solemn ceremony, and there it remains."—*Lossing.*

years, endured the miseries peculiar to an Indian war, of which no description can give an adequate idea. The enemy was at all times prowling about the frontier settlements, watching in concealment for an opportunity to strike a sudden blow, and to fly with safety. The women and children retired into the garrisons; the men left their fields uncultivated, or labored with arms at their sides, and with sentinels at every point whence an attack could be apprehended. Yet, notwithstanding these precautions, the Indians were often successful, killing sometimes an individual, sometimes a whole family, sometimes a band of laborers ten or twelve in number; and so swift were they in their movements, that but few fell into the hands of the English.

Determined to give the frontiers no respite, and probably animated by the success of Rouville at Deerfield, four hundred French and Indians marched from Canada, the same year, (1704,) across the Green Mountains, and, on the 31st of July, fell upon Lancaster in Massachusetts. Six fortified houses were simultaneously attacked, but the enemy met with so warm a reception that they were compelled to retire. Before they left the place, most of the other buildings were fired, and reduced to ashes. Three hundred men from the adjacent towns, hurried on to the place toward the close of the day, came up with and engaged the enemy, and several were killed on each side.

In the autumn, the French suffered a severe loss, by the capture of a large store-ship called the Seine, on her passage from France; on board of which were a number of ecclesiastics and laymen, of great fortunes.

The cargo was estimated at two hundred thousand dollars. The loss of this ship was a great embarrassment to the military operations of the French in Canada, and very few depredations were committed in 1705. Vaudreuil, the governor of Canada, made propositions to Governor Dudley of Massachusetts, for a treaty of neutrality between the hostile colonies. The latter, then contemplating the conquest of Canada, was opposed to the measure, but he had the address to protract the negotiation, under the pretense of consulting the other English governors. In the mean time, negotiations for an exchange of prisoners were carried on; and it was by this arrangement that a large portion of the Deerfield captives were finally released.

In 1707, Massachusetts, New Hampshire and Rhode Island dispatched an armament against Port Royal in Nova Scotia, then in possession of the French, which returned, however, without effecting its object; but in 1710, the troops of New England, assisted by a British fleet, succeeded in reducing the place, and in compliment to Queen Anne, changed its name to Annapolis.

The only effectual way to put an end to the depredations of the enemy, seemed to be the subjugation of Canada. Representations to this effect were acquiesced in by the British ministry early in 1709, and they promised to dispatch a squadron, containing five regiments, to Boston. The colonial governments east of Connecticut, were required to raise twelve hundred men, with suitable transports and provisions for three months, to accompany the British troops against

Quebec. The other colonies were to equip fifteen hundred men to proceed by the way of Lake Champlain, and make an attack upon Montreal. The latter were put under the command of Governor Nicholson, who, early in the summer, marched to Lake Champlain, to be in readiness to coöperate with the armament to be dispatched against Quebec. These were joined by six hundred Indians. While the latter were engaged in the construction of canoes, the former were cutting roads between the Hudson river and Lake Champlain, erecting forts, and supplying them with provisions. Every thing promised success. The Indians appeared to be heartily engaged in the enterprise. Joy and triumphant exultation pervaded the colonies. But the English squadron was delayed far beyond the appointed time, and at last intelligence arrived that, on account of reverses in Portugal, the fleet destined for this enterprise was directed to proceed to the relief of the British army in Portugal. In connection with this disappointment, a fatal epidemic broke out among the troops on Lake Champlain. Probably not less than a thousand men fell victims to this epidemic, which, with the non-arrival of the promised force from England, induced Nicholson to abandon the enterprise and to dismiss his troops. Thus terminated the second great effort for the subjugation of the French in Canada.

Encouraged, however, by the success of his expedition against Port Royal, Governor Nicholson visited England in 1710, to concert another campaign for the complete subjugation of Canada. His plans were adopted, and in June, 1711, Admiral Walker, with a fleet of fifteen ships of war, and forty transports, bringing an army of veteran troops, arrived at Boston. Taking on board two additional regiments, he sailed from that port about the last of July. At the same time, Governor Nicholson repaired to Albany, to take command of the troops that were to proceed by the way of Lake Champlain. When the fleet had advanced ten leagues up the St. Lawrence, the weather became tempestuous and foggy. A difference of opinion arose concerning the course to be pursued: the English pilots recommending one course, and the colonial another. The admiral, like most English officers, preferred the advice of his own pilots to the colonial. Pursuing the course they recommended, during the night, nine transports were driven upon the rocks and dashed to pieces. From every quarter cries of distress arose, conveying, through the darkness, to those who were yet afloat, intelligence of the fate of their comrades, and of their own danger. The shrieks of the drowning pleaded powerfully for assistance, but none could be afforded until the morning dawned, when six or seven hundred, found floating on the scattered wrecks, were rescued from death, more than a thousand having sunk to rise no more. Only one of the colonial vessels was wrecked, but all the persons on board escaped the watery grave in which so many of their brethren from the mother country were lost. Weakened by this terrible disaster, the admiral determined to abandon the enterprise and return to England.

The army designed to invade Canada by way of Lake Champlain, had not advanced far from Albany, before they received intelligence of the disaster which had attended the fleet. Nothing remained for Nicholson but to disband his troops and return. The Marquis de Vaudreuil, governor of Canada, had been at Quebec, preparing to repulse the British armament. He received intelligence from the fishermen, that several vessels had been wrecked, and that numerous dead bodies, with red coats, had drifted to the shore, but that there were no ships in the river. Vaudreuil, justly concluding that the English fleet had suffered so much as to induce them to abandon their attempt upon Quebec, ordered his united forces to Montreal and Lake Champlain, to oppose the advance of Nicholson's army. Three thousand French troops were posted at Chambly, to check his approach to Montreal. But Vaudreuil soon learned that he had nothing to fear from the colonial army; that it had been disbanded upon the intelligence of the disaster that had befallen the fleet; and that the people of Albany, instead of being engaged in any hostile attempts against Montreal, were in much anxiety concerning their own safety. But he was not prepared to take advantage of the calamities of the English, and invade the colonies. Such was the disastrous termination of the third systematic attempt to subjugate Canada.

In 1713, the treaty of Utrecht put an end to the wars between the French and English colonies, and for thirty years they enjoyed the benefits of peace. During this period of tranquillity, the earliest settlements in Vermont occurred, and were made almost contemporaneously by the English on the Connecticut river, and by the French on Lake Champlain. The boundaries between the two nations had never been defined, and as the outskirts of their respective settlements began to meet, disputes in regard to jurisdiction arose, and the red flames of war were again kindled.

The early discoveries of Cartier had turned the eyes of France toward the St. Lawrence and the neighboring territory, and established her claim to it, according to that peculiar code by which European powers had deemed it proper to apportion among themselves the rest of the world. Although Canada had scarcely any likeness to the smiling and luxuriant aspect of Florida, or even of Virginia, yet it opened into regions of vast extent; and the tracing to distant fountains the sea-like abyss of its waters, presented more than common attraction to curiosity and adventure. But for fifty years after their discovery, the French government gave but little encouragement to the plan of colonizing these northern regions, and after the project was undertaken, more attention was given to the consolidation and improvement of the colony, than to exploring the expanse of interior America. The Count de Frontignac, however, was of a more enterprising spirit. He extended the range of settlement to the shores of Lake Ontario, built there a fort to which his own name was given, and opened an intercourse with the tribes who roamed over the boundless plains westward of the Alleghanies. Not content with this, he determined to explore the mighty stream which was said to pour its stupendous current in a direction opposite to that of all the streams then known in America, but toward some distant ocean that lay far in the south and west. In the existing darkness as to the boundaries of the

continent, it was concluded that this could only be the
Mer Vermeio, or Gulf of California, by which it was
hoped that the long-sought passage might be found to
the golden regions of India. The strongest motives,
therefore, impelled the count to strain every effort for
its discovery. There was no want of bold and fitting
men ready to engage in the enterprise. M. Joliet, with
but six white men and two Indians for guides, setting
forth in two bark canoes, undertook to cross this great
continent. Proceeding to Lake Michigan, they passed
by way of the Fox and Wisconsin rivers to the Mississippi. Floating down the current, they heard in a few
days, from the right, the roar of a great stream, and
soon after saw another river, with even a more prodigious current than that of the Mississippi. Following
these two streams until they reached the mouth of the
Arkansas, they became convinced that the Mississippi
emptied itself into the Gulf of Mexico, and not, as they
had expected and hoped, into the Pacific. Fearing
that, by following farther on, they might fall into the
hands of the Spaniards who were exploring the gulf,
they determined to return to Canada. La Salle afterward followed the same route, and as early as 1699,
the French began settlements in lower Louisiana, and
in 1717 founded New Orleans.

Being in possession of the inland seas of Canada, as
they were called, and of the mouths of the two largest
rivers in North America, the French conceived the
magnificent idea of uniting their northern and southern possessions by a chain of forts along the banks of
the Ohio and Mississippi, and by that means of confining the English colonists to the eastern side of the

Alleghanies. In pursuance of this plan, in the year 1731, they ascended Lake Champlain with a considerable force, intending to erect fortifications at the most commanding positions. No measure could have been better adapted to promote their own interest. It was through Lake Champlain that their troops had marched in their expeditions against Schenectady, the Mohawk's castles, and Deerfield. It was through this lake that their scouting parties found the most easy and safe passage in their excursions against the English colonies. In all the attempts of the English to effect the conquest of Canada, the attacks upon Montreal it was always contemplated should be effected through the waters of Lake Champlain. To erect a fortress at the south end of this lake was to secure the whole navigation of it, and the command of a large portion of the English and Indian frontier. From this commanding situation, the French could not only defeat the attempts of the English to penetrate their own country, but would always have a magazine of arms and ammunition, to supply their own troops and scouting parties, and an asylum to which the Indians might readily retreat, from their plundering and scalping expeditions against the English frontiers. And by means of the river Sorel and the lake, the fort might always be reinforced in three or four days, or receive any supplies without difficulty or danger.

The French garrison was at first placed on the east side of the lake, and the settlement began in what is now the town of Addison. On the western side, a more convenient situation was found, however, in which the harbor was good, and the fortress would be encompassed by water on three of its sides. On this spot, now called Crown Point, the French erected a fort sufficiently strong to resist any force that could be suddenly or easily brought against it, and gave it the name of St. Frederick. The land on which it was erected properly belonged to the Six Nations; but it was claimed by the government of New York, and had been granted by one of their governors, so early as 1696, to Dellius, the Dutch minister of Albany. The designs of the French, and the dangerous consequences attending the erection of their new fort, were well understood in the English colonies. The Massachusetts government was not a little alarmed. Mr. Belcher, the governor, gave the first information to the government of New York, of the French proceedings. Still, through the passiveness of the council, the French were suffered to advance nearly two hundred miles toward Albany, and to erect a fortress which would enable them, in any future war, to make their assaults with safety and success upon the frontier settlements of New York, Massachusetts, and New Hampshire.

The war which had so long distressed the frontiers of Massachusetts and New Hampshire, effectually prevented the progress of settlements to the north and west. From 1703 to 1713, the inhabitants being constantly harassed by calls for military service, agriculture was suffered to languish, many people were killed or captured, a heavy public debt was incurred, and the population of the country was vastly below what it would have been, had an uninterrupted peace been maintained. According to Hutchinson, from 1675, the beginning of Philip's war, to 1713, five or six thousand of the youth of the country had been destroyed by the enemy, or diseases contracted by the war; nine in ten of these would have been fathers of families, and, in the course of forty years, must have multiplied to near one hundred thousand. The northern and western part of New York was a wilderness, little known to the English.

Nor was the war less embarrassing to the progress of settlements and population in Canada. In 1714, the whole number of inhabitants, from fourteen to sixty years of age, able to bear arms, was four thousand four hundred and eighty-four. The standing forces at that time were twenty-eight companies of marines, paid by the king, containing six hundred and twenty eight men; but the Indians were numerous, always ready to turn out on short notice, and as they were frequently led by daring French officers, their incursions were generally attended with distressing consequences.

Relieved from the war, the inhabitants of New England now turned their attention to their internal affairs, and the improvement of their plantations; and the settlers who had been shut up in fortified houses, or driven from their plantations, now flattered themselves that they should not again be molested by the Indians. But this was a vain hope, for a renewal of war between England and France must necessarily produce hostilities between their colonies, and all the horrors of savage war must be again sustained. A fleet sufficient to block up the St. Lawrence, and a small invading army by Lake Champlain under an able commander, would have put an end to the embarrassments so long suffered by the English colonies.

During the calm which followed the peace of Utrecht, the English colonies increased their settlements north and west. New York, Massachusetts, and New Hampshire extended their grants of land into the present limits of the state of Vermont. Fort Dummer was erected by Massachusetts in 1724, on the west bank of the Connecticut river, near the place where the village of Brattleborough has since grown up, and was thus named in compliment to Mr. Dummer, lieutenant-governor of Massachusetts. Other forts were built in its immediate vicinity on the east bank of the Connecticut, and many families settled near them on both sides of the river. These pioneers were considerably harassed by a war, which raged principally in New Hampshire, between the whites and Indians, and which was generally known as "Lovewell's war," from the name of a successful leader of the English. The Indians were said to have been instigated by Sebastian Rolle, a jesuit, who had long been settled among them, and possessed great influence with several tribes.* The war was begun in 1723, and concluded in 1725.

* Rolle was slain in battle, while fighting against the English. He had been a very active agent in, if not the principal cause of the war, and his death was considered a very auspicious event, by the English. It must be acknowledged, however, that he was a loss to the literary world. Previous to his residence at Norridgewock, he had spent six years in traveling among the various tribes in the interior of America, and he had learned most of their languages. He was nearly forty years a missionary, twenty-six of which he had spent at Norridgewock among the Indians; and with their manners and customs he had become intimately acquainted. His letters on various subjects, evince that he was a man of superior natural powers, which had been improved by an education in a college of jesuits in Europe. With the learned languages he was thoroughly acquainted, and by his assiduity, he had taught many

In 1744, England again declared war against France and Spain, which again involved the colonies in hostilities with the enemies of the mother country and their Indian allies. The savages took up the hatchet with great alacrity, and the frontier posts suffered severely. Commerce, in general, and especially the fisheries, suffered great injury from privateers fitted out at Louisbourg, a French port on Cape Breton. Its situation gave it such importance, that nearly six millions of dollars had been expended on its fortifications. The place was deemed so strong as to deserve the appellation of the Dunkirk of America. In peace, it was a safe retreat for the ships of France, bound homeward from the East and West Indies. In war, it gave the French the greatest advantages for ruining the fishery of the northern English colonies, and endangered the loss of Nova Scotia. The reduction of this place was, for these reasons, an object of the highest importance to New England; and Mr.

of his converts to read and write, and to correspond with him in their own language. With the principal clergymen of Boston, he held a correspondence in Latin. He possessed great skill in controversy, and made some attempts at Indian poetry. By a compliance with the Indian mode of life, and a gentle, condescending deportment, he had gained the affections of the savages. But he used the offices of devotion as incentives to Indian ferocity, and even kept a flag, on which was depicted a cross surrounded by bows and arrows, which he used to hoist on a pole at the door of his church when he gave the Indians absolution, previous to their engaging in any enterprise. A dictionary of the Norridgewock language, composed by him, was found among his papers, which is now deposited in the library of Harvard college. It is a quarto volume of five hundred pages. Rolle was in the sixty-seventh year of his age when he was killed. His natural son, by an Indian woman who had served him as a laundress, was also slain during the war.

Vaughan of New Hampshire, who had often visited that place as a trader, conceived the project of an expedition against it. He communicated it to Governor Shirley, and being ardent and enthusiastic, convinced him that the enterprise was practicable, and inspired him with his own enthusiasm. Early in January, 1745, before he received any answer to the communications he had sent to England on the subject, he requested of the members of the general court, that they would lay themselves under an oath of profound secrecy in regard to a proposal of very great importance. They readily took the oath, and he communicated to them the plan which he had formed of attacking Louisbourg. The proposal was at first rejected, but it was finally carried by a majority of one. Letters were immediately dispatched to all the colonies, as far as Pennsylvania, requesting their assistance, and an embargo on their ports. Forces were promptly raised, and William Pepperrell was appointed commander of the expedition. This officer, with several transports, sailed from Nantucket on the 24th of March, and arrived at Canso on the 4th of April. Here the troops, joined by those of New Hampshire and Connecticut, amounting collectively to upward of four thousand, were detained three weeks, waiting for the ice, which environed the island of Cape Breton, to be dissolved. At length Commodore Warren, agreeably to orders from England, arrived at Canso in the Superbe, of sixty guns, with three other ships of forty guns each; and, after a consultation with the general, proceeded to cruise before Louisbourg. The general soon after sailed with the whole fleet; and on the 30th of April, coming to anchor at Chapeaurouge Bay, landed his troops. Lieutenant-colonel Vaughan conducted the first column through the woods within sight of Louisbourg, and saluted the city with three cheers. At the head of a detachment, chiefly of the New-Hampshire troops, he marched in the night to the north-east part of the harbor, where they burned the warehouses containing the naval stores, and staved a large quantity of wine and brandy. The smoke of this fire, driven by the wind into the grand battery, so terrified the French, that, spiking the guns, they abandoned it and retired to the city. The next morning, Vaughan took possession of the deserted battery; but the most difficult labors of the siege remained to be performed. The cannon were to be drawn nearly two miles over a deep morass, within gun-shot of the enemy's principal fortifications; and for fourteen nights the troops, with straps over their shoulders, sinking to their knees in mud, were employed in this arduous service. The approaches were then begun in the mode which seemed most proper to the shrewd understandings of untaught militia. Those officers who were skilled in the art of war, talked of zig-zags and epaulements; but the troops made themselves merry with the terms, and proceeded in their own way. By the 20th of May, they had erected five batteries, one of which mounted five forty-two-pounders, and did great execution. Meanwhile, the fleet cruising in the harbor had been equally successful; it captured a French ship of sixty-four guns, loaded with stores for the garrison, to whom the loss was as distressing as to the besiegers the capture was fortunate. English ships of war were, besides, continually arriving, and added such strength to the fleet, that a combined attack upon the town was resolved upon.

Discouraged by these adverse events and menacing appearances, Duchambon, the French commander, determined to surrender; and, on the 16th of June, 1745, articles of capitulation were signed. After the surrender of the city, the French flag was kept flying on the ramparts, and several rich prizes were thus decoyed. Two East-Indiamen, and one South Sea ship, valued at six hundred thousand pounds, were taken by the squadron at the mouth of the harbor. This expedition was one of the most remarkable events in the history of North America. It was not less hazardous in the attempt, than successful in the execution. It displayed the enterprising spirit of New England; and though it enabled Britain to purchase a peace, yet it excited her envy and jealousy against the colonies, by whose exertions it was acquired. The intelligence of this event spread rapidly through the colonies, and diffused universal joy. Well might the citizens of New England feel somewhat elated. Without even a suggestion from the mother country, they had projected, and with but comparatively little assistance achieved, an enterprise of vast importance to her and to them. Their commerce and fisheries were now secure, and their maritime cities relieved from all fear of attack from a quarter recently so great a source of dread and discomfort.

Fired with resentment at their loss, the French made extraordinary exertions to retrieve it, and to inflict chastisement on New England. The next summer they dispatched to the American coast a powerful fleet, carrying a large number of soldiers. The news of its approach spread terror throughout New England; but an uncommon succession of disasters deprived it of all power to inflict injury. After remaining a short time on the coast, it returned to France, having lost two admirals, both of whom, it was supposed, put an end to their lives through chagrin; having also, by tempests, been reduced to one-half of its former force, without effecting any of the objects anticipated.

In former wars, several routes had been traversed by the enemy in approaching the frontiers of the New-England colonies from Canada. One by the river St. Francis through Lake Memphremagog,* thence over portages to the Pasumsic river, which empties into the Connecticut at Barnet. Another was through Lake Champlain by the present town of Whitehall, thence up Wood or Pawit creek, and over the Green Mountains to the Connecticut. Otter creek, the Winooski, Lamoille and White rivers, emptying into Lake Champlain, were also frequented routes in passing over the Green Mountains to the corresponding rivers on its eastern slope emptying into the Connecticut. All portions of that territory were therefore familiar to the

---

* This lake is thirty miles long, and two or three in width. It lies mostly in Canada, but the south end extends into Vermont. The Indian words from which its name is derived are *Mem-plow-bouque*, signifying a large expanse of water.— See *Thompson's Gazetteer.*

French, and as the scouting parties of the English were also penetrating northward to intercept the enemy, Vermont, which had been the highway of war parties, became the scene of many fierce and bloody affrays. The French fortress of St. Frederick, (called afterward, by the English, Crown Point,) afforded great facilities for sudden and successful attacks upon the English settlements. The history of a war on the frontiers is little else than the recital of the exploits, the sufferings, and the deliverance of individuals, of single families, or, at most, of small parties. The first incursion of the Indians was at the "great meadow," (now Putney, Vt.,) a few miles above Fort Dummer. They killed a few individuals at various times, and carried others into captivity. One case of heroism is mentioned with pride. Two Indians captured William Phipps in his field. After they had conducted him some distance, the Indians being some distance apart, Phipps knocked down the nearest Indian with his hoe, and, seizing his gun, shot the other. But, on returning to the fort, he fell into the hands of three other Indians, who killed him.

In August, 1746, a party of nine hundred French and Indians attacked Fort Massachusetts, near the south-west corner of Vermont. The garrison consisted of only twenty-two men, under the command of Sergeant Hawks. Notwithstanding the inferiority of his force, this brave officer, knowing the character of the French commander, resolved to defend the place to the last extremity. For twenty-eight hours, with small-arms only, and a scanty supply of ammunition, he resisted the efforts of the enemy, and kept them at a respectful distance. Habituated to sharp-shooting, the garrison singled out the assailants wherever they exposed themselves, and brought them down at long shot. Instances occurred in which the enemy were thus killed, at the extraordinary distance of sixty rods; and they often fell when they supposed themselves in perfect security. Having at length expended most of his ammunition, the brave commander reluctantly consented to submit, and a capitulation was agreed upon, by which the garrison were to remain prisoners of war until exchanged or redeemed, to be humanely treated, and to be shielded from the cruelty of the Indians. Vaudreuil, in violation of the articles of capitulation, delivered one half of the captives into the hands of the irritated Indians. Hawks[*] lost but one man during the siege, but the enemy, according to information afterward obtained, had forty-seven killed or badly wounded.

In the mean time, Shirley, having effected the conquest of Louisbourg, which must ever remain one of the hardiest enterprises recorded in military annals, determined on the conquest of Canada. His plan, like all previous ones for the accomplishment of that purpose, contemplated a simultaneous attack on Quebec by a fleet, and an expedition by the way of Lake Champlain against Crown Point and Montreal. Like the others, ill-success attended this enterprise.

[*] Sergeant Hawks rose to the rank of lieutenant-colonel in the army, in the war of 1755, and was at the attack on Ticonderoga in 1758, and with the army in the conquest of Canada. Bold, hardy, and enterprising, he acquired the confidence and esteem of his superior officers, and was intrusted with important commands. He was no less valued by the inhabitants of Deerfield, his native town, for his civil qualities.

Early in the year 1747, the fort at Number Four, (now Charlestown,) near Fort Dummer, was attacked by a party of three hundred French and Indians, under the command of a Frenchman named Debeline. It was defended by Captain Phinehas Stevens, and thirty men. The fort being constructed of combustible materials, the enemy believed it possible to set it on fire, and thereby compel the garrison to surrender without further opposition. To effect this, the neighboring fences, and a log hut about forty rods to windward, were soon set on fire, and as the wind was strong, the flames approached, and covered the fort with a dense body of smoke, through which was heard the terrifying yell of the savages, and a constant roar of musketry. Undaunted, the brave little garrison resolved to defend their post to the last extremity, and a novel scheme was adopted to extinguish the approaching flames, which now began to threaten its destruction. By great exertions, no less than eleven trenches, or subterranean galleries, were carried under the walls, of such a depth that men standing in them to extinguish the fire on the exterior walls, were completely protected from the shot of the enemy. Buckets of water, from a well within, were handed to the men, who kept the parapet constantly moistened. Several hundred barrels were thus expended, and the fort rendered perfectly secure from the approaching flames. In the mean time, a brisk fire was continued upon the enemy, when they could be distinguished through the smoke. Thus baffled in his plan, Debeline resolved to carry the place by other means; a sort of carriage was prepared, loaded with burning fagots, and forced toward the fort; flaming arrows were also tried, but his efforts to fire the place proved abortive. On the second day, Debeline proposed a cessation of hostilities until sunrise the next morning, to which Stevens assented; and in the morning, before the time had expired, Debeline approached with fifty men, under a flag, which he planted within twenty rods of the fort. A parley was then agreed on, and Stevens admitted a lieutenant and two men into the fort as hostages, and the same number were sent out to Debeline, who demanded that the garrison should lay down their arms, pack up their provisions in blankets, surrender the fort, and be conducted prisoners to Montreal; and Stevens was requested to meet him without the fort, and give an answer. Stevens accordingly met the French commander, but before he had time to return his answer, Debeline threatened that if the terms were rejected, the fort should be stormed, and in case any of his men should be killed, the garrison should be put to the sword. Stevens coolly replied, that as he had been intrusted by his government with the command of the fort, he should hearken to no terms, until he was satisfied that he could no longer defend it. Stevens returned to the fort and found his men unanimously determined to defend the place or die in the attempt. This resolution was communicated to the French commander about noon; the hostages were exchanged, and the firing was renewed with a shout from the Indians, and it continued until daylight the next morning, when Stevens was familiarly saluted with a "good morning" from the enemy, and a proposition was made for a cessation of arms for two hours. Soon after, two Indians approached with a flag, and promised that if Stevens would sell them provisions, they would leave the place without further efforts. In reply, they were told that five bushels of corn would be given for each captive in Canada, for whom they should give hostages, to remain until the captives should be delivered. In the attack which continued three days, thousands of balls were poured upon the fort, yet not a man of the garrison was killed, and only two wounded. Debeline, convinced that he could not operate upon the fears of his enemy, or gain possession of the place without an assault, continued a distant fire a short time; then reluctantly withdrew from the fort. When the intelligence of this brave defense was received at Boston, Commodore Sir Charles Knowles, who happened to be at that station, was so highly gratified at the conduct of Stevens, that he sent him an elegant sword; and Number Four, when incorporated into a town in 1753, was called after the commodore's name, Charlestown. It should have been named after its heroic defender.

Although baffled in their attempt on Number Four,* Debeline's forces remained on the frontiers, divided into small parties, and were engaged in several severe skirmishes with the hardy English pioneers. Fort Dummer, Bridgman's fort, and others, were the scenes of some of these affrays. Others occurred with bands

---

* This was one of the four townships granted on the east side of the Connecticut by Massachusetts, and then distinguished by no other name than their *number*.

of colonial rangers, who made frequent excursions over the Green Mountains, and sometimes to the vicinity of Crown Point. One of these bands of rangers, consisting of forty men, under the command of Captain Hobbs, met the enemy twelve miles west of Fort Dummer. The latter, one hundred and fifty in number, were commanded by a half-breed named Sackett. Confident of victory from their immense superiority in number, the enemy rushed up impetuously, but were checked by the well-directed fire of Hobbs. The two commanders had been known to each other in time of peace, and were celebrated for their intrepidity. Sackett, who could speak English, in a stentorian voice frequently called upon Hobbs to surrender, and threatened, in case of refusal, to rush in and sacrifice his men with the tomahawk. Hobbs, in tones which shook the forest, as often returned a defiance, and urged his enemy to put his threat in execution. The action continued with undaunted resolution, and, not unfrequently, the enemy approached Hobbs' line, but were driven back to their first position, by the fatal fire of his sharp-sighted marksmen; and thus four hours elapsed without either side giving up an inch of their original ground. At length, finding Hobbs determined on death or victory, and that his own men had suffered severely, Sackett ordered a retreat, carrying off his dead and wounded, and leaving his antagonist to continue his march without further molestation.

In November, 1747, a descent was made upon Saratoga, where about thirty families were collected. A party of French and Indians concealed themselves near the fort at night. In the morning, a few of the Indians approached the fort, and were fired upon by the garrison as soon as they were discovered. The Indians, pretending to be wounded, fell; then rose up, and, running a short distance, fell again. The English rushed out to take them prisoners, when the French, who had been concealed, surrounded and quickly disarmed them. Several were massacred and others were carried into captivity.*

The treaty of Aix-la-Chapelle, in 1748, again gave peace to the colonies. Prisoners were to be released on both sides without ransom, and all conquests mutually restored. This war had been extremely

* This expedition was led by the Abbe Picquet, a distinguished jesuit missionary. He was born in 1708. He became very celebrated in France, at an early age, and seemed rapidly winning his way to the highest distinction in the church; but the activity of his zeal induced him to become a missionary among the Indians. He came to America in 1733, and remained thirty years. He established a mission at La Presentation, (now Ogdensburg,) where he also erected a fort. Mills, workshops and trading-houses were completed in rapid succession. Beginning with only six families in 1749, there were ninety the year following, and four hundred in 1751. His industry and energy were remarkable. He labored from three o'clock in the morning until nine at night. His disinterestedness was extreme. He supported himself by his own exertions, having a daily allowance of only two pounds of bread and a half-pound of pork from the government; which caused the savages to say, on an occasion when they gave him a deer and some partridges, "We doubt not, Father, but that there have been disagreeable expostulations in your stomach, because you have had nothing but pork to eat. Here's something to put your affairs in order." Picquet had the address to attach the Six Nations to the French interests. Three thousand of these Indians were in his colony. He afterward distinguished himself in the war which resulted in the conquest of Canada. When, in 1760, he saw that all was lost, he went to New Orleans by the way of the lakes and the Mississippi, and about two years afterward he returned to France, and died in 1781.

disastrous to the colonies. Many lives were lost, the increase of population was checked, great losses were sustained in the commercial interests of the country, and a burdensome debt of several millions had been incurred. With the return of peace, however, commerce revived, the settlements began to extend, and public credit was restored.

But only a brief interval of repose was allowed to the colonies. In 1756, eight years from the peace of Aix-la-Chapelle, Great Britain again declared war against France, on the ground of the encroachments of the French upon the English territories in America. Some years previous to this war, the French had commenced a chain of posts, designed to extend from the head of the St. Lawrence to the Mississippi, with a view to maintain a communication between their northern possessions and Louisiana. In 1750, the English government granted a large tract of land on the Ohio river to an association called the Ohio company, formed for the purpose of settling the country, and carrying on a trade in furs with the Indians. The French governor of Canada, apprehending both the loss of the fur trade and the interruption of his communications with Louisiana, claimed the whole country between the Ohio and the Alleghanies, and prohibited the further encroachments of the English. He also opened a new communication between Lake Erie and the Ohio, and stationed troops at posts along the line. The Ohio company, thus threatened in their trade, persuaded Governor Dinwiddie of Virginia, in 1753, to send a remonstrance to the French commandant. GEORGE WASHINGTON was the bearer. The commandant returned for answer that he had taken possession of the country by order of the governor-general of Canada, whose orders alone he could regard. The British government, on learning the claim set up by the French, directed the Virginians to resist it by force. In 1754, an expedition was conducted against the French by Washington; but the superior force of the enemy obliged him to capitulate, with the privilege of returning with his troops to Virginia. This was properly the commencement of what is commonly styled the *French war*, although the formal declaration was not made till 1756. In the mean time, the British government recommended the colonies to unite for their common defense. A convention of delegates from all the northern colonies accordingly met at Albany in 1754, and adopted a plan of union; but it was rejected both by the provincial assemblies and by the home government: by the former because it gave too much power to the crown, and by the latter because it gave too little. The substance of the plan was the formation of a grand council, consisting of delegates from the several colonies, subject to the control of a president-general to be appointed by the crown, whose assent should be essential to the adoption of any measure of policy. This council, it was proposed, should have power to enact general laws, apportion the quotas of men and money to be raised by each colony, determine the building of forts, regulate the operations of armies, and concert all measures for their common protection and safety. It is worthy of remark that this plan of union was perfected on the fourth of July, the day which afterward became so memorable in our history. In the spring of 1755, vigorous preparations were made for carrying on the war. An expedition under General Braddock, directed against the French on the Ohio, was unfortunate. Owing to the arrogance and rashness of the commander, the British troops were surprised and defeated, with great loss, by a very inferior force of French and Indians. General Braddock was mortally wounded, and the conduct of the retreat devolved on Washington, who was in command of the colonial militia, and by whom the army was saved from total destruction.

In connection with Braddock's expedition against Fort Du Quesne, two others were concerted: one against Fort Niagara and Frontignac, to be commanded by Governor Shirley of Massachusetts, and one against Crown Point, to be commanded by General William Johnson. The former of these met with so many delays, that when it arrived at Oswego, the season was so far advanced, that prudence forbade the further prosecution of the enterprise.

The forces destined to attack Crown Point, with the requisite military stores, could not be collected at Albany until the last of August, 1755. Thence the army under command of General Johnson, proceeded to the south end of Lake George,* designing to proceed to the outlet of the lake at Ticonderoga, and there erect a fort to aid in the operations against Crown Point. There he learned that an armament, fitted out in France, had eluded an English squadron

* Until this time the lake had been called St. Sacrament, but Johnson gave it the name of Lake George. Recently, efforts have been made to restore to this beautiful lake the original Indian name of Horicon.

sent to intercept it, and had arrived at Quebec; and that Baron Dieskau, commander of the French forces, was rapidly advancing to the defense of Crown Point. Finding that no immediate attack would be made by the English, and being informed that Johnson's camp was not strongly fortified, Dieskau resolved on marching toward the English lines. An express that had been sent out by Johnson, returned about midnight, bringing word that the enemy was within four miles of Fort Edward, apparently intending to attack that post. It was probably only a detached party of Indians that had been seen by the express. This misinformation caused a severe disaster. A council of officers was assembled, who advised that a force should be sent to intercept the enemy, whether defeated or victorious, when on his way back from Fort Edward. Colonel Ephraim Williams, with a thousand troops, and Hendrick, a celebrated Indian chief, with two hundred Indians, were accordingly detached for this purpose, on the morning of September 8th. They had proceeded but four miles, when they encountered the enemy. Dieskau, informed by his runners of their approach, had halted and prepared for their reception, forming his forces in a semicircle, the ends of which were far in advance of the center, and concealed from view by the forest. Into this ambuscade the detachment marched, wholly unsuspicious that any enemy was within several miles. Suddenly the war-whoop resounded in every direction, and a galling fire was opened all along the front and left side of the column. Williams, to obtain a more defensible position, ordered his men to ascend the rising ground on their right. But this only brought them upon the other wing of the French line. Both Williams and Hendrick, with numbers of their followers, fell, and a confused retreat ensued. A large portion of these troops were from western Massachusetts, and there were few families in that district who did not mourn the loss of relatives or friends who were cut off in "the bloody morning scout at Lake George," as this encounter was familiarly designated.*

As the firing came nearer, it was manifest that Williams was defeated; and three hundred men under Colonel Cole, were sent out to cover the retreat. The discomfited soldiers soon began to arrive in large bodies, and at length, Dieskau's troops made their appearance. The order and regularity with which the grenadiers advanced in platoons, with their burnished muskets glittering in the sun, we can readily imagine caused no small trepidation among the raw troops of which Johnson's force was composed. Fortunately, a considerable pause was made by the French before commencing the attack, enabling the men measurably to recover from their panic, and when once engaged, they fought with the calmness and resolution of veterans. The camp was assailed by the grenadiers in front, and by the Canadians and Indians upon both flanks. But a few discharges of artillery against these last, caused them to fall back and secrete themselves behind logs and trees, from whence they afterward maintained only an irregular and nearly harmless fire. General Johnson being wounded, was compelled to retire to his tent, and

* Fitch's History of Washington County.

the command subsequently devolved upon General Lyman, who several times stationed himself in front of the breastwork, the better to inspirit the men and direct their movements. For nearly four hours the battle lasted; and the assailed still standing firm at every point, Dieskau was constrained to order a retreat. This order appears to have been obeyed with more alacrity than any that had been given for some time previous. So hastily did the men withdraw, that their leader, having been wounded in his foot, was unable to keep pace with them. Reclining against a stump to obtain temporary relief from his pain and fatigue, he was discovered by a provincial soldier. Dieskau, to propitiate the soldier, was about drawing out his watch to present to him; whereupon the soldier, deeming he was searching for a pistol, discharged his musket at the baron, giving him a grievous wound in the hip, of which he died twelve years afterward. The French retreated to the ground where the forenoon engagement had occurred, and there paused for the night, searching out the bodies of the slain, and rifling them of whatever they found of value upon them.*

This victory revived the spirits of the colonists, depressed by the recent defeat of General Braddock; but the success was not improved by General Johnson. With an apathy quite unaccountable, he failed to follow up his victory, and drive the French from Lake Champlain, as he might easily have done. The remainder of the campaign was employed in the erection of Fort William Henry, at the head of Lake

* Fitch's History of Washington County.

George. In the fall his army was discharged, with the exception of six hundred men who occupied the forts on the frontier. The French retained possession of Ticonderoga,* and fortified it. Thus ended the campaign of 1755. It opened with the brightest prospects: immense preparations had been made, yet not one of the objects of the three principal expeditions had been attained; and, by this failure, the whole frontier was exposed to the ravages of the Indians, which were accompanied by their usual acts of barbarity. The expedition under Braddock had been conducted with extreme imprudence and rashness, and had terminated in defeat and disgrace. The movement against Niagara, under Shirley, had been too extensive in its plan to be concluded in one campaign; and at the northward, Baron Dieskau had given Johnson an opportunity to gain a victory without leaving his camp or exposing himself to danger.

The army under General Johnson, on the frontiers of New York, although it checked incursions to the north-west quarter of Massachusetts, afforded but little security to the frontiers on Connecticut river. The St. Francis tribe of Indians, commanding an easy route through Lake Memphremagog and several neighboring streams, made frequent inroads, and killed many persons. But the most disastrous affair that occurred on Connecticut river, was at Bridgman's

* The original Indian name was *Cheonderoga,* signifying *noisy,* in reference to the rush of waters at the outlet of Lake George. It was at first called by the French *Carillon,* a word having the same signification as the Indian name.

Fort. A fortified house had been destroyed at the same place in 1747, and another was built soon after, and is still standing in Vernon, Vt. The Indians found the men belonging to this fort at work in a field, and shot them. Three women, with eleven children, were taken prisoners and carried to Crown Point.

Another band of Indians, the year previous, had captured several persons at Number Four, and had taken them to Canada. Among these prisoners was a Mrs. Johnson, who, on the second day's journey, gave birth to a daughter, and named her *Captive*.* In this critical situation, she had little hope of escaping the hatchet; but, contrary to their usual conduct, the Indians treated her and her infant with tenderness, carrying them part of their route on a litter, and they took much pains in nursing the infant. After a painful captivity, this little band of sufferers was ransomed, and returned again to their friends.

The colonies, considerably encouraged by the results of the campaign of 1755, determined to renew and increase their exertions. General Shirley, to whom the superintendence of all the military operations

---

* Captive Johnson was married to Colonel George Kimball, and was still living a few years ago. At Vernon, near where she was born, a monument has been erected, on which is the following inscription : "This is near the spot that the Indians encamped the night after they took Mr. Johnson and family, Mr. Labaree and Mr. Farnsworth, August 30th, 1754, and Mrs. Johnson was delivered of her child half a mile up this brook.
"When trouble is near the Lord is kind,
  He hears the Captive's cry;
  He can subdue the savage mind,
  And learn it sympathy."
[*See Thompson's Gazeteer.*

had been confided, assembled a council of war at New York, to concert a plan for the ensuing year. He proposed that expeditions should be carried on against Du Quesne, Niagara, and Crown Point, and that a body of troops should be sent, by the way of the rivers Kennebec and Chaudiere, to alarm the French for the safety of Quebec. This plan was unanimously adopted by the council. Shirley, on the last of January, returned to Boston to meet the assembly of Massachusetts, of which colony he was governor. He endeavored to persuade them to concur in the measures proposed; but, disgusted with the proceedings of the last campaign, and especially at General Johnson for neglecting to pursue his advantages, they were unwilling to engage in offensive operations, unless the command of their forces should be given to General Winslow, who had acquired popularity by his success in Nova Scotia. Their wishes were complied with, and their concurrence was then granted. In April, news arrived from Great Britain, that the conduct of General Johnson, instead of being censured, was considered highly meritorious; that, as a reward for his success, the king had conferred upon him the title of baronet, and parliament a grant of five thousand pounds sterling; that his majesty disapproved of the conduct of Shirley, and had determined to remove him from command. This information not being official, General Shirley continued his preparations with his usual activity and zeal. While engaged in collecting at Albany, the troops from the different colonies, General Webb brought from England, official information of his removal. On the 25th of June, General Abercrombie arrived and took command of the army. It now consisted of about twelve thousand men, and was more numerous, and better prepared for the field, than any army that had ever been assembled in America.

The change of commanders delayed the operations of the English army. The French were active; and on the 12th of July, General Abercrombie received intelligence that they meditated an attack upon Oswego, a post of the utmost importance. General Webb was ordered to prepare to march with a regiment for the defense of that place. In the mean time, Lord Loudon, who had been appointed commander-in-chief over all the British forces in the colonies, arrived in America. Amidst the ceremonies which followed, the affairs of the war were forgotten. General Webb did not begin his march until the 12th of August. Before he had proceeded far, he learned that Oswego was actually besieged by a large army of French and Indians. Alarmed for his own safety, he proceeded no further, but employed his troops in erecting fortifications for their defense. General Montcalm, the commander of the French troops in Canada, began the siege of Oswego on the 12th of August. On the 14th, the English commander having been killed, terms of surrender were proposed by the garrison, and were agreed to. These terms were shamefully violated. Several of the British officers and soldiers were insulted, robbed, and massacred by the Indians. Most of the sick were scalped in the hospitals, and the French general delivered twenty of the garrison to the savages, that being the number they had lost during the siege. Those unhappy persons were, doubtless, according to the Indian custom, tortured and burnt. In this expedition the French took fourteen hundred prisoners, and an immense quantity of provisions and munitions of war. General Webb was permitted to retreat, unmolested, to Albany. Lord Loudon pretended it was now too late in the season to attempt any thing further, though the troops under General Winslow were within a few days' march of Ticonderoga and Crown Point, and were sufficient in number to justify an attack upon those places. He devoted the remainder of the season to making preparations for an early and vigorous campaign the ensuing year. This spring had opened with still more brilliant prospects than the last; and the season closed without the occurrence of a single event that was honorable to the British arms, or advantageous to the colonies. This want of success was justly attributed to the removal of the provincial officers, who were well acquainted with the theater of operations, but whom the ministry, desirous of checking the growth of talents in the colonies, were unwilling to employ. Yet the several assemblies, though they saw themselves thus slighted, and their money annually squandered, made all the preparations that were required of them for the next campaign.

In the campaign of 1756, two persons, who were destined to win imperishable honor in the war of the Revolution, received their first military discipline. These were Israel Putnam and John Stark. There were no great engagements during the year in which they could distinguish themselves; but in the arduous duties of *scouts* or rangers, they were eminently useful, and were soon found to be foremost among the skillful, active and daring. In January, 1757, Major Rogers, in whose company of rangers Stark * was a lieutenant, was ordered on a reconnoitering expedition down Lake George toward Ticonderoga. Traveling now on the

* Stark was born in New Hampshire, August 28th, 1728. His early life was one of great hardship. In 1752, he was taken prisoner by the Indians. While on a hunting excursion with three other persons, far to the north of the English settlements on the Connecticut, and while separated from his companions, he was seized by a party of ten Indians.

being questioned about his companions, he pointed in a direction opposite to that which they had taken, and thus succeeded in leading the Indians two miles out of the way. His companions, unfortunately, becoming alarmed at his absence, and ignorant of its cause, fired several guns as a signal to him. This betrayed them to the savages. But John had the courage, as the Indians were coming up to them, to hail them and urge them to escape. While they were retreating, four Indians fired upon them, but, at the moment of the discharge, John struck the guns of two, and his brother William was by this means enabled to escape. John was severely beaten for this. When the Indians returned to St. Francis, the captives were compelled to "run the gauntlet." One of them was severely beaten; but Stark snatched a hatchet from the nearest Indian, and attacked with great fury all who attempted to strike him. This pleased the old men of the tribe, and won Stark much favor. He appears to have caught the humor of the Indians, and to have known how to approach them on the side of their prejudices. On one occasion, he was ordered by them to hoe their corn. Well aware that they regarded labor of this kind as fit only for squaws and slaves, he took care to cut up the corn and spare the weeds, in order to give them a suitable idea of his want of skill in unmanly labor. As this experiment upon their good nature did not answer its desired object, he threw his hoe into the river, declaring "it was the business not of warriors, but of squaws to hoe corn." This spirited deportment gained him the title of "young chief," and the honor of adoption into the tribe.—*See Everett's Life of Stark.*

ice and now on snow-shoes, they, on the third day, crossed to Lake Champlain, and seeing some sleds approach, hastened toward and captured some of them. From the prisoners they learned there was a large force at Ticonderoga. Knowing that those who escaped would convey intelligence which would speedily bring out an overwhelming company in pursuit of him, Rogers directed an immediate return to Fort William Henry. On their way back, tramping over the snow in single file, as the foremost men gained the summit of a hill, they unexpectedly found themselves close upon two hundred of the enemy, who were drawn up in a semicircle to receive them. The rangers recoiled before the fire that blazed in their very faces, and crimsoning the snow with their blood, they reached the rear under Stark, who was fifteen rods distant on the summit of another hill. They here formed their line, and firmly stood, in snow four feet in depth, and repelled every attack of the enemy from two o'clock until nightfall. Rogers, wounded upon the head, and by a bullet through his wrist, was so disabled that the entire command devolved on Stark. At sunset, some of the men suggested that they ought to make their escape before the piercing cold of the winter's night closed upon them; but Stark, standing himself where the shot fell thickest, and knowing that their safety depended on maintaining their ground till after dark, threatened to shoot the first man who should attempt to fly. Evening came, and the French now abandoned the combat, and withdrew, leaving half their number scattered upon the trampled and blood-stained snow of the hill-side, sleeping that sleep that knows no waking. Forty-eight of the rangers remained unwounded, and the company now dragged themselves through the woods and snow the livelong night, reaching the shore of Lake George in the morning. All were now quite exhausted with their fatigues, and the wounded were wholly unable to advance further on foot. Stark hereupon generously offered to travel with two others to Fort William Henry, at the opposite end of the lake, and obtain sleds for conveying the wounded. He accordingly departed, and reached the fort in the evening. The sleds being procured, he immediately set out with them to return to his comrades, traveling all night and arriving at their bivouac upon the following morning. And finally he drew a loaded sleigh back to the fort, reaching there in the evening. He thus stood out three days and two nights of severe and incessant toil, engaged for nearly four hours in a hot combat, and the remainder of the time in traveling over snow and ice. Such was the future hero of Bennington.

At the commencement of the year 1757, a council was held at Boston, composed of Lord Loudon and the colonial governors. At this council, his lordship proposed that New England should raise four thousand troops for the coming campaign, and that New York and New Jersey should supply a proportionate number. These requisitions were complied with, and in the spring he found himself at the head of a very considerable army. Admiral Holborn arrived at Halifax in July, with a powerful squadron, and a reinforcement of five thousand men under the command of Lord Howe. Lord Loudon sailed from New York with six thousand regulars to join these troops at the place of their arrival. Instead of the complex operations undertaken in previous campaigns, he limited his plan to a single object. Leaving the posts on Lake Champlain strongly garrisoned, he resolved to direct his whole disposable force against Louisbourg; Halifax having been determined on as the place of rendezvous for the fleet and army destined for the expedition. Information was soon received, however, that a French fleet had lately sailed from Brest; that Louisbourg was garrisoned by six thousand regulars exclusive of provincials; and that it was also defended by seventeen line-of-battle ships which were moored in the harbor. There being no hope of success against so formidable a force, the enterprise was deferred until the next year; Loudon proceeded to New York, and the colonial troops were dismissed.

The Marquis de Montcalm, availing himself of the absence of the principal part of the English force, advanced with an army of nine thousand men, and laid siege to Fort William Henry. Montcalm had won a distinguished reputation on the continent of Europe, and had met with extraordinary success in America. The conquest of Oswego had raised his fame among the Indians, and given him the command of almost all their tribes and commerce. He pursued the advantages he had gained, with much discretion. The garrison at Fort William Henry consisted of between three and four thousand regulars under the command of Colonel Monroe, and its fortifications were strong and in good order; and for the additional security of this important post, General Webb was stationed at Fort Edward with an army of four thousand men. The French commander, however, urged his approaches with such vigor, that, within six days after the investment of the fort, Colonel Monroe, the commandant, having in vain solicited succor from General Webb, found it necessary to surrender by capitulation. The garrison was to be allowed the honors of war, and to be protected against the Indians until within the reach of Fort Edward; but the next morning, a great number of Indians, having been permitted to enter the lines, began to plunder; and meeting with no opposition, they fell upon the sick and wounded, whom they immediately massacred. Their appetite for carnage being excited, the defenseless troops were attacked with fiend-like fury. Monroe in vain implored Montcalm to provide the stipulated guard, and the massacre proceeded. All was turbulence and horror. On every side savages were butchering and scalping their wretched victims. Their hideous yells, the groans of the dying, and the frantic shrieks of others shrinking from the uplifted tomahawk, were heard by the French unmoved. The fury of the savages was permitted to rage without restraint until fifteen hundred were killed, or hurried captives into the wilderness. The day after this awful tragedy, Major Putnam* was sent with his rangers to watch

---

* Israel Putnam was born at Salem, Massachusetts, January 7th, 1718. Courage, enterprise, activity and perseverance were his prominent characteristics. He was also distinguished for a faithful discharge of all the duties of his station, and for the most undeviating principles of honor, humanity and benevolence. In 1739, he removed to Pomfret, Connecticut, where he applied himself to agricultural pursuits until the opening

the motions of the enemy. When he came to the shore of the lake, their rear was hardly beyond the reach of musket shot. The prospect was horrible in the extreme; the fort demolished; the barracks and buildings yet burning; innumerable fragments of human carcasses still broiling in the decaying fires; and dead bodies, mangled with tomahawks and scalping-knives, in all the wantonness of Indian barbarity, were everywhere scattered around. Who can forbear exclaiming with the poet,

"Man is to man the surest, sorest ill!"

Thus ended the third campaign in America; happily forming the last of a series of disasters resulting from folly and mismanagement, rather than from want of means and military strength. The successes of the French left the colonies in a gloomy state. By the acquisition of Fort William Henry, they had obtained full possession of the Lakes Champlain and George; and by the destruction of Oswego, they had acquired the dominion over those other lakes which connect the St. Lawrence with the waters of the Mississippi. The first afforded the easiest admission from the northern colonies into Canada, or from Canada into those colonies; the last united Canada to Louisiana. By the continued possession of Fort Du Quesne, they preserved their ascendancy over the Indians, and held undisturbed

of the war with the French in 1755, when he was appointed to the command of a company of rangers. His hardy and adventurous disposition always led him to the post of the greatest fatigue and danger, and he often came near falling into the hands of the enemy, or being slain in his frequent skirmishes with them. His services during the campaign of 1756, had been rewarded by promotion to the rank of major.

control of the country west of the Alleghany mountains. The British nation was alarmed and indignant, and the king found it necessary to change his councils. At the head of the new ministry, he placed the celebrated William Pitt, afterward earl of Chatham, who was raised by his talents from the humble post of ensign in the guards, to the control of the destinies of a mighty empire; under his administration public confidence revived, and the nation seemed inspired with new life and vigor. He was equally popular in both hemispheres; and so promptly did the governors of the northern colonies obey the requisitions of his circular letter of 1757, that by May, in the following year, Massachusetts had seven thousand, Connecticut five thousand, and New Hampshire three thousand troops, prepared to take the field. The zeal of Massachusetts was particularly ardent. The people of Boston endured taxes which took away two-thirds of the income on real estate; one-half of the effective men in the province were on some sort of military duty; and the transports for carrying the troops to Halifax were ready to sail in fourteen days from the time of their engagement. The mother country was not less active. While her fleets blockaded or captured the French armaments, she dispatched Admiral Boscawen to Halifax with a formidable squadron of ships, and an army of twelve thousand men. Lord Loudon was replaced by General Abercrombie, who, early in the spring of 1758, was ready to enter upon the campaign at the head of fifty thousand men, the most powerful army ever yet seen in America.

In the winter of 1757, when Colonel Haviland was

commandant at Fort Edward, the barracks adjoining the north-west bastion, took fire. They stood but twelve feet from the magazine, which contained three hundred barrels of powder. On its first discovery, the fire raged with great violence. The commandant endeavored in vain, by discharging some pieces of heavy artillery against the supporters of this range of barracks, to level them with the ground. Putnam arrived from an island where he was stationed, at the moment when the blaze approached that end which was contiguous to the magazine. With the promptness, energy and daring that always characterized him, Putnam at once made a vigorous attempt to extinguish the conflagration. A way was opened by the postern gate to the river, and the soldiers were employed in bringing water, which he, having mounted on a ladder to the eaves of the building, received and threw upon the flame. It continued, notwithstanding their utmost efforts, to gain upon them. He stood, enveloped in smoke, so near the sheet of fire, that a pair of blanket mittens was burnt entirely from his hands. He was supplied with another pair dipped in water. Colonel Haviland, fearing that he would perish in the flames, called to him to come down; but he entreated that he might be suffered to remain, since destruction must inevitably ensue if their exertions should be remitted. The gallant commandant, not less astonished than charmed at the boldness of his conduct, forbade any more effects to be carried out of the fort, animated the men to redoubled diligence, and exclaimed, "If we must be blown up, we will all go together." At last, when the barracks were seen to be tumbling, Putnam descended, placed himself at the magazine, and continued, from an incessant rotation of replenished buckets, to pour water upon its blazing walls. The outside planks were already consumed by the proximity of the fire, and as only one thickness of timber intervened, the trepidation now became general and extreme. Putnam, still undaunted, covered with a cloud of cinders, and scorched with the intensity of the heat, maintained his position until the fire subsided, and the danger was over. He had contended for one hour and a half with that terrible element. His legs, his thighs, his arms, and his face were blistered; and when he pulled off his second pair of mittens, the skin from his hands and fingers followed them. It was a month before he recovered. The commandant, to whom his merits had before endeared him, could not stifle the emotions of gratitude due to the man who had been instrumental in preserving the magazine, the fort, and the garrison.

Three points of attack were involved in the campaign of 1758: Louisbourg, Ticonderoga, and Du Quesne. General Amherst conducted the enterprise against Louisbourg with an army of fourteen thousand men. Preparations had been made on such an extensive scale, that the commander at Louisbourg soon saw that all resistance would be in vain, and he accepted terms of capitulation. The command of the St. Lawrence was by this surrender placed in the hands of the English. The expedition against Fort Du Quesne was equally successful; the garrison escaping down the Ohio, the evening before the arrival of the British army.

The army destined to execute the plans against

Ticonderoga, was commanded by General Abercrombie, and consisted of more than fifteen thousand men, attended by a formidable train of artillery. Early in July, the general embarked his troops on Lake George, and commenced operations against Ticonderoga. After debarkation at the landing-place, in a cove on the west side of the lake, the troops were formed into four columns, the British in the center, and the provincials on the flanks. In this order they marched toward the advanced guard of the French, which, consisting of one battalion only, posted in a logged camp—destroyed what was in their power, and made a precipitate retreat. While Abercrombie was continuing his march in the woods toward Ticonderoga, the columns were thrown into confusion, and in some degree entangled with each other. At this juncture, Lord Howe, at the head of the right center column, fell in with a part of the advanced guard of the enemy, which had been lost in the wood in retreating from Lake George, and immediately attacked and dispersed it, killing a considerable number, and taking one hundred and forty-eight prisoners. This success was attended by the loss of the gallant nobleman, who fell in leading the attack. The English army, without further opposition, took possession of a post within two miles of Ticonderoga. Abercrombie, having learned from the prisoners the strength of the enemy at that fortress, and, from an engineer, the condition of their works, resolved on an immediate storm, and made instant disposition for an assault. The troops having received orders to march up briskly, rush upon the enemy's fire, and reserve their own till they had passed a breastwork, marched to the assault with great intrepidity. Unlooked-for impediments, however, occurred. In front of the breastwork, to a considerable distance, trees had been felled with their branches outward, many of which were sharpened to a point, by means of which the assailants were not only retarded in their advance, but, becoming entangled among the boughs, were exposed to a very galling fire. Finding it impracticable to pass the breastwork, which was eight or nine feet high, and much stronger than had been represented, General Abercrombie, after a contest of near four hours, ordered a retreat, and the next day resumed his former camp on the south side of Lake George. In this brave but ill-judged assault, nearly two thousand of the assailants were killed and wounded, while the loss of the enemy, who were covered during the whole action, was inconsiderable. General Abercrombie immediately recrossed Lake George, and entirely abandoned the project of capturing Ticonderoga.

In the month of August, five hundred men were employed, under the orders of Majors Rogers and Putnam, to watch the motions of the enemy near Ticonderoga. At South Bay they separated the party into two equal divisions, and Rogers took a position on Wood creek, twelve miles distant from Putnam. Upon being, some time afterward, discovered, they formed a reunion, and concerted measures for returning to Fort Edward. Their march through the woods was in three divisions, by files: the right commanded by Rogers, the left by Putnam, and the center by

Captain D'Ell. At the moment of moving, the famous French partisan, Molang, who had been sent with five hundred men to intercept their party, was not more than one mile and a half distant from them. Major Putnam was just emerging from the thicket, into the common forest, when the enemy rose, and, with discordant yells and whoops, commenced an attack upon the right of his division. Surprised, but undismayed, Putnam halted, returned the fire, and passed the word for the other divisions to advance to his support. D'Ell came. The action, though widely scattered, and principally fought between man and man, soon grew general, and intensely warm.

Major Putnam, perceiving it would be impracticable to cross the creek in his rear, determined to maintain his ground. Inspired by his example, the officers and men behaved with great bravery; sometimes they fought collectively in open view, and sometimes individually under cover: taking aim from behind the bodies of trees, and acting in a manner independent of each other. For himself, having discharged his fusee several times, at length it missed fire, while the muzzle was pressed against the breast of a large and well-proportioned savage. This warrior, availing himself of the indefensible attitude of his adversary, with a tremendous war-whoop, sprang forward with his lifted hatchet, and compelled him to surrender; and, having disarmed and bound him fast to a tree, returned to the battle.

The intrepid Captains, D'Ell and Harman, who now commanded, were forced to give ground, for a little distance; the savages, conceiving this to be the certain harbinger of victory, rushed impetuously on, with dreadful and redoubled cries. But the two partisans, collecting a handful of brave men, gave the pursuers so warm a reception, as to oblige them, in turn, to retreat a little beyond the spot at which the action had commenced. Here they made a stand. This change of ground placed the tree to which Putnam was tied, directly between the hottest fire of the two parties. Human imagination can hardly figure to itself a more deplorable situation. The balls flew incessantly from either side; many struck the tree, while some passed through the sleeves and skirts of his coat. In this state of jeopardy, unable to move his body, to stir his limbs, or even to incline his head, he remained more than an hour — so equally balanced, and so obstinate was the fight! At one moment, while the battle swerved in favor of the enemy, a young savage chose an odd way of displaying his humor. He found Putnam bound — he might have dispatched him at a single blow — but he loved better to excite the terrors of the prisoner, by hurling a tomahawk at his head; or rather, it would seem, his object was to see how near he could throw it without touching him. The weapon stuck in the tree a number of times, at a hair's breadth distance from the mark. When the Indian had finished his amusement, a French officer, perceiving Putnam, came up to him, and, leveling a fusee within a foot of his breast, attempted to discharge it — it missed fire. Ineffectually did the intended victim solicit the treatment due to his situation, by repeating that he was a prisoner of war. The degenerate Frenchman, dead to sensibility, violently and repeatedly pushed the muzzle of the gun against Putnam's ribs, and finally gave him a cruel blow on his jaw with the butt-end of his piece. After this dastardly deed he left him.

At length, the active intrepidity of D'Ell and Harman, seconded by the persevering valor of their followers, prevailed. They drove from the field the enemy, who left about ninety dead behind them. As they were retiring, Putnam was untied by the Indian who had made him prisoner, and whom he afterward called master. Having been conducted for some distance from the place of action, he was stripped of his coat, vest, stockings, and shoes; loaded with as many packs of the wounded as could be piled upon him; strongly pinioned, and his wrists tied as closely together as they could be pulled with a cord. After he had marched through no pleasant paths, in this painful manner, for many a tedious mile, the party (who were excessively fatigued) halted to breathe. His hands were now immoderately swelled from the tightness of the ligature, and the pain had become intolerable. His feet were so much scratched that the blood dropped fast from them. Exhausted with bearing a burden above his strength, and frantic with torments exquisite beyond endurance, he entreated the Irish interpreter to implore, as the last and only grace he desired of the savages, that they would knock him on the head at once, or loose his hands. A French officer, instantly interposing, ordered his hands to be unbound, and some of the packs to be taken off. By this time, the Indian who captured him, and who had been absent with the wounded, coming up, gave him a pair of moccasins, and expressed great indignation at the unworthy treatment his prisoner had suffered.

That savage chief again returned to the care of the wounded, and the Indians, about two hundred in number, went before the rest of the party to the place where the whole were that night to encamp. They took with them Major Putnam, on whom, besides innumerable other outrages, they had the barbarity to inflict a deep wound with a tomahawk in the left cheek. His sufferings were, in this place, to be consummated. A scene of horror, infinitely greater than had ever met his eyes before, was now preparing. It was determined to roast him alive. For this purpose they led him into a dark forest, stripped him naked, bound him to a tree, and piled dry brush, with other fuel, at a small distance in a circle around him. They accompanied their labors, as if for his funeral dirge, with screams and sounds inimitable but by savage voices. They then set the piles on fire. A sudden shower damped the rising flame. Still they strove to kindle it, until, at last, the blaze ran fiercely round the circle. Major Putnam soon began to feel the scorching heat.

His hands were so tied that he could move his body. He often shifted sides as the fire approached. This sight, at the very idea of which all but savages must shudder, afforded the highest diversion to his inhuman tormentors, who demonstrated the delirium of their joy by corresponding yells, dances, and gesticulations. He doubted not that his final hour was inevitably come. He summoned all his resolution, and composed his mind as far as circumstances could admit, to bid an eternal farewell to all he held most dear. To quit the world would scarcely have cost him a single pang, but for the idea of home, but for the remembrance of domestic endearments, of the affectionate partner of his soul, and of their beloved offspring. His thoughts were ultimately fixed on a happier state of existence, beyond the tortures he was beginning to endure. The bitterness of death, even of that death which is accompanied with the keenest agonies, was in a manner past — nature, with a feeble struggle, was quitting its last hold on sublunary things, when a French officer rushed through the crowd, opened a way by scattering the burning brands, and unbound the victim. It was Molang himself, to whom a savage, unwilling to see another human sacrifice immolated, had run and communicated the tidings. That commandant spurned and severely reprimanded the barbarians whose nocturnal powwows and hellish orgies he suddenly ended. Putnam did not want for feeling or gratitude. The French commander, fearing to trust him alone with them, remained until he could deliver him in safety into the hands of his master.

The next day he was allowed his blanket and moccasins, and permitted to march without carrying any pack, or receiving any insult. To allay his extreme hunger, a little bear's meat was given him, which he sucked through his teeth. At night the party arrived at Ticonderoga, and the prisoner was placed under the care of a French guard. The savages, who had been prevented from glutting their diabolical thirst for blood, took another opportunity of manifesting their malevolence for the disappointment, by horrid grimaces and angry gestures; but they were no more suffered to offer violence or personal indignity to him. Colonel Peter Schuyler was then a prisoner among the French. No sooner had he heard of Major Putnam's arrival, than he went and found him, in a comfortless condition, without coat, waistcoat or hose; the remnant of his clothing miserably dirty and ragged; his beard long and squalid; his legs torn by thorns and briers; and his face gashed with wounds and swollen with bruises. Through Colonel Schuyler's intervention, Putnam was treated according to his rank, and clothed in a decent manner. The following year an opportunity was afforded for an exchange of prisoners, and Putnam was released.*

* On his return from Canada, Putnam was accompanied by Mrs. Howe, known as the "fair captive," who had been taken at Bridgman's Fort in 1756. Her history was very affecting. Her first husband was William Phipps, an account of whose death, after having slain two of his Indian captors, near Fort Dummer, has already been related. Her second husband was Mr. Howe, who was also slain at the time of her captivity. On the march to Canada, she had endured extreme suffering, the poignancy of which was increased by the cruel treatment which her children received from the Indians. She was taken to Crown Point, and from thence, by the way of Montreal, to the village of St. Francis; her master having failed to sell her. "Our provisions," she says, in her deeply affecting narrative, "were so scanty, as well as insipid and unsavory, the weather was so cold, and the traveling so very bad, that it almost seemed as if I must have perished on the way. The lips of my poor child were sometimes so benumbed, that, when I put it to my breast, it could not, till it grew warm, imbibe the nourishment requisite for its support. While we were at Montreal, we went into the house of a certain French gentleman, whose lady, on being sent for, and coming into the

The campaign of 1758 had been highly honorable to the British arms, and the result of it was very important. Of the three expeditions, two had completely succeeded, and the leader of the third had

room where I was, to examine me, seeing I had an infant, exclaimed suddenly in this manner: 'D—— it, I will not buy a woman that has a child to look after.' There was a swill-pail standing near me, in which I observed several crusts and crumbs of bread swimming on the surface of the greasy liquor it contained. Sorely pinched with hunger, I skimmed them of with my hands and ate them; and this was all the refreshment which the house afforded me." Mrs. Howe's children, being claimed by different Indians, were separated from their mother and from each other. Even her babe was snatched from her. "This," she says, in her narrative, "was a severe trial. The babe clung to my bosom with all its might; but I was obliged to pluck it thence, and deliver it, shrieking and screaming enough to penetrate a heart of stone, into the hands of those unfeeling wretches, whose tender mercies may be termed cruel." It was taken to Missisco, where, some weeks after, Mrs. Howe was permitted to visit it. "I had preserved my milk," she says, "in hopes of seeing my beloved child again. And here I found it, it is true, but in a condition that afforded me no great satisfaction — it being greatly emaciated and almost starved. I took it in my arms, and put its face to mine, and it instantly bit me with such violence, that it seemed as if I must have parted with a piece of my cheek. I was permitted to lodge with it that and the two following nights; but every morning that intervened, the Indians, I suppose on purpose to torment me, sent me away to another wigwam, which stood at a little distance, though not so far from the one in which my distressed infant was confined, but that I could plainly hear its incessant cries, and heart-rending lamentations." During her rambles with the Indians, she was frequently on the point of perishing with hunger, and as often subjected to hardships seemingly intolerable. On one occasion she was informed by a friendly Indian, that one of her children was in a wigwam seven miles distant, and she determined to visit him. "While I was busy in contemplating this affair," she says, "the Indians obtained a little bread, of which they gave me a small share. I did not taste a morsel of it myself, but saved it all for my poor child, if I should be so lucky as to find him. At length, having obtained leave of my keepers to be absent for one day, I set off made an important conquest. To the commanding talents of Pitt, and the confidence which they inspired, this change of fortune must be chiefly attributed; and in no respects were these talents more strikingly displayed than in the choice of men to execute his plans. The advantages of this campaign

early in the morning, and beheld, as I drew nigh, my little son without the camp. He seemed to be nearly starved. I took him in my arms, and he spoke to me these words in the Indian tongue : 'Mother, are you come?' I took him into the wigwam with me, and observing a number of Indian children in it, I distributed all the bread which I had reserved for my own child, among them all; otherwise I should have given great offense. My little boy appeared to be very fond of his new mother, kept as near me as possible while I stayed, and when I told him I must go, he fell as though he had been knocked down with a club." Two of Mrs. Howe's daughters were of marriageable age, and to add to the number of her miseries, the Indians selected a couple of their young men to marry them. The fright and disgust which the intelligence of this intention occasioned to these poor young creatures, added infinitely to the sorrows and perplexities of their frantic mother. But she found an opportunity of conveying to the governor a petition that her daughters might be received into a convent, for the sake of securing the salvation of their souls. Happily, this expedient succeeded. After Mrs. Howe had been a year with the Indians, she was purchased by an old Frenchman, in whose family new trials awaited her. She was still beautiful, and both her master and his son, who held a commission in the French army, became passionately fond of her, and she was greatly embarrassed by their importunities, from which she saw no way of escape. Finally, she found an opportunity of telling the story of her woes to Colonel Peter Schuyler, who was then a prisoner at Montreal. He immediately endeavored to procure her liberty ; but the Frenchman who had purchased her from the savages, unwilling to part with so fair a purchase, demanded an immense ransom. Colonel Schuyler, however, obtained from the governor an order that she should be given up for the price that had been paid for her; nor did his active goodness rest, until he had restored every one of her five sons to her. One of her daughters subsequently married a French officer, and the other returned home. Such is a brief narrative of the sufferings of one of the early Vermont matrons.

had, however, been purchased by an expensive effort, and corresponding exhaustion of provincial strength; and when, by his persuasion, the colonies resolved upon making the most vigorous preparation for the next, they soon discovered that their resources were by no means commensurate with their zeal.

Notwithstanding these difficulties, it was resolved to signalize the year 1759 by the complete conquest of Canada. The plan of the campaign was, that three powerful armies should enter the French possessions by three different routes, and attack all their strongholds at nearly the same time. At the head of one division, Brigadier-general Wolfe, a young officer who had signalized himself at the siege of Louisbourg, was to ascend the St. Lawrence, and to proceed against Quebec, escorted by a strong fleet to coöperate with his troops. The central and main army, composed of British and provincials, was to be conducted against Ticonderoga and Crown Point, by General Amherst, the new commander-in-chief, who, after making himself master of these places, was to proceed on Lake Champlain, and by the way of the Richelieu river to the St. Lawrence, and, descending that river, form a junction with Wolfe before Quebec. The third army, to be composed principally of colonial troops, reinforced by a strong body of friendly Indians, was to be commanded by General Prideaux, who was to lead this division first against Niagara, and, after the reduction of that place, to embark on Lake Ontario, and proceed down the St. Lawrence against Montreal. The second of these expeditions properly belongs to the scope of this narrative; while the others can only be described sufficiently to show their influence upon the military operations carried on by way of Lake Champlain.

Early in the year 1759, General Amherst commenced preparations for his part of the enterprise. But so many difficulties occurred to retard the operations of his army in that unsettled part of the country, that the summer was already far advanced, before he could pass Lake George with his troops and artillery. Aware of the danger of surprise, and not unmindful of the disaster that the British troops had sustained the year before, this able and judicious officer proceeded with the greatest circumspection: leaving nothing to chance, but making provision for every difficulty or opposition that could be foreseen. At length, in the latter end of July, he arrived in the vicinity of Ticonderoga, with his army of regulars and provincials in excellent order, and amply supplied with artillery, military stores, and provisions. The enemy had watched all his motions, in the hope of finding an opportunity to gain some advantage; but they ventured to make no opposition to his troops, either when crossing the lake, or effecting their landing. Having passed the lake and landed his stores, Amherst immediately began to make preparations to reduce the fortress by a regular siege. At first the enemy appeared determined to make a stubborn defense. They soon found that they had an able officer to oppose; that Amherst was cautious, resolute, well prepared for undertaking the siege, and not disposed to subject anything to unnecessary risk or hazard. Despairing of making a successful defense, and having orders to retreat from place to place toward the center of operations at Quebec, rather than to run the risk of diminishing the French force by surrendering prisoners of war, they set about dismantling the fortifications; and, having done some small injuries to the works, abandoned them and retired to Crown Point; leaving their heavy artillery, several sunken boats, and the works but little damaged, though on fire.

Having succeeded in his attempts against Ticonderoga, Amherst began to repair and enlarge the fortifications; and to prepare his bateaux and other vessels for an expedition against Crown Point. Scouting and ranging parties were constantly employed, hovering in the neighborhood of that place, and watching all the motions of the enemy. One of these parties brought intelligence that the French had also abandoned Crown Point and were gone down the lake without destroying the works. Amherst detached a body of rangers to take possession of the place; and on the 4th of August embarked with his army, landed the same day, and placed his troops within the enemy's works. Thus was effected the reduction of Ticonderoga and Crown Point. No sooner was their conquest completed, than Amherst undertook the erection of new works, strengthened and enlarged the old ones, and began another fort: determined that the enemy should never again obtain possession of a post which had been so dangerous and distressing to the British provinces. The French troops retired to the Isle Aux Noix at the north end of Lake Champlain.

Crown Point had been in the possession of the French for thirty years, and from the time of its erection had afforded facilities for predatory excursions into the English colonies; and many were the prisoners who had there suffered all the barbarities that savage ingenuity could devise. Its conquest insured safety to the frontiers of New England from incursions by way of Lake Champlain; but another channel, through which the settlements on the Connecticut had been harassed, remained still open. This was the Indian village of St. Francis, situated at the mouth of the river of that name. This place the Indians had enriched with the pillage of the New-England settlements, and they had garnished it with the scalps of many hundreds of their victims. Passing up the St. Francis river to Lake Memphremagog, and from thence to the Connecticut, these Indians had been enabled to make sudden and successful incursions into the colonies of New Hampshire and Massachusetts, and to return to their homes in safety. Amherst resolved to attempt the destruction of this village. Major Rogers, of the New-Hampshire rangers, was selected for this arduous duty. Two hundred of the most hardy and resolute men in the army were placed under his command. The massacre at Fort William Henry, and the numberless other atrocities which their kindred and friends had suffered from these Indians, were fresh in the minds of all; and they exulted in the expectation that the time for retribution had now come. The orders which they received from Amherst were little calculated to restrain their ferocity. "Remember," said he, "the barbarities that have been committed by the enemy's Indian scoundrels on every occasion, where they had an opportunity of showing their infamous cruelties on the king's subjects, which they have done without mercy. Take your revenge, but forget not that though these villains have dastardly and promiscuously murdered the women and children of all ages, it is my orders that no women or children are killed or hurt." The only practical route to the Indian village was by way of Missisco bay, near where the French were encamped. The utmost circumspection being necessary to avoid a discovery of the enemy, Rogers was seven days in reaching the bay. Concealing his boats he pushed forward through the woods, to the village of St. Francis. On the 2d of October, after having forded many streams and passed through many swamps, with incredible labor, Rogers reached the St. Francis river, and succeeded in fording it, although it was five feet in depth with a strong current. October 4th, in the evening, they came in sight of the Indian village. Disguised as Indians, Rogers, with two other officers, went forward to reconnoitre the place. They discovered that the Indians were wholly unsuspicious of danger, engaged in a dancing frolic. Their revelry was continued till four o'clock in the morning, when they retired to their huts, and all became still. The troops, relieved of their packs, had refreshed themselves, and were now led up; and, half an hour before sunrise, in three divisons, made a simultaneous attack on three sides of the village. So completely were the savages surprised and confounded, that they made but little resistance, and an indiscriminate massacre in true Indian style now took place. The cabins were forcibly entered, and their inmates knocked down, or shot dead in their attempts to fly, few escaping. In the obscure light, and confusion of the onset, it was impossible to distinguish age or sex. As the sun arose, it revealed to their view a scene so horrid that the men might have relented, but for the sight of the scalps of their murdered countrymen, six or seven hundred of which, suspended on poles, were waving in the air in all parts of the village. This steeled their hearts to all emotions of compassion, and they continued to dispatch all alike; and about seven o'clock the work was terminated by a general conflagration of the village. Of its three hundred inhabitants, two hundred were slain. Twenty women and children were taken prisoners, but most of them were soon after liberated. Five English captives were found in the place, and were set free. Two hundred guineas in coin were found, and a silver image weighing ten pounds, together with a large quantity of clothing and some provisions. Collecting the provisions, and such articles as they could easily transport, they set fire to the town, and reduced it to ashes. At seven o'clock in the morning, the affair was completely over; Rogers then assembled his men, and found that one was killed, and six slightly wounded. Having refreshed his men for one hour, the major made no further delay, but set out on his return. To avoid his pursuers, Rogers now took a different route, and marched up St. Francis river: meaning to have his men collect, and rendezvous at Coos on the Connecticut. On their march, they were harassed by some of the enemy, and several times attacked in the rear. In these encounters they lost seven of their men. At length, Rogers, favored by the dusk of evening, formed an ambuscade, and fell upon the enemy where they least expected it; by this stroke, he put an end to any further annoyance from them.

For about ten days the detachment kept together till they had passed the eastern side of Lake Memphremagog. It was then thought best to scatter into smaller parties, and make the best of their way to some of the English settlements. Their sufferings now began to be severe, not only from the excessive fatigues they had undergone, but from hunger. Their provisions were expended, and they were yet at a distance from any place of relief. Some were lost in the woods, and others perished at Coos, being unable to hold out any further. But Rogers, with most of his men, persevered amidst all their sufferings, till they arrived at Number Four. This enterprise had been dangerous and fatiguing to the men who had been engaged in it; but it made a deep impression on the enemy. It carried alarm and consternation into the heart of Canada, and convinced the Indians that the hand of vengeance was now come upon them.

During the operations of Amherst at Lake Champlain, General Wolfe prosecuted his daring and important expedition against the capital of Canada. Strong naturally, and still stronger by art, Quebec had obtained the appellation of Gibraltar of America; and every attempt against it had failed. It was now commanded by Montcalm, an officer of distinguished reputation; and its capture must have appeared chimerical to any one but Pitt. He judged rightly, however, that the boldest and most dangerous enterprises are often the most successful, especially when committed to ardent minds, glowing with enthusiasm and emulous of glory. Such a mind he had found in Wolfe, whose conduct had attracted his attention. In June, 1759, Wolfe landed with eight thousand troops a few miles below Quebec. From this position, he could take a near and distinct view of the obstacles to be overcome. These were so great, that even the bold and sanguine Wolfe perceived more to fear than to hope. But he resolved to do his best. He declared he would rather die than to fail in the enterprise. Various attempts were made against the French, but besides his superior position, Montcalm's forces were much more numerous than those of Wolfe, and the latter was several times repulsed with the loss of many men. Nothing, however, could shake the resolution of this valiant commander, or induce him to abandon his purpose.

Baffled and harassed in all his previous assaults, General Wolfe seems to have determined to finish the enterprise by a single bold and desperate effort. This was to surmount the heights of Abraham, which overlooked Quebec, and were then deemed inaccessible. To mislead the French, the English fleet sailed several miles up the river, making occasional demonstrations of a design to land troops; while on the night of September 12th, a strong detachment of flat-bottomed boats was dispatched down the St. Lawrence, to a point a mile above the city. The army landed about an hour before daybreak, clambered up a precipitous steep, three hundred feet high, and by sunrise, five thousand troops were marshaled on the heights of Abraham — a position which commanded the city. Montcalm would not at first believe the intelligence of this movement; but, as soon as he was aware of its truth, he made all prudent haste to decide a battle which it was no longer possible to avoid. About nine in the morning, the main body of the French advanced briskly to the charge, and the action soon became general. Montcalm having taken post on the left of the French army, and Wolfe on the right of the English, the two generals met each other where the battle was most severe. The English troops reserved their fire until the French had advanced within forty yards of their line, and then, by a general discharge, made terrible havoc among their ranks. The fire of the English was vigorously maintained, and the enemy everywhere yielded to it. General Wolfe, who, exposed in the front of his battalions, had been wounded in the wrist, betraying no symptoms of pain, wrapped a handkerchief round his arm, and continued to encourage his men. Soon after, he received a shot in the groin; but, concealing the wound, he was pressing on at the head of his grenadiers with fixed bayonets, when a third ball pierced his breast.* The army, not disconcerted by his fall,

* On receiving his mortal wound, Wolfe was conveyed into the rear, where, careless about himself, he evinced, in the agonies of death, the most anxious solicitude concerning the fate of the day. "Support me," he said to an officer near him; "let not my brave soldiers see me drop. The day is ours—keep it." From extreme faintness, he had reclined his head on the arm of an officer, but was soon aroused by the cry of "They fly, they fly!" "Who fly?" exclaimed the dying hero. "The French," answered his attendant; "they give way everywhere." "What!" feebly exclaimed Wolfe, "do they run already? Go to Colonel Preston and tell him to march Webb's regiment immediately to the bridge over the St. Charles so as to cut off the fugitives' retreat. Now, God be praised, I die happy." These were his last words, and in the midst of sorrowing companions, just at the moment of victory, he expired. A death more full of military glory has seldom been recorded by the pen of the historian, or celebrated by the pencil of the painter. General Wolfe was only thirty-three years of age. He possessed those military talents, which, with the advantage of years and opportunity of

continued the action under Monckton, on whom the command now devolved, but who, receiving a ball through his body, soon yielded the command to General Townshend. Montcalm, fighting in front of his battalions, received a mortal wound about the same time; and General Senezergas, the second in command, also fell. The British grenadiers pressed on with their bayonets. The center of the French army was broken. The Scottish highlanders, drawing their broadswords, completed the confusion of the enemy. An attempt was made by them to rally, but after a brief and fierce conflict, they retired, leaving the British undisputed masters of the field. The loss of the French was much greater than that of the English. Although Quebec was strongly defended by its fortifications, General Townshend had scarcely prepared to get his heavy artillery upon the heights for a siege, when the inhabitants capitulated on condition that, during the war, they might enjoy their civil and religious rights. A garrison of five thousand English troops was placed in the city, and the fleet sailed out of the St. Lawrence.

The fall of Quebec did not produce the immediate submission of Canada. The main body of the French

---

action to moderate his ardor, expand his faculties, and give to his intuitive perception and scientific knowledge the correctness of judgment perfected by experience, would have placed him on a level with the most celebrated generals of any age or nation. Montcalm was every way worthy to be a competitor of Wolfe. He had the truest military genius of any officer whom the French had ever employed in America. After he had received his mortal wound, he was carried into the city; and when informed that it was mortal, his reply was, "I am glad of it." On being told that he could survive but a few hours, "So much the better," he replied, "I shall not then live to see the surrender of Quebec."

army retired to Montreal. There they remained during the winter, making extensive preparations for the recovery of Quebec. In the month of April, 1760, the French army sailed down the St. Lawrence, and effected a landing near Quebec. General Murray, to whom the care of maintaining the English conquest had been intrusted, had taken every precaution to preserve it; but his troops had suffered so much from the extreme severity of the winter, that instead of five thousand, the original number of the garrison, there were scarcely three thousand fit for service. But with this small army he resolved to meet the enemy in the field, and marched out to the heights of Abraham, to defend that important location against the French; but after a fierce encounter, Murray was obliged to retreat into the city. But before the French could prepare their batteries, and bring their guns to bear upon the fortifications, a British fleet most opportunely arrived, and the French precipitately retreated to Montreal. There the Marquis de Vaudreuil, governor of Canada, had fixed his headquarters, and determined to make his last stand. For this purpose he called around him the whole force of his colony.

While Vaudreuil was thus preparing for resistance, General Amherst was concerting and executing measures to bring all the British armies in America, to act in concert against Montreal. He had sent instructions to General Murray, at Quebec, directing him, as soon as the season would permit, to advance up the river St. Lawrence by water, toward Montreal, with all the troops that could be spared from the garrison of Quebec. He appointed Colonel Haviland to command a body of troops, which were to proceed from Crown Point, through Lake Champlain, to take possession of the Isle Aux Noix; and from thence they were to advance by the shortest practicable route, to the banks of the river St. Lawrence. For himself, he proposed to go with the main body of his army by the way of the Mohawk to Lake Ontario; to embark his troops at Oswego, sail over the lake, and down the river St. Lawrence, to the Island of Montreal. By this plan, he proposed to bring all his troops against that place, and to inclose and surround the enemy on that island. Almost on the same day, the armies from Quebec, from Lake Ontario, and from Lake Champlain, were concentrated before Montreal, and Vaudreuil was speedily compelled (September 8, 1760) to capitulate. In 1763, peace was ratified between England and France, by which all the possessions of the French in Canada were ceded to the English.

Thus terminated a war, which originated in an attempt on the part of the French to surround the English colonists, and chain them to a narrow strip of country along the coast of the Atlantic; and ended with their giving up the whole of what was then their only valuable territory in North America. The immediate advantage the colonies derived from the successful issue of the contest was great and apparent. Although, for a short period after the conquest of Canada had been effected, they were subject to attacks from the Indian tribes attached to the French, they were soon enabled to visit their cruelties with severe retribution, and to procure a lasting repose, as the Indians had no forts to which to repair for protection or aid. But the indirect results, though almost unperceived at first, were far more important, and prepared the way for those momentous efforts which resulted in the loss to Great Britain of the fairest portions of her colonies, and the establishment of her vassal as a rival. The colonies became inured to the habits and hardships of a military life, and skilled in the arts of European warfare; while the desire of revenge for the loss of Canada, which France did not fail to harbor, was preparing for them a most efficient friend, and making way for the anomalous exhibition of a despotic sovereign exerting all his power in the cause of liberty and independence.

CHAPTER II.

THE NEW-HAMPSHIRE GRANTS.

"Look now abroad — another race has filled
 These populous borders — wide the wood recedes,
And towns shoot up, and fertile plains are tilled;
 The land is full of harvests and green meads;
Streams, numberless, that many a fountain feeds,
 Shine disembowered, and give to sun and breeze
Their virgin waters; the full region leads
 New colonies forth, that toward the western seas
Spread, like a rapid flame among the autumnal leaves."
Bryant.

Up to the close of the French war in 1760, the territory now composing the state of Vermont, was an uncultivated wilderness. The only considerable settlement within its limits was at Fort Dummer, now Brattleborough. This fort had been built under the authority of Massachusetts, in 1724, and gave protection to a few families in its immediate vicinity. The region between Lake Champlain and the Connecticut river is not known to have been the permanent habitation of the Indian tribes, although it was often traversed by them in their hunting excursions, and in their warlike expeditions against each other. The constant warfare which was maintained between the Indians on the St. Lawrence, and those on the Mohawk, as well as the subsequent wars between the French and English colonies, were carried on chiefly through Lake Champlain and its vicinity, rendering the settlement, by Indians or whites, extremely hazardous. To prevent the unwelcome incursions of the Indians attached to the French interests, and to give protection to the frontier settlements, Fort Dummer was erected; as was also, about twenty years afterward, Fort Hoosic or Massachusetts, the site of which is now pointed out between the villages of Williamstown and North Adams. For a series of years previous to 1759, the French had held possession of the forts at Ticonderoga and Crown Point, and their vicinity had been the scene of many bloody and destructive battles between them and their Indian allies on the one hand, and the English colonists on the other. In these warlike operations, as well as in the incursions of the savages, much of the best blood of New England had been spilt, and many of its most valuable inhabitants had been carried into captivity. In their retaliatory expeditions against Canada, the English colonists had traversed the greater portion of Vermont, and had become charmed with its beauties and fertility. The French also regarded this region as an attractive portion of their possessions, and while, in the intervals of peace, the English colonists were gradually spreading their settlements northward on the Connecticut, French adventurers as eagerly sought homes along the borders of Lake Champlain.

The war having terminated in the conquest of Canada, the frontiers of New York, Massachusetts and New Hampshire were no longer exposed to the inroads of the French, or the ravages and depredations of the Indians. The prospect was that the unsettled parts of the country would now afford pleasant and safe abodes for a large body of farmers, who might wish to advance their fortunes by establishing settlements along the frontiers. No portion of the country appeared more inviting than that situated between Lake Champlain and the Connecticut, and it was eagerly explored by adventurers and speculators. The soil was, in many places, of uncommon fertility, favorable to the production of grain, and in all, to grazing and the raising of cattle. It was plentifully watered by numerous streams, and abounded with excellent timber. In such a soil and situation, it was thought by the hardy pioneers, the labor and hardships of a few years could scarcely fail to secure for them valuable farms, with the ease and independence which are the proper rewards of industry and frugality. Encouraged by such prospects, many people began to settle, or to speculate in those lands. As early as 1696, indeed, Governor Fletcher, of the province of New York, bestowed a considerable portion of the present state of Vermont upon Godfrey Dellius, one of his favorites, who was the minister of the Dutch church in Albany. Dellius was one of the commissioners for Indian affairs, and had previously obtained from the Mohawk Indians, fraudulently, as they said, a deed of their title to the same lands. This singular and very liberal donation, conveyed to Dellius eight hundred and forty square miles of territory. The avarice of the minister, and the generosity of the governor, are equally entitled to a smile, if it is permissible to smile at any transaction between so venerable a prelate as "our Loving Subject the Reverend Godfredius Dellius, Minister of the Gospel att our city of Albany," and so august a magistrate as "his Excellency, the Honorable Benjamin ffletcher, his Majesty's Governor and Commander in Chief of the Province of New Yorke and the territories depending thereon in America." The conveyance was made upon the following condition: "He Yielding Rendering and Paying therefore Yearly and every Year unto us our Heirs and Successors on the feast Day of the Annunciation of our blessed Virgin Mary at our city of New Yorke the Annuall Rente of one Raccoon Skinn in lieu and stead of all other Rents Services Dues Dutyes and Demands whatsoever. for the said Tract of Land and Islands and Premises." The Earl of Bellamonte, who succeeded Fletcher, justly regarding these and other large grants as calculated to impede the settlement of the country, recommended the annulment of these grants or patents by the legislature. This was accordingly done, and the assembly, exercising ecclesiastical as well as civil authority, also passed a resolution, suspending Dellius from the ministry for "deluding the Maquaas [Mohawk] Indians, and illegal and surreptitious obtaining of said grants." Dellius returned to Holland, and, regarding his title as still valid, transferred his claim to the Rev. John Lydius, his successor in the ministry at Albany, whose descendants long afterward attempted the enforcement of the claim. From 1731, until the conquest of Canada in 1760, the French governors of that province made grants of nearly all the lands contiguous to Lake Champlain, and various settlements were begun; but they were all abandoned during the last French war.

In the charters granted by the sovereigns of England

to the early colonists on the continent, so little was known of the geography of the country, and so trifling was the value of the grants considered, that their definition of boundaries was extremely vague, as they well might be, the crown having no precise notions of the extent or situation of the territories it was ceding to its favorites. Accordingly, as the importance of the colonies increased, and the people became interested in knowing the exact limits of their possessions, it was found that there were, in several instances, conflicting claims to the same tract of country. Hence arose many imbittered controversies between the colonies, some of which were not finally settled until long after the Revolution. The territory comprising the state of New York is an example of the difficulty attendant upon these questions. By the terms of the charters to Massachusetts and Connecticut, the possessions of each were to extend westward to the South sea or Pacific ocean. Although the Dutch had for several years been in possession of the Hudson river, it does not seem to have been fully known that the above grants conflicted with their interests, although they contained the following condition: "Provided always, that the said lands, islands, or any of the premises by the said letters patent intended or meant to be granted, were not then actually possessed or inhabited by any other Christian power or State." After the conquest of "New Netherlands," as the Dutch possessions were called, Charles II. granted them to his brother, the Duke of York. The terms of this charter, (the controversy respecting which resulted in the admission of Vermont as a separate state of the Union) will interest the reader.

THE CHARTER OF NEW YORK. 121

"CHARLES THE SECOND, by the Grace of God, King of England, Scotland, France and Ireland, Defender of the Faith, &c. To all to whom these presents shall come, Greeting: Know ye, that we, for divers good causes and considerations, have, of our especial grace, certain knowledge and mere motion, given and granted, and by these presents, for us, our heirs and successors, do give and grant unto our dearest brother, James, Duke of York, his heirs and assigns, all that part of the main land of New England, beginning at a certain place, called or known by the name of St. Croix, next adjoining to New Scotland in America; and from thence extending along the sea coast, unto a certain place called Petuaguine, or Pemaquid, and so up the river thereof to the furtherest head of the same, as it téndeth northwards; and extending from the river of Kenebeque, and so upwards, by the shortest course of the river Canada, northwards: And all that island or islands, commonly called by the several name or names of Matowacks or Long Island, situate, and being towards the west of Cape Cod, and the Narrow Highgansetts, abutting upon the main land, between the two rivers there, called or known by the several names of Connecticut and Hudson's River, together also with the said river called Hudson's, *and all the lands from the west side of Connecticut river to the east side of Delaware Bay:* and also, all those several islands, called or known by the names of Martin's Vineyard, and Nantuckes, otherways, Nantucket; together with all, &c. Dated the twenty ninth day of June, in the twenty sixth year of the reign of King CHARLES the Second."

The boundary between New York and Connecticut was ultimately fixed at a distance of twenty miles east of the Hudson, it being found that lands had been granted by the Connecticut authorities, and settlements made, thus far westward; and, for a similar reason, the same arrangement was made in regard to the boundary between Massachusetts and New York. The governor of New Hampshire, thinking it probable that the jurisdiction of his government, the charter being somewhat ambiguous, was designed to extend as far westward as that of Massachusetts and Connecticut, took prompt measures, as soon as the importance of the territory seemed to justify the step, to establish this boundary. During the peace which preceded the last French war, Benning Wentworth, then governor of New Hampshire, wrote to Governor George Clinton, of New York, in regard to the subject. He said, "I have it in command from his Majesty, to make grants of the unimproved lands within my government, to such of the inhabitants and others as shall apply for grants of the same, as will oblige themselves to settle and improve, agreeable to his Majesty's instructions. The war, hitherto, has prevented me from making so great a progress as I hoped for on my first appointment; but as there is a prospect of a lasting peace with the Indians, in which your Excellency has had a great share, people are daily applying for grants of land in all quarters of this government, and particularly some for townships to be laid out in the western part thereof, which will fall in the neighborhood of your government. I think it my duty to apprise you thereof, and to transmit to your Excellency the description of New Hampshire, as the king has determined it in the words of my commission, which, after you have considered, I shall be glad if you will be pleased to give me your sentiments in what manner it will affect the grants made by you or preceding governors; it being my intention to avoid, as much as I can, consistent with his Majesty's instructions, interfering with your government." Governor Clinton placed this letter before the council; they "humbly advised his Excellency to acquaint Governor Wentworth, in answer to his said letter, that this province [New York] is bounded eastward by Connecticut river; the letters-patent from King Charles II. to the Duke of York, expressly granting 'all the lands from the west side of the Connecticut river to the east side of Delaware bay.'" This resolution of the council was transmitted to Governor Wentworth.

Previous to receiving a reply from the governor of New York, Wentworth granted (January 3d, 1749) to William Williams and sixty-one other persons, a township, six miles square, which, in allusion to his own name, was called Bennington. It was situated twenty-four miles east of the Hudson river, and six miles north of the Massachusetts line. Wentworth gave information to Clinton of this grant, and promised to make no further cessions of land in that vicinity until the question of jurisdiction should be decided. Both governors consented to make representations of the matter to the king, and await his decision. Notwithstanding this, Wentworth, during the ensuing four or five years, continued to make grants of lands on the west side of the Connecticut, amounting, in all, to fourteen townships in 1754. That year hostilities commenced between the English and French colonies, and until the final conquest of Canada, no further applications were made for lands within the disputed limits. During the continuance of the war, the New-England troops cut a road from Number Four, on the Connecticut, to Crown Point, on Lake Champlain. From the summits of the Green Mountains they looked admiringly upon the smiling and luxuriant valleys beneath them, and many a hardy volunteer selected the place where, at the close of the war, he should wish to establish a home. Upon the conquest of Canada, these persons applied for grants to the governor of New Hampshire, within whose jurisdiction the lands were generally supposed to be. By the advice of his council, Wentworth directed a survey to be made of Connecticut river for sixty miles; and three lines of townships to be laid out, on each side. The applications for lands increased, and new surveys were made. So rapid was the progress, that during the year 1761, not less than sixty townships, of six miles square, were granted on the west of Connecticut river. The whole number of grants, in one or two years more, amounted to one hundred and thirty-eight; and their extent was from Connecticut river, to what was considered twenty miles east of Hudson river, so far as that extended to the northward; and after that, as far west as the eastern shore of Lake Champlain. The cultivation of the country, and the number of the settlers, increased with surprising rapidity; and Mr. Wentworth had an opportunity to accumulate a large fortune, by the fees and donations which attended the business, and by a reserve of five hundred acres, which he made in every township, for himself.

To check the proceedings of New Hampshire, and to intimidate the settlers, Mr. Colden, lieutenant-governor of New York, issued a proclamation, setting forth the charter to the Duke of 'York, asserting its validity, claiming that the jurisdiction of New York extended eastward to the Connecticut river, and commanding the sheriff of the county of Albany to make a return of all persons who, under color of grants from Governor Wentworth, had taken possession of any lands west of the Connecticut. To counteract the influence of this proclamation, Mr. Wentworth also published one, pronouncing the charter to the Duke of York to be obsolete; asserting that New Hampshire extended as far westward as Massachusetts and Connecticut; and assuring the settlers upon his grants that they would be confirmed by the crown, even should the jurisdiction be transferred to New York. The people were exhorted not to be intimidated, but to be industrious and diligent in the cultivation of their lands; and the civil officers were required to exercise jurisdiction as far westward as grants had been made, and to punish all disturbers of the peace. After such assurances from a royal governor, they entertained no suspicion that a contest between two provinces, respecting the extent of their jurisdiction, would ever affect the rights of those who had fairly purchased their lands from a governor appointed by the king.

Hitherto, the claim of New York to the territory in question had been founded on the grant to the Duke of York. But when application was made to the crown for a confirmation of the claim, it was supported by a petition, purporting to be from a large number of the settlers on the New-Hampshire grants, representing that it would be for their advantage to be annexed to the colony of New York, and praying that the western bank of Connecticut river might be established as the eastern boundary of that province.

The application from New York was referred to the board of trade, and upon their recommendation, seconded by a report of a committee of the privy-council, an order was made by the king, (July 20, 1764,) declaring "the western banks of Connecticut river, from where it enters the province of Massachusetts Bay, as far north as the forty-fifth degree of latitude, *to be* the boundary-line between the two provinces of New York and New Hampshire."

This decree, like many other judicial determinations, while it closed one controversy, opened another. The jurisdiction of the governor of New Hampshire, and his authority to grant lands, were circumscribed on the west by Connecticut river; but the grantees of the soil found themselves involved in a dispute with the government of New York. From the words "*to be*," in the royal declaration, adverse conclusions were drawn. The government assumed that they referred to time past, and construed them into a declaration that the Connecticut always had formed the eastern boundary of New York; consequently, that all the grants made by Mr. Wentworth were illegal, and that the lands might be granted again. The grantees understood the words as simply designed to affect the future, and not to annul the validity of past transactions. They regarded it as merely extending the jurisdiction of New York, from that period, over their territory. But they had no apprehension that it could in any way affect the title to their lands. Having purchased and paid for those lands, under grants from the crown, they did not understand by what perversion of justice they could be compelled, by the same authority, to repurchase or abandon them. To the change of jurisdiction they were willing to submit, although, at first, the governor of New Hampshire remonstrated against it. However, he was at length induced to abandon the contest, and issued a proclamation "recommending to the proprietors and settlers due obedience to the authority and laws of the colony of New York." In this state of things, the government of New York proceeded to extend its jurisdiction over the New-Hampshire grants, dividing the territory into four counties, and establishing courts of justice in each." The settlers were called on to surrender their charters, and repurchase their lands under grants from New York. Most of them peremptorily refused to comply with this order. New grants of their lands were, therefore, made to others; in whose names actions of ejectment were commenced, and judgments obtained, in the courts at Albany. The attempts to execute these judgments, by dispossessing the settlers, met with a determined and obstinate resistance. For the purpose of rendering this resistance more effectual, various associations were formed; and at length, a convention of representatives from the several towns on the west side of the mountains was called. This convention, after mature deliberation, appointed Samuel Robinson, of Bennington, an agent, to represent to the court of Great Britain the grievances of the settlers, and obtain, if practicable, a confirmation of the New-Hampshire grants. Mr. Robinson proceeded to London, and laid the subject before his Majesty.

By this means he obtained an order from the king,

(July 24, 1767,) as follows: "His Majesty, taking the said report [a report of the board of trade] into consideration, was pleased, with the advice of his private council, to approve thereof, and doth hereby strictly charge, require and command, that the Governor or Commander in Chief of his Majesty's Province of New York, for the time being, do not, upon pain of his Majesty's highest displeasure, presume to make any grant whatsoever, of any part of the lands described in the said report, until his Majesty's further pleasure shall be known, concerning the same."

Notwithstanding this explicit prohibition, the governor of New York continued to make grants; and writs of ejectment continued to be issued, returnable to the supreme court at Albany. On trial of these actions, it was decided that duly authenticated copies of the royal orders to the governor of New Hampshire, and of the grants made in pursuance of those orders, should not be read in evidence. Thus, compelled to abandon a legal defense, the settlers were driven to the last resort. A convention of the people assembled at Bennington, and "resolved, to support their rights and property under the New-Hampshire grants, against the usurpation and unjust claims of the governor and council of New York, by force, as law and justice were denied them."

Conspicuous among those who were, by their resistance to New York, laying the foundation upon which the independent state of Vermont has been reared — indeed the leader and champion of that resolute band of husbandmen who first planted themselves in the wilderness of the Green Mountains — was

ETHAN ALLEN. Joseph Allen, the father of Ethan, was a native of Coventry, Connecticut; but afterward, on his marriage to Mary Baker, removed to Litchfield, where Ethan was born, January 10, 1737. The father of Ethan Allen was a sober, industrious farmer, of good character, and in moderate circumstances. After the birth of Ethan, his parents removed to Cornwall, where other children were born, making, in all, six sons and two daughters: Ethan, Heman, Lydia, Heber, Levi, Lucy, Zimri and Ira. All the brothers grew up to manhood, and four or five of them emigrated to the territory west of the Green Mountains, among the first settlers, and were prominent members of the social and political compacts into which the inhabitants gradually formed themselves. Bold, active and enterprising, they espoused with zeal and defended with energy, the cause of the settlers against what were deemed the encroaching schemes of their neighbors, and, with a keen interest, sustained their share in all the border contests. Nothing is known of the early life of Ethan Allen, previous to his removal to Bennington, Vermont. This was about the year 1772, although, being interested in a considerable portion of the New-Hampshire grants, he had spent much of his time in exploring the lands in the vicinity of the Green Mountains, for the purpose of locating townships, and had taken an active part in the controversy with New York for three or four of the previous years. Next to Ethan, Ira, the youngest, was the most energetic of the brothers, and entered into the land speculation with more zeal than the others. While thus engaged, he kept a journal of his proceedings, and a few extracts from it cannot be uninteresting; for they depict, in a lively manner, the nature of the transactions in which he was engaged, and are illustrative of his character. His foresight in the choice of the location where the beautiful and flourishing town of Burlington has grown up, will perhaps excite quite as much admiration as the shrewdness he displayed in disposing of worthless lands.*

1772. "My next object was to make a map of the township of Mansfield with the allotments and survey-bills thereof, agreeable to the bond, &c., I had given the Proprietors of said town the preceding summer. I soon completed the map, but turning my attention to the field-books that Captain Remember Baker and I had kept, a difficulty arose in my mind, for my object was to sell out of Mansfield at all events, and if possible, to get the ninety pounds for the survey, &c. A great proportion of the corners of said lots were made on Spruce or Fir timber, and if I described them as such, it would show the poorness of the town, and raise many questions I wished to avoid. I made use of a stratagem that answered my purpose. In my survey-bills I called Spruce and Fir, Greenwood, a name not known by the people of Sharon, (the place where the Proprietors lived.) They asked what kind of timber Greenwood was. I told them full, straight trees, that had a gum much like the gum on Cherry-trees, &c. While the Proprietors were busy in inspecting the map, survey-bills, &c., I took aside the Brother of one of the principal Proprietors, who was an ignorant fellow, and owned two rights of land in the town. I tried to buy his rights, but he dare not sell them without first consulting his Brother. By this the Proprietors all got the alarm that I wished to purchase, and Land in Mansfield was

* The original manuscript of Ira Allen's journal is in the possession of Henry Stephens, Esq., of Barnet, Vermont, the distinguished antiquary of that state. The extracts are given *verbatim*, and are now, for the first time, placed before the public.

considered of consequence. I was urged to sell back to the Proprietors the twenty rights I had bought, which I did, and obtained the ninety pounds for the survey, &c., which I considered of more consequence than the whole town. Having closed this business satisfactory to myself, I returned to my Brothers, and had a hearty laugh with the Brothers Heman and Zimry, on informing them respecting the Greenwood, &c.

1772. "Some lands were owned by Edward Burling and others at the White Plains, twenty-one miles from New York which we wanted. Col. Ethan Allen, Capt. Remember Baker and myself armed with hatchets and pistols, a good case of pistols each in our pockets, with each a good hanger set out to purchase the aforesaid and other lands in the colony of New York. We traveled under the character of British officers, going from Canada to New York to embark for London, and made no small parade. My brother Heman being then in a mercantile line, set out for New York, but was seldom in company with us as he was too much known on that road. We put up at a tavern near Mr. Burling's, having previously concerted measures with Heman to acquaint Mr. Burling of our intentions and the reason of our traveling in that manner, the time we should call on him &c. We proceeded according, bought great part of Mr. Burling's lands and bought of others, spent three days there without the suspicion who we were. The evening before we left there after closing our business, Heman came & putting up at the same house, as it was necessary to be together as we should part next morning, for Heman was to make purchases in New York (Zimry was also occasionally to purchase Lands) it was with much difficulty Heman could get introduced to our company that evening by the diffidence of the Landlord, and after questions of the supposed British Officers, questioning the character of the Connecticut merchant &c. But Heman got leave by bringing in his hand a liberal Bowl to be introduced. It was with difficulty we could all keep our countenances till the Landlord retired, which was very soon. It was curious to see the astonishment of the Landlord the next morning, when we called in our bill all together, and declared who we were, informing a Pedler who was present, going direct to New York, that bounties were offered for us, giving our names &c. We saw the Pedler set out at full speed to New York to raise a party against us, as he supposed we were going to continue speculating in lands, depending on our own arms for defence. On his arrival in New York he went to the Governor and Council, and gave his deposition of our being purchasing Lands &c. at the White Plains. At first it was proposed to send a party of light horse men after us, and preparations were made for that purpose; but James Duane, Esq. observed that we were daring fellows and no doubt well mounted, and had gone directly out of the colony in hopes of being pursued to laugh at our pursuers, that it was in vain to pursue Green Mountain Boys on their guard &c. Mr. Duane was perfectly right, for within two hours after the express arrived in New York we were in the colony of Connecticut, in hopes of being pursued, to gain a greater opportunity to satarize our adversaries.

1773. "I went and pitched a number of hundred-acre lots contiguous to Burlington Bay. The land in itself was great part poor-looking Pine plains. This move of mine, astonished my friends, who had observed me to be very enterprising in pitching good lands, and that much good land remained untouched in Burlington; and I gave no reasons for my conduct, which raised many questions and disputes; indeed I did not but in part explain myself to my worthy friend and partner, Baker; for I found he had but little opinion of that place, but looked for good lands, more than situations; observing that good lands would certainly be of consequence, but it was hard to determine where places of consequence would arise in a country so extensive and new, that after securing the best of the lands by pitches, we might in consequence of settlements, &c., be [a few lines illegible in the original manuscript] of situations, and pitch or purchase any lands we might think of consequence. These remarks were of much good sense, but Baker had not explored the country so much as I had, and I had settled my opinion from which I was determined not to depart, nor give any further reasons. Frequent satires passed on me respecting Burlington Pine Plains. One rainy day Stephen Lawrence, Joshua Stanton and others had been fishing at the Falls, the rain proving too hard came into the fort where Baker kept spirits &c. for sale & over a bowl of Punch began severely to bulragg me for pitching Burlington pitch pine plains (by knic name I was called Stub) they carried the joke so far as to call Stub a fool for pitching such lands that he could not give any good reason for it. Stub as cheerfully answered to that name as to any other, resolved to take them a little in and give no satisfactory reasons neither, observed that he was surprised that they could not see use for such lands considering its situation &c., that for a double bowl of punch he would give his reasons. This they agreed to give, but Stub would have the punch in and take a good drink before he began to give his reasons. This was done with so much apparent candor that the company complied, the punch was brought in and Stub took the first drink and passed it round. All attention was then paid for Stub to give his reasons for pitching Burlington Pine Plains. When Stub putting on a serious countenance began. That the life of man was by sacred writ estimated at three score years and ten, that although some survived that period of life, yet many fell short and none could tell the time of their dissolution, that dry Pine plain was easy digging and good burying ground, and if as suggested by some, the spirits of the deceased conversed with each other and viewed the conduct of posterity it would be convenient passing from Tomb to Tomb through that light dry earth and to see from the high sand bank the multitude carry on commerce in Burlington Bay &c. This serious satire and having first got a double bowl of punch, induced Stub's neighbors to say very little more to him about Burlington Pine Plains for considerable time." *

* The following amusing narrative of Ira Allen's adventure with a ghost, as told by him in the autobiography from which the above extracts

SETH WARNER was second only to Ethan Allen in that energetic resistance to the claims of Governor Tryon, which ultimately led to the independence of Vermont. He was born in Woodbury, Connecticut,

are taken will doubtless be interesting, as illustrative of the character of the Allens: "Mr. and Mrs. McIntire were from Scotland, and had two daughters about twenty-four years of age. The old lady and her daughters used to amuse me by telling many frightful stories respecting ghosts, apparitions, &c., appearing to people in Scotland, &c., amongst which was many stories respecting an old woman appearing without a head. One evening I challenged the old woman without a head, and all the ghosts, &c., to meet me at any time and place they chose. This exceedingly alarmed my honest landlady and daughters, and they all seemed exceeding anxious for my safety for being so presumptuous as to make such a challenge, and not doubting but that I should meet with difficulty the first time belated and in the woods in the evening. The next day I found a part of the hogs that had been strayed away and become wild, with all the art I had, could not get them so gentle as to come to them till near dark, at which time I was at least three miles in the wilderness. There was then a snow on the ground about four inches deep. I made the best of my way to gain a foot-path from Mr. McIntire's to a beaver meadow. In the way I passed a thicket of Hemlock, &c., under which it was dark. I cut a staff about three feet long to defend my eyes &c. from limbs that might come in my face. In this way I found the foot path, in which several loads of hay had been carried from the meadow to the house which had mixed leaves, snow, &c., so that I could discover the foot path for twenty rods before me. At this time for the first time that night I thought of the old woman without any head at which I had a hearty laugh to think whether I should turn out if she met me in that narrow path. I thought no more of the matter till I had walked about one mile, when to my no small surprise at about eight rods distance, I discovered the perfect appearance of a woman in the path without any head; her shoulders, waist, arms akimbo, her hands on her hips, women's clothes & feet below were in perfect shape before me which I viewed with astonishment.

I reasoned to myself is this appearance fictitious or real. If the God of Nature authorises such apperations then there is no flying from them. What injury can they possibly do me? I had been promised faithfully in 1743. His father, Dr. Benjamin Warner, removed to Bennington in 1763, only one year after the first settlement was made in that town. Although quite young, Seth at once took a prominent part in the various controversies and struggles which were incident to the early settlement of a new state. He was distinguished in his youth, as he was afterward in his manhood, for the solidity and extent of his understanding. With no other scholastic advantages than such as a common school education afforded, yet those advantages were employed to the best possible purpose; and, at his majority, he was possessed of a fund of knowledge, which was as serviceable as if it had been obtained in the classic walks of Harvard, or under the elms of Yale.

Coming to the state of Vermont, as Seth Warner did, while the soil was yet but poorly tilled, while the

not to flinch at any such appearance I will see it out: on this determination, kicked the snow away that I might know where I made the discovery, and advanced with my cane in my hand for a blow as soon as I arrived near enough. With trembling approaches I came within about thirty yards, before I discovered the cause of such an appearance. The facts were that a tree had been broken by the wind leaving a stump, which the woodcocks had pecked the bark off in that shape so long that the wood had become whitish and the bark of the other part fallen off. The darkness of the night prevented me from seeing the darker colour, while the reflection of snow shone the other part of the stumps forming the size and figure of a woman without a head. Had it been a little lighter the whole stump would have been seen, or a little darker and no part could have been seen. To satisfy myself, I went back to where I kicked away the snow, and the old woman again appeared in perfect shape. I occasionally passed that place frequently after, but not at a time when such an opportunity could be discovered. Had I been frightened and ran away, I might like others have believed in such appearances."

forests were uncleared, while no school-house or church had been erected, there was, it would seem, but little to encourage the mind of that Connecticut boy to become a resident among the Green Mountains. But the rivers, lakes and ponds were filled with large quantities of excellent fish. The forests abounded with every variety of game, and in the dells and on the hills could be seen flowers of rare excellence and beauty. "Solomon in all his glory was not arrayed like one of these." Young Warner was a skillful botanist. He sought, partly from necessity but chiefly from choice, to render himself familiar with such plants and roots as were indigenous to Vermont. We are assured that no man acquired more information touching the nature and properties of such natural productions than he. With such invaluable knowledge, he was exceedingly useful in new settlements, where he could administer relief when medical assistance could not easily be obtained.

Young Warner was a huntsman, too. The ready pen of that romance-writer who cordially sympathizes with every effort to learn the character of the early settlers of this state, represents him, under the character of "Colonel Warrington," as a successful lover of the pleasures of the chase. Traveling back eighty years, if we wish to see him as he was, we find him an inhabitant of one of the rude cabins that were thinly scattered through the wilderness. We observe him felling the forest, or tilling the soil which had never been touched by any hand before. There will be found around his cabin, unbroken silence, save when the stroke of his ax awakens the echo, or the howl of the wolf disturbs the dull ear of midnight. In the midst of all his labors, as well as his pastime, he is compelled to be ready with the loaded musket to repel the lurking savage. "You see a man of a very fine and even majestic appearance. Though tall and muscular so compactly and finely set are his limbs, that his contour presents nothing to the eye in the least disproportioned or ungainly. His features seem to correspond in regularity of formation to the rest of his person, while his countenance is rather of the cool and deliberate cast, indicative, however, of a mild, benevolent disposition, as well as a sound and reflecting intellect. Every development, indeed, whether of his shapely head or manly countenance, goes to show a strong, well-balanced character, and one capable of action beyond the scope of ordinary men."*

It is said by contemporaries who have seen him at the head of his brave "Green-Mountain Rangers," armed and equipped for duty, that no man could bestride a horse with more grace and dignity than he. With a broad and intellectual forehead, relieved by a profusion of nut-brown hair, and with sparkling blue eyes beaming forth under eye-brows most beautifully arched, his physiognomy gave unmistakable signs of an intelligent, courageous and energetic man.

Such was the skillful huntsman and the practical botanist, before the blast of war blew in the ears of the early settlers of the New-Hampshire grants. Continuing to use his quick eye-sight and steady arm in hunting after game in the forests, and indulging his scientific taste in the dells and dingles where medica

* See the "Green Mountain Boys," by Daniel P. Thompson, Esq.

plants were most abundant, he became widely known as one upon whose usefulness and humanity reliance could be reposed. And thus was laid the basis of that reputation which, in after times, rendered him so influential and powerful for good when "the slings and arrows of outrageous Fortune" were hurtled at those who, like himself, had pitched their tents among the green hills of Vermont.

Captain REMEMBER BAKER, who was early associated with Allen and Warner, was, like the latter, a native of Woodbury, Connecticut. He was born about the year 1740. In his youth he was deprived of his father, who was accidentally shot by a neighbor, while on a hunting excursion. Young Baker, being thus left an orphan, was sent to live with, and learn the trade of a joiner, by whom he was taught to read and write, and was made acquainted with figures. In the year 1757, he enlisted as a soldier in an expedition against Canada. He also served in the ensuing campaign as a non-commissioned officer, and gained much applause for his intrepidity. He was also at the storming of the French lines when Abercrombie was defeated before Ticonderoga, and his bravery in that fatal action, as well as his discretion on the retreat of the colonial forces, gave him considerable distinction. He continued a third year in the service, but returned to Connecticut after the conquest of Canada. In the year 1763, he removed to the New-Hampshire Grants, as the country which afterward received the name of Vermont was then called, where he spent considerable time in exploring the wild lands, and in hunting the game with which the Green Mountains then abounded.

He finally removed with his family to Arlington, where he built the first mills that were erected north of Bennington. This afforded great encouragement to the settlers, and the population in the vicinity of Arlington increased with much rapidity.

The charter of Bennington, although dated January 3d, 1749, was not actually issued until March, 1750. The survey, however, was made in 1749—and it was no doubt designed that the actual occupancy of the territory would, as in the case of Connecticut and Massachusetts, result in settling whatever controversy might arise, respecting jurisdiction, in favor of New Hampshire. The charter of the town had been granted in sixty-four equal shares, or "rights," as they were called, of three hundred and sixty acres each. The grantees resided principally, if not wholly, at Portsmouth, New Hampshire. But none of them, it is believed, ever removed to the town. The first settlers were purchasers under the original proprietors, and were from Massachusetts. Samuel Robinson, of Hardwich, who had been for several years a captain in the French war, on his return from Lake George to Fort Massachusetts, while proceeding up Hoosic river, mistook the Walloomscoik* for that stream, and followed it up to the tract of country which had been granted under the name of Bennington. There he discovered that he had missed his way, and directed his course to the fort. He was much pleased with the country, and returned to his family with a determination to begin a settlement upon it. He accordingly repaired to New

* See Thompson's Gazetteer of Vermont—an invaluable work to all Vermonters.

Hampshire, made purchases of a considerable portion of the "rights," and then sought for persons who would undertake to occupy the lands. These were readily found, and the settlement of the town was commenced in the spring of 1761. The first emigrants were Harwoods, Robinsons and Pratts, and, with their families, consisted of about twenty persons. They traveled on horseback, and in that way transported all their household effects, of which, it may be imagined, there was no considerable variety or quantity. They reached the town on the 18th of June. Benjamin Harwood, (who was still living a few years ago,) was the first person born in the town, (January 12th, 1762.) In the fall of 1761, many other families settled in Bennington, and the place rapidly grew in importance. Among the first cares of the people, after the erection of suitable habitations, was the establishment of a church and a school. The first meeting of the proprietors, of which a record has been kept, was held February 12th, 1762. A committee was then appointed "to look out a place for a meeting-house;" and soon after a site was agreed upon, and a church was immediately constructed, which was paid for, partly by individual contributions, and partly by a tax on the proprietors of the town. Upon the organization of the church, the "Cambridge platform" was adopted, except such parts as admitted, according to the New-England fashion of that day, the aid of the civil magistrates in enforcing the support of the ministry, and their coercive power over the church in other matters. They denominated themselves "Congregationalists," but being in advance of the great majority of their brethren of that period in the liberality of their views of religious freedom, were for some time called "Separatists." In the fall of 1763, the Rev. Jedediah Dewey, of Westfield, Massachusetts, became pastor of the church, and in addition to the encouragement he obtained from voluntary contributions, he received from the proprietors of the town a donation of three hundred and sixty acres of land, eligibly situated, which was called "the minister's right." Mr. Dewey continued to reside with the congregation at Bennington until his death, in 1778. In 1763, the proprietors voted a tax for building a schoolhouse, and sixty dollars were contributed toward supporting a school "to be kept in these parts of the town."

The early settlers suffered great inconvenience for the want of roads, bridges and mills. To overcome these difficulties, the inhabitants taxed themselves liberally — opened roads in various directions, and constructed bridges where necessary. For the erection of each saw and flouring mill, a bounty of forty dollars was paid by the proprietors. Meantime, among the inhabitants of the New-England colonies, a market had been found for the lands granted by Governor Wentworth, and settlers were flocking over the mountains from various quarters. The easy terms upon which the townships had been patented, enabled the original purchasers to dispose of shares and single farms at very low prices, thus holding out strong allurements to settlers. Apprehensions as to the validity of their title, may also have induced the first proprietors to prefer a quick sale with small profits, to the uncertain prospect of larger gains at a future day. By this union of policy and interest, the lands were rapidly sold, in tracts of various dimensions, to practical farmers, who resolved to establish themselves as permanent residents on the soil. Many settlements were begun, and when, after enduring almost incalculable hardships and the severest toil, they began to realize the blessings for which they had labored so indefatigably, the alarming intelligence reached them, that they must repurchase their lands from the government of New York, at exorbitant prices, or be expelled from their homes and deprived of their possessions. To pay a second time for their lands at their original value, would have been regarded as grossly unjust; but to be required to purchase the improvements which they had made in effort and self-denial, was a demand which they felt that they could meet only with armed resistance.

In regard to the jurisdiction of the government of New York, which had been established by order of the crown in July, 1764, as heretofore stated, they were not disposed to have any serious controversy. They were, indeed, familiar with the laws and institutions of New Hampshire, and preferred them to those of New York. New Hampshire, as well as the other New-England provinces, recognized the townships as little republics, in which the people, at annual town-meetings appointed their own legal officers, and, in conformity with established laws, made their own municipal regulations. In New York, most of these matters were then either subjects of direct provincial legislation, or came under the still more anti-republican superintendence of the governor and council, or of the judges of the courts, who were the creatures of their appointment.

The people contemplated with regret the withdrawal of power from themselves which early education had made dear to them, and long experience had proved to be convenient and just. Besides, the division of New York into large tracts of territory termed manors, of which individuals denominated landlords or patroons, were the owners, and all who cultivated the soil were their tenants, subject to the payment of quit-rents, alienation fees, and other acknowledgments of dependence and subjugation, accorded ill with their New-England notions of personal equality and independent ownership of the soil. But notwithstanding this strong preference to the government of New Hampshire, the jurisdiction of New York, had jurisdiction been the sole aim of Governor Tryon, would have been quietly acquiesced in.

But the governor of New York had other objects in view, than that of simply extending the powers of his government over the people inhabiting the "New-Hampshire Grants." Those grants contained a large quantity of fertile lands, much of which had been made highly valuable by the improvements of the settlers; and the temptation to derive a pecuniary profit from them was too strong to be resisted.* He therefore called on the settlers, by proclamation, to surrender their grants and repurchase their lands from him. A few of the towns near Connecticut river complied; but most of them, including all those west of the Green Mountains, refused. Upon this refusal,

* The fees to the governor of New Hampshire, for granting a township, were about one hundred dollars; under the government of New York they usually amounted to between two and three thousand dollars.

Governor Tryon made new grants of the town to others: principally to his friends and dependents, including some belonging to his council, and also judges of the courts, members of the bar, and of the colonial assembly. The limitation of these grants to a favored class who were connected with the government, will account for the pertinacity with which the New-York claims were afterward prosecuted by the rulers of the province, as well as the apathy with which their successive efforts to eject the original settlers were seconded by the people at large.

The New-York purchasers caused their lands to be surveyed preparatory to making sales or leases of them. This proceeding was quite unacceptable to the actual occupants of the land, and whenever the surveyors were discovered, they were roughly driven from their employment. One of the surveyors, in attempting to run a line across the farm of Samuel Robinson, of Bennington, was attacked by him with a hoe and driven off. For this, Robinson was apprehended; but after being confined for two months in the jail at Albany, was released, on the payment of a fine. Others who resisted were indicted, but the sheriff of Albany county, (which then extended to the Connecticut river,) was generally unsuccessful in his attempts to arrest them. The people were alarmed by these and other demonstrations by the governor of New York, but having a strong reliance upon the justice of their cause, and being confident that the crown had been deceived in regard to the subject, or that a wrong construction had been placed upon the order of the king, prepared a remonstrance against the proceedings of New York, and in the fall of 1766, at a convention of the several towns on the west side of the Green Mountains, appointed Samuel Robinson as their agent to present the remonstrance, and to advocate their application for relief, by his personal solicitations. They could not conceive that a parental government, in which character they were disposed to view that of the mother country, could possibly desire to deprive them of their hard-earned property, for the benefit of a few land-speculators. By some of the towns, their share of the expense of the embassy was levied in the form of a tax upon the proprietors; while in others, resort was had to individual subscriptions. An order from the king was obtained, as heretofore stated, forbidding the issue of further grants by the governor of New York; but before the purpose of his mission had been fully accomplished, Mr. Robinson was seized with the smallpox, and died.

The progress of Governor Tryon, in his efforts to obtain possession of the disputed lands, underwent some interruption from the order of the king in regard to making grants. It was, however, soon discovered, that the order did not, technically, prohibit his taking possession of lands which he had already granted, but only forbade the issue of new grants. In October, 1769, the governor's council advised him that the king's order "did not extend to prevent the governor from the granting of any lands which had not previously been granted by New Hampshire." He therefore proceeded to issue new patents, and in effect wholly neglected the king's order, and continued giving lands to his friends, without regard to their having been previously granted by New Hampshire. Thus, the mission of Mr. Robinson to England, although attended with apparent success, had no other effect upon the New-York government, than to impose a temporary check upon its operations. However, it inspired the settlers with new confidence in the justice of their cause, and gave them strong reasons to hope that their rights would eventually be acknowledged and protected by the "home government," which was then recognized as the supreme authority that would finally decide the question.

In 1769, the efforts of the New-York claimants to obtain possession of the disputed lands, were again commenced with great vigor. In October of that year, a number of the inhabitants of Bennington were assembled on the farm of James Brackenridge, in the western part of the town, for the purpose of assisting him in harvesting his corn. While they were thus employed, a number of surveyors came upon the farm, and appeared to be running a line across it. Mr. Brackenridge, and Mr. Samuel Robinson left their work, and entered into conversation with them. The surveyors declared that they were acting under the authority of the state of New York, for the purpose of dividing among the proprietors the patent of Wallumschaik.* Brackenridge and Robinson forbade their proceeding further, stating, at the same time, that it

* It was asserted that, about ten years previous to the grant of the township of Bennington by Governor Wentworth, a Dutchman, named Wallum, had obtained from the governor of New York, a grant, covering nearly all of the same territory, although he took no measures

was not their intention to use violence, but merely to protest against the proceeding, for the purpose of preserving their legal rights. Much conversation took place, and finally the party desisted from their survey, and retired. Upon this, Abraham Ten Brook, one of the proprietors of the patent, petitioned the governor and council of New York on the subject; stating, that the commissioners and surveyors for dividing the patent of Wallumschaik, had been "violently opposed by sundry persons, and prevented by their threats from executing the trusts reposed in them." Upon which a proclamation was issued by the governor "for apprehending and securing the principals and ringleaders;" and at the following January term of the court at Albany, several persons who had been present were indicted as rioters. Among them was the Rev. Jedediah Dewey, Joseph Robinson, Elijah Fay, Thomas Henderson, Ebenezer Robinson, and John Stewart. None of them, however, were arrested or brought to trial. Other attempts, of a similar character, were attended with the same results, and actions of ejectment were brought by the New-York grantees against the settlers. Affairs were approaching a crisis. Upon the actions of ejectment depended the title to the lands, so far as the courts of New York could determine the question. Although the people had but little confidence in these tribunals, they resolved to appear and

to occupy it. The grant was called Wallumschaik — the termination "chaik" meaning scrip or patent. This gave name to the stream passing through it; the orthography of which, in accordance with the pronunciation. was changed to Walloomscoik.

make the best defense in their power. The management of the business was intrusted to Ethan Allen. Bold, enterprising, ambitious, and having extreme confidence in his powers, both of body and mind, he entered zealously upon his task. His aid was rendered the more valuable, by reason of his extensive acquaintance in New England and New York. Although laboring under the disadvantages of a defective early education, he possessed considerable general information, and he could write a letter or an argument in strong and intelligible, if not accurate and polished language; and he could address a multitude, and, when occasion required, a court, with skill and effect. Upon his selection as an agent to defend the suits brought against the settlers, he went to New Hampshire, and obtained copies of Governor Wentworth's commission and instructions from the king, under which he had acted in making the grants. He next proceeded to Connecticut, and engaged the services of Mr. Ingersoll, an eminent counselor of that time. In June, 1770, they appeared before the court in Albany. An action of ejectment against Josiah Carpenter, of Shaftsbury, came on for trial; and the defendant's counsel offered in evidence the documents above mentioned, together with the charter of the township, and a deed of the land in question from the original proprietor to the defendant. This evidence was rejected by the court, on the ground that the New-Hampshire charters were illegal and void, and the jury were directed to find a verdict for the plaintiff. Two other actions were tried with the same result. As all the cases were precisely like these, their decision was regarded as a precedent for the residue, and no further attempts at a defense were made, in the various trials which ensued.* The defendants and their friends did not, however, contemplate that the matter would end at Albany. After Allen retired from the court, several gentlemen, interested in the New-York grants—one of whom was the king's attorney-general for the colony—called upon him, and urged him to go home and advise his friends to make the best terms they could with their new landlords; intimating that their cause was now desperate, and reminding him of the proverb, that "might often prevails against right." Allen coolly replied: "The gods of the valleys are not the gods of the

* In 1779, Allen published a work, entitled, "A Vindication of the opposition of the Inhabitants of Vermont to the governor of New York, and of their right to form into an independent state, humbly submitted to an impartial world, by Ethan Allen." From this work, the following characteristic account of these trials is taken: "In the year 1769, the claimants under the subsequent grants from New York, and not residing on the controverted premises, brought actions of ejectment in the supreme court held at Albany, against sundry actual settlers, who claimed the soil by virtue of prior grants from New Hampshire. But most, if not all the judges and attornies, particularly Messrs. Duane and Kemp, which attended the court, were patentees under New York; and some of them interested in the very patents on trial. The plaintiffs appearing in great state and magnificence, which, together with their junto of land thieves, made a brilliant appearance; but the defendants appearing but in ordinary fashion, having been greatly fatigued by hard labor wrought on the disputed premises, and their cash much exhausted, made a very disproportionate figure at court. In fine, interest, conviction and grandeur, being all on one side, easily turned the scale against the honest defendants, and judgments without mercy, in favor of the claimants under New York, was given against them," &c.

hills;" and when asked by Kemp, the attorney-general, to explain his meaning, he replied: "If you will accompany me to the hill of Bennington, the sense will be made clear."

The purpose of his mission being thus brought to a close, Mr. Allen returned and reported the particulars to his constituents. The news spread from habitation to habitation, and created a sudden and loud murmur of discontent among the people. Seeing, as they thought, the door of justice shut against them, and having tried, in vain, all the peaceable means of securing their rights, they resolved to appeal to the last arbiter of disputes. The inhabitants of Bennington immediately assembled, and came to a formal determination to defend their property by force, and to unite in resisting all encroachments upon the lands occupied by persons holding titles under the warrants granted by the governor of New Hampshire. This was a bold step; but it was promptly taken, and with a seeming determination to adhere to it, at any hazard, and without regard to consequences. Nor was this decision changed or weakened by a proposition on the part of the New-York patentees, made about this time, which allowed to each occupant a fee-simple of his farm, at the same price for which the unoccupied lands in his neighborhood were sold. The first purchasers still insisted that this was requiring them to pay twice for their lands; and that, in any view, the proposal was not just, inasmuch as the value of the unoccupied lands depended mainly on the settlements which had been made in their vicinity, by the toil, and at the expense, of the original occupants. In short, the time for talking about charters, and boundaries, and courts of judicature, was past, and the mountaineers were now fully bent on conducting the controversy by a more summary process.

Actions of ejectment continued to be brought before the Albany courts; but the settlers, despairing of success, after the decision of the first cases, did not appear in defense, nor give themselves any more trouble in the matter. Next came sheriffs and civil magistrates to execute the writs of possession, and by due course of law to remove the occupants from the lands. At this crisis, the affair assumed a tangible shape. The mountaineers felt themselves at home on the soil which they had subdued by their own labor, and in the territory over which they had begun to exercise supreme dominion, by meeting in conventions and committees, and taking counsel of each other on public concerns. To drive one of them from his house, or deprive him of his hard-earned substance, was to threaten the whole community with an issue, fatal alike to their dearest interests, and to the rights which every man deems as sacred as life itself. It was no wonder, therefore, that they should unite in a common cause, which required their combined efforts to maintain. But the results of the trials at Albany had given additional confidence to the New-York claimants, and they determined on renewed efforts to obtain possession of the disputed lands. The proprietors of the Wallumschaik patent made another attempt to survey the township of Bennington; but, as in previous instances, the endeavor was unsuccessful. The surveyors had not proceeded far, when they were met by a body of twenty or thirty of the settlers, who warned them to desist, in so decided a tone, that they abandoned the undertaking. This was in September, 1770. Abraham Ten Brook, one of the proprietors of the patent, in behalf of himself and the other proprietors, petitioned the governor and council of New York on the subject; stating "that the proclamation which the governor had issued on the 11th of December, 1769, for apprehending rioters, had been attended with no effect — that actions of ejectment had been tried at the last summer-assizes at Albany, against the settlers, and three different verdicts obtained against them, and that another defendant had made default — that these judgments had induced the petitioners to believe the commissioners might proceed unmolested; but that they had been opposed by a riotous and tumultuous body, who armed themselves with clubs, and warned them to desist from their business; threatening them with violence, &c. The petition also stated that the commissioners did not think it safe to proceed further, and prayed the governor and council for aid and relief in the premises." The petition was taken into consideration, and in October, 1770, the council advised the governor "to issue a proclamation for apprehending Simeon Hatheway, Moses Scott, Jonathan Fisk, and Silas Robinson, principal authors and actors in said riot, and to insert in the proclamation, the declaration that the governor had orders from the king, to protect the New-York claimants with his whole power and authority."

At this period, and for some time afterward, one of the most active and efficient advocates and supporters of the New-York government, was John Munro, proprietor of a patent under that province, lying upon White creek and extending into the present town of Shaftsbury. He held the office of justice of the peace for Albany county, and resided on his patent. He had a number of tenants and dependents about him, and by his boldness and energy of character, was very troublesome to the occupants of the New-Hamsphire grants. In obedience to the governor's proclamation, Henry Ten Eyck, sheriff of the county of Albany, in company with Munro and others, repaired to the house of Silas Robinson, in Bennington, early on the morning of the 29th of November, and arrested him. By attacking him unexpectedly, and returning precipitately to Albany, they succeeded in committing him to the jail, before any attempt could be made by his neighbors to rescue him. The sheriff was much elated by his success, and wrote an account of it to the governor, who returned a highly complimentary letter, and directed him to keep the prisoner in custody until he should be released by due course of law. Robinson was afterward indicted, but was finally released, on giving bail for his appearance at court. Fourteen others were indicted with Robinson, but no attempt was made to arrest them.

From the time judgments were rendered in the ejectment suits at Albany, in the spring of 1771, various efforts were made by the sheriff to put the plaintiffs in possession of the premises which had been adjudged to them, but without success. Wherever he went, he was sure to be met by a party larger than that which accompanied him, and was told that any attempt to execute a writ of possession would certainly be resisted by force. These facts being reported to the governor, he directed them to summon the militia of the county to his aid. This was accordingly done, and in July, 1771, an attempt was made to arrest James Brackenridge. The following account of this expedition is from Ira Allen's History of Vermont:*

"The sheriff of Albany county summoned the *posse* to aid him in serving a writ of possession upon James Brackenridge. The sheriff was followed by seven hundred and fifty men well armed, and three hundred settlers assembled to resist him. The settlers had full notice of his approach, and had completed their arrangements for defence. An officer with eighteen men was placed in the house — one hundred and twenty behind trees in a wood near a road through which the sheriff must march and would naturally halt his men. The other division was stationed behind a ridge of land in a meadow, within gunshot of the house, and out of sight of the sheriff's men. Thus an ambuscade was formed to have a crossfire on the sheriff's men without endangering themselves, and to be ready against the sheriff forced the door, which was to be known by hoisting a red flag above the top of the chimney. When the sheriff approached, all were silent: he and his men were completely within the ambuscade before they discovered their situation. Mr. Ten Eyck, the sheriff, went to the house and demanded entrance as the sheriff of Albany county, and threatened on refusal to force the door. The answer was 'Attempt it and you are dead men.' He repeated his demand and threat without using any force, & received for a second answer hideous groans from within! At this time the two divisions exhibited their hats on the points of their guns, which appeared to be more numerous than they really were. The sheriff and his

---

* This is a small work, published by Allen in London, in 1798. It is now rarely to be met with.

posse seeing their dangerous situation, and not being interested in the dispute, made a hasty retreat, so that a musket was not fired on either side, which gave satisfaction to and cemented the union of the inhabitants, & raised their consequence in the neighboring provinces."

Although the New-York claimants had been foiled in their attempts to execute their writs of possession, they did not abandon their determination to substantiate their claims by other means. Finding that the militia of Albany county could not be relied upon to act effectually against the settlers, they sought to accomplish their object by less direct means. The old practice of indictment for riots was again resorted to; favorable offers of titles under New York were made to prominent individuals residing on the grants; offices were conferred on others; and persons from New York were encouraged to make settlements on unoccupied lands which had been granted by New Hampshire. By these means it was hoped divisions would be created among the people, and the New-York interest so much strengthened as to secure its predominance. In order effectually to resist these movements of the New-York authorities, committees of safety were appointed by the several towns west of the Green Mountains, who met in convention, passed resolutions, and adopted regulations which had the potency of laws with their constituents. It was decreed, among other things, that no officer of New York should convey any person from the New-Hampshire Grants without permission of the committee of safety; and that no surveys should be made, or settlements attempted by people from New York, upon any portion of the territory originally in dispute between New York and New Hampshire. For a violation of this law, the offender was to be punished according to the judgment of the committees of safety, or "the ideas of the people." Nevertheless, the civil officers of New York were to be allowed the exercise of their proper functions in the collection of debts, and also in other matters not connected with the controversy in regard to lands. That a force might be ready to act in any emergency, a military association was formed, of which Ethan Allen was appointed commandant, with the title of colonel, and Seth Warner, Remember Baker, Robert Cockrane, Gideon Warner, and some others were appointed captains. The men were armed, and occasionally met for military exercise. John Munro, in a letter to Governor Tryon, stated that "the rioters had established a company at Bennington, commanded by Captain Warner—and that on New Year's day (1772) his company was reviewed and continued all day in military exercise and firing at marks."

In pursuance of the policy heretofore mentioned, the grantees made attempts to establish settlements on the western borders of the grants. Whenever this was done, Ethan Allen, at the head of a detachment of the "Green-Mountain Boys," as the men under his command were called, promptly met the intruders and drove them off. The New-York sheriffs continued to be pursued with unremitting eagerness, whenever they dared to set their feet on the forbidden ground. With these various affairs on his hands, it will readily be imagined that the commander of the Green-Mountain Boys was not idle; nor was it surprising that he should attract the particular notice of the New-York government. So many complaints were made of the riotous and disorderly proceedings of his volunteers and associates ; such was the indignation of the New-York party on account of the harsh measures adopted by them toward the persons whom they seized as trespassers upon their property ; and so entirely did they set at defiance the laws of New York, to which their opponents accounted them amenable, that the governor was tempted to try the virtue of another proclamation, in which he branded the deed of dispossessing a New-York settler with the opprobrious name of felony, and offered a reward of twenty pounds to any person who would apprehend and secure Allen, or either of eight other persons connected with him, and mentioned by name.

Whether this proclamation was thought too mild in its terms, or whether new outrages had added to the enormity of the offense, it is not easy to decide; but another was promulgated, enlarging the bounty for Allen to one hundred and fifty pounds, and for Seth Warner and five others to fifty pounds each. Not to be outdone by the authority of New York in exercising the prerogatives of sovereignty, Colonel Allen and his friends sent out a counter-proclamation,* offering a

---

* Advertisement. £25 Reward. Whereas James Duane and John Kempe of New York, have by their menaces and threats greatly disturbed the public Peace and Repose of the honest Peasants of Bennington and the settlements to the Northward, which Peasants are now, and ever have been in the Peace of God & the King, and are patriotic and liege subjects of George the Third,— Any person that will apprehend those common disturbers, viz., James Duane and John Kempe, and bring them to Landlord Fays at Bennington, shall have £15 Reward for James Duane, and £10 for John Kempe, paid by   ETHAN ALLEN,
                                                                     REMEMBER BAKER,
Dated at Poultney, Feb. 5th 1772.   ROBERT COCKRANE.

reward for the apprehension of the persons who had become most obnoxious to the inhabitants of the New-Hampshire Grants. Notwithstanding the frequency of proclamations, it is believed that no person was apprehended in consequence of them, which is a proof that the people of the parts of New York adjoining the New-Hampshire grants were more favorable to the settlers than were prominent men of the colony; otherwise, the allurement of the reward would have induced combinations for seizing individual offenders, particularly as the people were required by law to assist the sheriff in the execution of his office. Allen never denied that the conduct of himself and his mountaineers, interpreted by the laws of New York, or the laws of any well-ordered society, was properly called riotous; but he contended that they were driven to this extremity by the oppression of their stronger neighbors; that no other means were left by which they could defend their property; and that, under such circumstances, they were perfectly justified in resorting to these means. They encroached not upon the possessions of other people; they remained on their own soil; and, if riots existed, they were caused by those who came among them for molestation and injury. Viewing things in this light, he thought it hard, and with reason, that he should first be called a rioter, then a criminal rioter, and last of all be denounced to the world as a felon, with a price set upon his liberty, and threats of condign punishment if he should be taken.*

But Allen, who was brave even to rashness, was in no degree intimidated by the reward offered for his

* See Sparks' Life of Ethan Allen.

apprehension, and this he designed that those who had advised that measure should fully understand. Much anxiety was felt by his friends for his safety, on account of the many opportunities which his indifference to danger afforded for arresting him. Allen, however, laughed at their fears, and offered a bet that he would proceed to Albany, alight at the most prominent house of entertainment, drink a bowl of punch, and finally escape unharmed. This was accepted. Having made the necessary arrangements, Allen proceeded to Albany, and, after deliberately alighting from his horse, and entering the house with a haughty air, called for a bowl of punch, according to the terms of his bet. The intelligence that "Ethan Allen was in the city," spread rapidly, and a large concourse of people collected around the house, among whom was the sheriff of Albany county. Allen was wholly unmoved. Having finished his punch, he went to the door, mounted his horse, and giving a hearty "Huzza for the Green Mountains," departed unharmed. Those who were disposed to arrest him felt that the enterprise would not be unaccompanied with danger.

On another occasion, Allen's temerity very nearly proved his ruin. While traveling upon the shores of Lake Champlain, opposite Crown Point, with a single companion, he stopped at the house of a Mr. Richards. It happened that, at the same time, a party of six soldiers from the neighboring fortress, fully armed, were at the house, with the intention of remaining during the night. Knowing Allen, they determined on arresting him, and obtaining the tempting reward offered by the government of New York for his apprehension.

Mrs. Richards overheard their conversation, and when lighting Allen and his companion to their room, informed them of the design of the soldiers; and silently raising a window, advised them to escape. When the soldiers discovered that Allen had left the house, they threatened Mrs. Richards with punishment, for conniving at the escape of the heroic leader of the Green-Mountain Boys; but she apologized, on the ground that if she had failed to do so, the people would have torn down her house, and driven herself and family from their possessions.

John Munro, who has been heretofore mentioned as an active and determined partisan of New York, in the hope of receiving the reward offered by Governor Tryon, and to enjoy the honor which would attend the success of such an undertaking, resolved on capturing and carrying to Albany one of the persons who had been outlawed by the proclamation. He accordingly assembled ten or twelve of his friends and dependents, and, on the morning of March 22d, 1772, before daylight, surrounded the house of Remember Baker, of Arlington, for the purpose of arresting him. Armed with swords and pistols, they burst open the door and entered the house. Baker was severely wounded upon the head and arm by a sword. His wife, and a son about twelve years of age, were also treated with great inhumanity, the one being wounded upon the head and neck by the blow of a sword, and the other receiving a dangerous cut upon his arm. Baker, being overpowered by numbers, was bound, thrown bleeding into a sleigh, and driven rapidly toward Albany. The alarm was spread with great rapidity, and in a short time ten well-armed men mounted their horses, and started in pursuit of the captors. Others, as speedily as preparations could be made, hastened to their assistance. As Munro, with his prisoner, reached the Hudson river, the party in pursuit also arrived at the ferry. Munro and his party abandoned their prisoner and fled. Captain Baker, who was nearly exhausted from loss of blood, needed the immediate care of his hardy friends. They dressed his wounds, and carried him back to his family, to the extreme joy of the entire community. Munro, in the report of this transaction to the governor of New York, represented the conflict at Baker's house as a very desperate one, and said "he had reason to be thankful to divine Providence, for the preservation of his life, and that of the whole party." An account of the scene, written, as it was understood, by Ethan Allen, was published in the Connecticut Courant, of June 9, 1772, with the ensuing title: "The following contains a true narrative of the sufferings and abuses received by Mr. Remember Baker, his Wife and Family, on the 22d day of March, A. D. 1772, at his own dwelling-house in Arlington, and on the lands granted by his late Excellency Benning Wentworth, Esq., late Governor of the Province of New Hampshire." *

"This wicked, inhuman, most barbarous, infamous, cruel, villainous and thievish Act was perpetrated, committed, and carried into execution by one John Munro, a reputed Justice of the Peace, living near that place, with a number of ruffians, his neighbors — who,

* This curious document, the style of which was well suited to the feelings and comprehension of the uneducated Green-Mountain Boys, is republished *verbatim.*

after a Lords day consultation in plotting this wicked and horrid design, surprised the said Baker in his said dwelling-house, about the first appearance of morning light, on the said 22d day of March, and, after making an attempt to discharge their fire-arms through the said Baker's house, and finding their fire-arms missing fire, said Munro with his attendants, did with axes forcibly break and enter the said Baker's house, and with weapons of death, spread destruction round the room, cutting with swords and bruising with fire-arms and clubs men women and children, swearing by —* he would have Baker dead or alive, and that he would burn the house, Baker Wife & Children and all the effects, and to compass and bring this villainous scheme into execution, did with his own wicked and rebellious hand convey fire from the hearth in the said house to a cupboard in the room, it being the most convenient place to answer his intentions, when all on a sudden, as quick as a flash, a Judas spirit, that of gain and plunder, overballanced his wicked noddle. This being agreed on, he instantly thrust his sword at Mrs. Baker with an intention to have ended at that instant her life (as he has since confessed) when her right arm, near her elbow joint, for that time, happily preserved her from the intended *murder*. Others, in the mean time, his attendants, were mauling and beating and bruising his children. Mr. Baker, having at that time posted himself in his Chamber for the better security of himself, family and effects, finding their malice oaths and imprecations principally levelled at his person, thought most proper to leave his chamber, thinking thereby to draw the murderers after him and so give his family in their wounded circumstances a better opportunity to save themselves from impending ruin and utter destruction, accordingly burst a board from the gable end of the house and leaped out of the window he had by that means made, when part of the ruffians, by the

---

* Wherever oaths occur in the original narrative of the assault upon Mr. Baker, as well as other documents republished in these pages, their place will be supplied with a dash.

said Justice's command, were ordered (after firing on said Baker, and saying three times successively, —— him he is dead) to set on him a large spiteful wilful and very malicious dog, educated and brought up agreeable to their own forms and customs who being like those other servants of the devil at that time all obedience, seized the said Baker, and being instantly joined by those his cruel partners, bound and pinioned him so fast that he was unable to use or make even the least resistance in defence of himself, his unhappy wounded wife, or his poor helpless distressed children.

"And not being as yet satisfied with their own unlawful proceedings, and their thirst for blood not being quenched, the better to enhance & increase their horrid crime and procure a fell draught of human blood, to quench their unnatural thirst, did convey the said Baker to the carriage in which they rode; where in his confined state, the said John did with his attendants, Tomahawk, cut and slash in spots, that their eyes might see a life languish out by degrees in streams of blood, while they did with a —— —— at almost every breath, laugh him in the face, to express their satisfaction in his agonizing groans.

"In this awful and lamentable situation, almost on the verge of eternity, by means of the bruises, cuts, and great effusion of blood, said Baker with a voice according to his strength, called for his clothes as he was yet naked from his bed, who was denied them by the said Justice, which after several strokes with his naked sword over said Baker's naked face and eyes, and breaking the same in three pieces and gave him this reflection, that —— —— him he would cloath him as a —— —— traitor; which aggravating threats, gave them a new sip to their beloved revenge.—Thus they continued him in his naked journey, for the space of four miles and a half, with many cruel words, and hard blows stopping his breath with handkerchiefs, till almost suffocated, lest he should apply to some person for relief.

"The said Justice and attendants had taken what of the effects belonged to the house, he and they thought worthy their present affrighted notice; although they would in probability have been more faithful in the prosecution of self and worldly gain, had not they have feared a surprise in so unchristian an act.—They pursued their journey with severe words and cruel threats as though resolved to take a full swing and make an ample feast of human cruelty, until pursued by three persons loyal and faithful subjects to the Crown of Great Britain, whose banner they mean ever more to live and die under, and, after inquiring for the preservation of the life of said Baker, were immediately fired on by several of Munro's party and robbed of what interest he had with him, to the value of forty dollars, as a fresh sip and recruit to their hellish demand. These distressing tidings being soon spread on the premises, enhanced the innocent inhabitants, and for the preservation of Baker his family & their own persons, families and effects, some of them did pursue the said carriage about thirty miles, and when said John with his attendants, being savage like, conscience struck and condemned, run and hid themselves so private that it is not known by his or their acquaintances where they have been ever since; leaving the said Baker with very little remains of life, unable to fight for himself, who willingly in his capacity accepted of mercy, which he had been so long a stranger to.

"The foregoing contains but a very short, though true account of the barbarous conduct of the said John towards the said Baker and family, and such conduct exercised by a pretended civil magistrate, or such a magistrate rather must be dishonorable, a reproach, shame, disgrace &c. on the laws, restrictions, regulations, peace, manners, good order and economy, both of the Laws of God and Man. The above and much more can be attested with good authority, as many worthy persons were eye witnesses of the said tragedy. The robbery has since been confessed by the said Justice and he has promised to make amends."

But to return to the spring of 1772. The attack upon Captain Baker, as might have been anticipated, produced a strong feeling of indignation among his friends and partisans. This was still further increased by a subsequent attempt of Munro to arrest Captain Seth Warner. The latter, with a single friend, was riding on horseback in the vicinity of Munro's residence. Munro, with several of his dependents, met them, and entered into conversation. Suddenly, Munro seized the bridle of Warner's horse, and commanded those present to aid in his arrest. Warner, after advising the New-York magistrate to desist, struck him over the head with his cutlass so powerfully, that he fell to the ground insensible. The spectators, intimidated by this energetic action, made no attempt to interfere; and Warner rode off, without further molestation. Munro received no permanent injury, and speedily recovered. He wrote to the governor, however, giving a most dismal account of the state of affairs in his vicinity; stating, among other things, that the "rioters," by their number and boldness, were "striking terror into the whole country—that he was in a continual fear of them, as he could not find a single magistrate or officer that would speak or act against them—that he was almost worn out with watching, and that nothing but the most vigorous measures for the defense of his property, would save it from destruction."

It now became the fixed determination of the settlers, at all hazards, to maintain their position by expelling from the New-Hampshire Grants every person who should attempt to act under the authority of the New-York claimants. While the feelings of the people were highly exasperated by the occurrences which have been narrated, intelligence reached Bennington that Governor Tryon was ascending the Hudson, with a body of British troops, who were on the way to subdue the refractory Green-Mountain Boys. This news was the more readily credited, as the royal troops had recently been employed at "Bateman's Patent," in the colony of New York, to quell an insurrection founded on a dispute in regard to the title or rents of lands; and it was also known that the New-York claimants to the New-Hampshire Grants, had applied to the governor to send the troops of the regular army against the Green-Mountain Boys. The report of the approach of Governor Tryon at first produced alarm. The committees of safety, with the military officers, met in convention, to consult on the measures proper to be taken. Their perilous situation was anxiously discussed, and on full consideration it was finally resolved, that "it was their duty to oppose Governor Tryon and his troops to the utmost of their power." This resolution being taken, every practical measure was adopted to make their resistance effectual. Two pieces of cannon and a mortar were procured from Fort Hoosic and taken to Bennington, and a general rally of all persons capable of bearing arms was instituted. A plan of operations was devised, by which a few sharp-shooters were to be stationed in a narrow pass on the road leading from Albany to Bennington, who were to remain in concealment, and shoot down the officers as they approached with their troops. The same marksmen were then to return through the woods, and join another party of their comrades in a similar position, where they were to exercise their unerring skill in the use of the rifle, and, when they could no longer maintain their position, retreat to the main body, who would be prepared to receive the invading troops, disordered and dispirited as it was supposed they would be by the loss of their officers. A trusty person was dispatched to Albany, with instructions to await the arrival of Governor Tryon's army; to observe the officers particularly, that he might distinguish them again; and to ascertain as many particulars as he should be able in regard to the number of the enemy, the time of marching, and their intended movements. The messenger returned with the welcome information, that the troops were bound for Ticonderoga and Crown Point, and that they had no intention of marching toward Bennington. Although the people were happily relieved from the necessity of putting their valor to the test, their prompt and bold preparations for the onset were a pledge that in no event would it have terminated in their dishonor. The increased number of troops stationed within their immediate vicinity, could have no other effect than to strengthen their apprehensions as to the ultimate designs of the governor of New York.

Information of the proceedings of the Green-Mountain Boys, during this alarm, soon reached the governor of New York, in letters from Munro, and also from several individuals, who, in consequence of having repurchased their lands from New York, had excited the animosity of their neighbors, and deemed it prudent to flee to Albany, during the preparations to resist Governor Tryon. This magistrate, from the number and determined spirit of the settlers, as indicated during their apprehension of an invasion, seems to have been impressed with the difficulty of subduing them by force, and to have come to the determination of trying what could be done by negotiation. He accordingly prepared a letter, addressed to the Rev. Mr. Dewey and other principal inhabitants of Bennington, in which, after censuring the illegality of their conduct, he expressed a strong desire to do them justice, and invited them to send a deputation of such persons as they might choose, to lay before him a full statement of their grievances, and the reasons for their resistance to his authority. "That there may be no obstruction," continued the governor, "to your laying before me, in council, as soon as possible, a fair representation of your conduct, I do hereby engage full security and protection to any persons whom you shall choose to send on this business to New York, from the time they leave their homes to the time of their return, except Robert Cockrane, as also Allen, Baker and Sevil, mentioned in my proclamation of the 10th of December last, and Seth Warner, whose audacious behavior to a civil magistrate has subjected him to the penalties of the laws of his country."

This letter was duly delivered to the occupants of the New-Hampshire Grants by the sheriff of Albany county. On receiving this invitation to negotiate, the people of Bennington and the neighboring towns assembled by their committees, took the subject into consideration, and promptly acceded to the proposal. They returned a firm and respectful answer to Governor Tryon, detailing the oppressions which they had suffered, and urging him to discontinue all violent proceedings against them, until a full representation of the matter could be made to the king, and his full decision of all the points involved in the controversy could be obtained. Captain Stephen Fay, with his son, Dr. Jonas Fay, were appointed delegates to return this answer to Governor Tryon, with authority to make particular explanations, in case that functionary should wish them to do so.

Neither was the opportunity to be passed over by Allen and his proscribed friends, of vindicating themselves against the aspersions cast upon them by their enemies, and the stigma of being pointed out to the world as rioters, abettors of mobs, and felons. They sent a joint dispatch to Governor Tryon, in the nature of a protest against the treatment they had received, and in justification of their motives and acts. Allen was again the penman for his brethren; and, considering their provocations, and the degree of excitement to which they had been wrought up, their remonstrance was clothed in language sufficiently respectful — breathing the spirit of men conscious of their dignity, and resolute in the defense of their rights, but ready to meet the awards of justice, and abide by the decision of a fair and impartial tribunal.* Some of their arguments are put in a forcible manner. "If we do not oppose the sheriff and his posse," say they, "he takes immediate possession of our houses and farms; and when others oppose officers in taking their friends so indicted, they are also indicted, and so on, there being no end of indictments against us, so long as we act the bold and manly part, and stand by our liberty. And it comes to this at last: that we must tamely be dispos-

* See Life of Ethan Allen, by Jared Sparks.

sessed, or oppose officers in taking possession; and as a next necessary step, to oppose the taking of rioters, so called, or run away like so many cowards, and quit the country to a number of cringing, polite gentlemen, who have ideally possessed themselves of it already." Again: "Though they style us rioters for opposing them, and seek to catch and punish us as such, yet in reality themselves are the rioters, the tumultuous, disorderly, stimulating faction, or in fine the land-jobbers; and every violent act they have done to compass their designs, though ever so much under pretense of law, is in reality a violation of law, and an insult to the constitution and authority of the crown, as well as to many of us in person, who have been great sufferers by such inhuman exertions of pretended law. Right and wrong are eternally the same to all periods of time, places and nations; and coloring a crime with a specious pretense of law, only adds to the criminality of it, for it subverts the very design of law, prostituting it to the vilest purposes." "We beg leave to observe," says Allen, "that as, on the one hand, no consideration whatever shall induce us to remit, in the least, of our loyalty and gratitude to our most gracious sovereign, nor of a reasonable submission to your Excellency; so, on the other hand, no tyrannical exertions of the powers of the government, can deter us from asserting and vindicating our undoubted rights and privileges as Englishmen." "No person or persons," continues the sturdy patriot, "can be supposed to be under any particular compact or law, except it presupposeth, that that law will protect such person or persons in his or their properties; for otherwise the subject would, by law, be bound to be accessory to his own ruin and destruction, which is inconsistent with the law of self-preservation; but this law being natural as well as eternal, can never be abrogated by the law of men." And again: "The transferring or alienation of property is a sacred prerogative of the true owner — kings and governors cannot intermeddle therewith."* Had kings and governors, in those days, possessed much foresight, they would have been more reluctant to drive men like Ethan Allen to the utterance and armed maintenance of such principles.

Governor Tryon received the agents who were the bearers of these communications, with affability and kindness. He invited them to meet with his council and discuss freely the subjects in dispute. Afterward, a committee of the council made a report to the governor respecting the controversy, and made the following recommendations: "The committee are desirous your Excellency should afford the inhabitants of those townships all the relief in your power, by suspending, till his Majesty's pleasure shall be known, all prosecutions in behalf of the crown, on account of the crimes with which they stand charged, by depositions before us; and to recommend it to the owners of the contested lands under grants from this province, to put a stop, during the same period, to all civil suits concerning the lands in question." This report of the committee was approved by the governor and council, and with this intelligence the Fays returned to their constituents, and were hailed as the harbingers of peace and joy.

* This letter is published entire in Slade's Vermont State Papers — a collection of historic documents of great interest.

The people had never asked for more than was implied in these terms, being well persuaded that, however the question of jurisdiction might be settled, the king could never sanction a course of proceeding which would deprive them of their property. Gladness was diffused rapidly throughout the cabins of the remotest settlers. A large public meeting was held at Bennington, where the minutes of the governor's approval of a peaceful policy were read amid loud acclamations, and for the moment, the memory of all former griefs was swept away by the overflowing tide of enthusiasm in favor of Governor Tryon. The following account of the proceedings of this meeting was sent to Albany by the Fays:

"We, as messengers, laid before the above committee an extract of the minutes of his Majesty's council of the province of New York of the 2d instant, together with his Excellency Governor Tryon's letter of the same date, directed to the inhabitants of Bennington, &c., and after reading the same, the above committee and a numerous concourse of the inhabitants of the adjacent country and other spectators, gave a full and unanimous vote in favor of the papers aforesaid; and the thanks of the people were presented to us for our diligence in procuring these papers. Peace was also recommended on the whole New Hampshire Grants, by all who were present; when the whole artillery of Bennington, with the small-arms, were several times discharged in honor of the governor and council of New York.— Health to the king — Health to Governor Tryon — Health to the council of New York — Universal peace and plenty, liberty and prosperity, by

sundry respectable gentlemen, some of whom were from neighboring provinces. STEPHEN FAY,
JONAS FAY."

This season of rejoicing was of but short continuance. The reconciliation was not so complete as the people imagined. The seeds of contention had not been eradicated, and it was but a short time before the former animosity between the Green-Mountain Boys and the governor of New York resumed its wonted vigor. The conciliatory resolve of the governor and council contained an ambiguity which had escaped the notice of a people eager to believe that they were to receive justice. The New-York grantees were requested to refrain from prosecuting their claims until the king's pleasure could be known; but nothing was said in regard to suspending executions where suits had already been decided in their favor. There was no prohibition of their claiming possession of the lands which had been awarded to them by such decisions, nor were they required to desist from surveying the lands and determining their situation or boundaries. Hence, many actual sources of dissension and tumult still remained open. Unfortunately, an act of violence on the part of the inhabitants of the Grants, hastened the interruption of the friendly feeling which it was hoped had been established. During the absence of the commissioners in New York, intelligence was received at Bennington that Mr. Kockburn, a surveyor who was especially odious to the people, was busily engaged in some of the northern townships, in the survey of lands. A small party, with Colonel Allen at their head, went in pursuit of Mr. Kockburn, and succeeded in capturing him and in destroying his instruments. He was taken to Castleton, tried by a court-martial, and threatened with death should he ever again enter the interdicted territory. But at this juncture, the result of the mission of the Fays to New York was learned, and Mr. Kockburn was released, and the sentence against him withdrawn. During the expedition in search of Mr. Kockburn, Ethan Allen and his party dispossessed the tenants of an intruder in New Haven, near the mouth of Otter creek. The charter of the townships had been granted by New Hampshire in 1763, and as early as 1769, a settlement was commenced under the charter, and a saw-mill erected. Soon afterward, Colonel Reid, of New York, who claimed under a subsequent patent from that province, forcibly turned out the New-Hampshire settlers and put his own tenants in possession. They erected additional log-houses and a grist-mill. Allen gave these persons a short time to remove their effects, and then burned the houses, requiring the people to repurchase under New Hampshire, or leave the district. Pangburn, the former proprietor, was put in possession of his saw-mill, but the machinery of the grist-mill was destroyed. Governor Tryon, on hearing of these exploits, was much exasperated. He wrote a letter to the inhabitants of the Grants, complaining of this conduct as an insult to the government, and a violation of public faith. This letter was taken into consideration by the committees of the several townships, assembled at Manchester, who returned a bold and decisive, though conciliatory answer. They asserted that their conduct could be no breach of faith, because none was plighted until the 15th of July, when the proposition of Governor Tryon was accepted by the people in convention at Bennington, and that the transactions complained of had happened before that time; that if there had been any violation of the compact, the New-York claimants had been the aggressors in undertaking to survey and occupy the territory in dispute. If such conduct, contended they, was not forbidden by the agreement proposed by Governor Tryon and accepted by the people, they had wholly misunderstood the character of his proposition, and had been deceived in regard to the compact which had received their approval. They assured him that they had never consented, and never would consent to abandon their property to the land speculators of New York. Although the forms of civility were retained in the correspondence, it was evident that the situation of the people was precisely what it had been previous to any attempt at negotiation. Indeed, as is usual in cases of unsuccessful efforts at reconciliation, the animosity of the parties was increased, and the prospect of a peaceful termination of the difficulties was much diminished.

A meeting of deputies, from the towns on the west side of the Green Mountains, was held at Manchester, on the 21st of October, 1772, which not only confirmed all previous resolutions to resist the New-Yorkers, but adopted others still more belligerent. For the purpose of strengthening their interest on the Grants, the New-York government renewed the policy of appointing several of the most conspicuous and influential settlers to office. In some instances these appointments were attended with the anticipated results, and the individuals thus distinguished became the adherents of the government by which they had been honored. To counteract the tendency of this policy, it was decreed by the convention, that no person residing within the limits of the disputed territory should hold or accept office under New York. On conviction before a proper tribunal of Green-Mountain Boys, the offender was to be punished at the discretion of the "court." The punishment under this decree, which continued in force for several years, was commonly whipping and banishment — the whipping was quaintly denominated "the application of the *beech-seal*," or, as Ethan Allen sometimes had it, "a castigation with the twigs of the wilderness." The New-Hampshire Grants were thus actually separated from New York, and thenceforward acted as an independent republic, the people making and administering their own laws, and yielding only a nominal allegiance to the authority of the British crown. Indeed, the people of Bennington seem never to have fully acknowledged the jurisdiction of New York. Until near the beginning of 1770, the notifications of all town-meetings were usually headed, "Province of New Hampshire;" but after that time they were simply entitled "Town of Bennington," without any allusion to the province in which it was situated. This was continued until 1778, when the inhabitants of the Grants formally announced their independence, and adopted a written constitution. During the intermediate period they existed as a thorough democracy; all laws and regulations, as well as the time and manner of their enforcement in particular instances, being decided upon in general meetings of the people. The convention at Westminster, it is true, had sent Jehiel Hawley and James Brackenridge as commissioners to London, to seek redress of their grievances from the governor of New York; but the subject of taxing the colonies then engrossed the entire attention of the home government, and prevented any decisive action being taken in regard to the matter.

From the fall of 1772 until the commencement of the Revolution, the controversy with New York was carried on with increasing vigor and animosity. Its history is one of repeated attempts on the part of the New-York authorities to take possession of the disputed lands; of indictments against the occupants of the New-Hampshire Grants as rioters for resisting these attempts; of laws and proclamations for their apprehension and punishment; of the forcible expulsion of the New-York intruders; and of the arrest, punishment or banishment of persons on the Grants who countenanced the New-York titles or jurisdiction. Only a few of the most important incidents of this period need be mentioned. The settlement at New-Haven Falls, the scene of Ethan Allen's summary manner of awarding justice, became the subject of further difficulties. In July, 1773, Colonel Reid, who then resided in New York, induced a number of Scotch emigrants, who had recently landed in that city, to accompany him to New Haven, and become his tenants upon the lands which he claimed under a patent from New York. This party took immediate possession of the improvements — a second time expelling the New-Hampshire settlers. Having repaired his mills, Colonel Reid returned to New York, leaving the Scotchmen to retain possession of the premises and to continue the improvements. Intelligence of this invasion was sent to Bennington, and Allen, Warner, Baker and others immediately repaired to the scene of action, and forcibly reinstated the New-Hampshire claimants. The machinery of the flouring mills was broken, and the miller was warned not to repair it, "on pain of suffering the displeasure of the Green-Mountain Boys." The Scotchmen, who were accompanied by their families, on being informed of the nature of the controversy, declared that they had been deceived by Colonel Reid, removed from the place, and finally settled near the Mohawk river. To prevent further intrusions, Allen and his party caused a block-fort to be erected at the place, and supplied it with a small garrison, which thenceforward afforded full protection to the people in that vicinity. A similar fort was built on the Winooski, amply furnished with arms and ammunition. Further defensive measures were contemplated, and an agent was actually sent abroad to purchase the necessary munitions of war.

In consequence of information received at New York, of these and other occurrences of a similar character, the council advised Governor Tryon, "that the frequency of riots and the boldness of rioters made it necessary to employ a military force;" and unanimously requested him to demand of General Haldimand, the commander of the regular forces, "a sufficient number of troops to occupy Ticonderoga and Crown Point, to aid the magistrates in the performance of their duty." This requirement was made by the governor, but was not well received by the general, who did not appear to be convinced of the propriety of assenting to the use of the regular troops for such a purpose. A voluminous correspondence ensued between the two officials, which was protracted until so late in the season that it became impracticable to transfer the troops to the proposed stations.

The town of Clarendon and its vicinity was the theater of repeated disturbances. The first settlers of the town, which they called Durham, had purchased from the heirs of Lydius. They favored the claims of New York, although they declined to repurchase their lands of either New York or New Hampshire. Governor Tryon, in the hope of obtaining their aid against the claimants of lands under New-Hampshire grants, acquiesced in the validity of their title from the heirs of Lydius. Some of their principal men were appointed magistrates, and they recognized the jurisdiction of New York. This defection, in the midst of the New-Hampshire Grants, gave much uneasiness to the Green-Mountain Boys, and various measures were adopted to induce the "Durhamites," as they were called, to recognize the validity of the titles from Governor Wentworth. In order either to terrify or force them into a compliance with the views of the Green-Mountain Boys, Allen and Baker, with one hundred armed men, marched to Clarendon in the autumn of 1773. The persons against whom the expedition was chiefly undertaken, having notice of the approach of the hostile force, effected their escape. Allen and his party remained in the town several days, "visiting the inhabitants, and exhorting them to repent of their New-York attachments." After committing several acts of violence, and threatening still severer measures should their requirements be disregarded, they returned to their homes. The persons who had fled from Clarendon proceeded to New York, and placed before the governor and council a full statement of the alledged outrages of Allen and his party, which they denominated "the Bennington mob."

In the winter of 1774, the New-York grantees combined their influence, and applied to the assembly for legislative aid against the Green-Mountain Boys. The result was a law purporting to be an act for the prevention of tumultuous and riotous assemblies, and the punishment of rioters, which may safely be pronounced to be one of the most extraordinary specimens of legislative despotism that ever disgraced a statute-book. After naming Ethan Allen, Seth Warner, Remember Baker, Robert Cockrane, Peleg Sunderland, Silvanus Brown, James Brackenridge, and John Smith as the principal leaders in the riots, the law empowered the governor and council to issue a proclamation requiring those persons, or any others who should be indicted for a similar offense, (that of resisting the sheriff,) to surrender themselves for commitment to any justice of the peace, within seventy days from the date of such requirement; and in case this summons should be disobeyed, the person neglecting to surrender himself was to be "adjudged and deemed" convicted, and to suffer death without further trial; and the supreme court was authorized to pass a judicial sentence in the same manner as if an actual trial had been had, and a verdict of guilty duly rendered! This law was enacted on the 9th of March, 1774, and on the same d[ay the] governor, never weary of offering rewards for the apprehension of Allen and his associates, issued a proclamation promising a reward of one hundred pounds for the arrest of Ethan Allen, and fifty pounds for either of the other persons accused as "the principal ringleaders of the Bennington mob." The purpose of these proceedings was to inflict a punishment so severe upon these persons, as would overawe the opposition to the authority of New York. The effect was far otherwise. "They may," said Allen laughingly, "*sentence* us to be hung for refusing to voluntarily place our necks in the halter; but how will the fools manage to hang a Green-Mountain Boy before they catch him?" The committees of the several townships assembled in convention, and took up the subject with more calmness than could have been anticipated under circumstances so irritating. They reviewed the causes of the controversy, asserted anew their rights, affirmed that they were not the aggressors, that all the violence to which they had been accessory was fully justified by the laws of self-preservation, and that they were determined to maintain the ground they had taken, without fear or favor, at every hazard and every sacrifice. They closed their public proceedings by a resolve, that all necessary preparations should be made, and that the inhabitants should hold themselves in readiness at a minute's warning to defend those among them "who, for their merit in the great and general cause, had been falsely denominated rioters;" declaring, at the same time, that they would act only on the defensive, and that in all civil cases, and criminal prosecutions —

really such — they would assist the proper officers to enforce the execution of the laws.

In addition to these public doings of the people at large by their representatives, the proscribed persons, at the head of whom was Ethan Allen, published a manifesto, to which they jointly affixed their names, containing a defense of themselves, and free remarks on the New-York act and proclamation. To look for moderation as a prominent quality in a paper of this kind, is perhaps more than would be authorized by the nature of the case, or the character of the individuals concerned; yet it expressed sentiments which we should be sorry not to find in men whom we would respect, and in whom we would confide in the hour of peril. It spoke in a tone of deep complaint of the injuries they had suffered from the vindictive persecutions of their enemies, protested against the tyrannical abuse of power which would arraign them as criminals for protecting their own property, and threatened death to those who "should be tempted by the wages of unrighteousness offered in the proclamation," and undertake to put in execution against them the sanguinary edict of the New-York assembly. After these decisive manifestoes of the belligerent parties, acts of violence might be anticipated. These were, however, not numerous, nor of a decisive character. There were a few cases in which the "beech-seal" was applied to the partisans of New York with considerable energy; but this punishment was reserved for the most incorrigible offenders. Milder measures were adopted with the less dangerous and active, and usually with success. Ridicule was often employed, and constituted the principal ingredient of the punishments inflicted upon them. An instance of this is found in the case of Doctor Samuel Adams, of Arlington. He openly declared himself a partisan of New York, and was accustomed to speak disrespectfully of the conventions and committees, and advised the public to peaceably purchase the title to their lands from New York. He was informed by his neighbors that his conversation was unacceptable, and they admonished him to be more prudent in the expression of his views. Far from producing a reform, their hints served only to stimulate the anger of the courageous doctor, who forthwith armed himself with pistols and other weapons, and proclaimed his opinions more loudly and decidedly than ever. He announced his full determination to defend himself to the best of his ability against any person who should approach him with any unfriendly design. Such a threat was not likely to be disregarded, and the doctor was seized in an unguarded moment, and compelled to surrender. He was taken to the "Green-Mountain Tavern" in Bennington, (then kept by Captain Stephen Fay, and now occupied as a private residence by his grandson, Samuel Fay, Esq.,) where he was arraigned before the committee, who, not satisfied with his defense, sentenced him to a novel punishment, which was immediately inflicted. Before the door of the tavern stood a sign-post, twenty-five feet high, the top of which was adorned with the skin of a catamount stuffed to the size of life, with its head turned toward Albany, its jaws distended, and its formidable teeth portending destruction to all who should approach from that direction. The contumacious doctor was tied into a chair, and drawn up to the top of the sign-post, where, according to the decision of the court, he was to remain suspended for two hours. This occasioned great merriment to the large assemblage which was present to witness the affair, and so mortified Doctor Adams that he returned to his house in silence, and thenceforward took no part in the controversy.

It will be borne in mind, that the resolutions adopted by the conventions of the people were regarded as the law of the New-Hampshire Grants. Offenses against the dearest rights of the people, when they threatened to be attended with any degree of success, were punished with commensurate severity. The case of Benjamin Hough will serve as an example of this. He was among those who applied to the assembly of New York for legislative aid against the Green-Mountain Boys, and was commissioned as a justice of the peace, on the very day that the assembly passed its sanguinary law and the governor issued his offensive proclamation against the defenders of their mountain homes. Taking with him these documents, he returned to his residence in Clarendon, and undertook to establish the authority of New York. He was repeatedly warned not to act as a magistrate, but, being found incorrigible, was taken before the committee of safety at Sunderland. The committee ordered the resolution of the convention of the New-Hampshire Grants to be read, in which the holding of any office, civil or military, under the colony of New York, within that district, was declared to be penal. The prisoner confessed that he had been active in procuring the passage of the odious New-York law, and in exercising his authority as a magistrate, but pleaded the jurisdiction of New York in justification of his conduct. The sentence of the committee was as follows : " That the prisoner be taken from the bar of this committee of safety, and be tied to a tree, and then, on his naked back, receive two hundred stripes; his back being dressed, he should depart out of the district, and on return, without special leave of the convention, to suffer death." This sentence was carried into execution in the presence of a large concourse of people; and at his request the following certificate was furnished for his future reference :—

" SUNDERLAND, 30th January, 1775.

"This may certify the inhabitants of the New-Hampshire Grants, that BENJAMIN HOUGH hath this day received a full punishment for his crimes committed against this country; and our inhabitants are ordered to give him, the said HOUGH, a free and unmolested passport toward the city of New York, or to the Westward of our Grants, he behaving himself as becometh.

"Given under our hands the day and date aforesaid.
ETHAN ALLEN,
SETH WARNER."

When this paper was handed to Hough, Allen observed that the certificate, together with the receipt on his back, would, no doubt, be admitted as legal evidence before the supreme court and the governor and council of New York, although, in several instances, to his knowledge, the king's warrant to Governor Wentworth and his excellency's sign-manual, with the great seal of the province of New Hampshire, would not. Living, as we now do, in the enjoyment of just and equal laws, and in times when such penalties are never inflicted, it is no slight task to form a proper estimate of the measures now under review. Those who regard them as severe must bear in mind that, aside from the alternative of surrendering their farms, which their industry had made to blossom as the rose, or a determined resistance by force, the settlers on the New-Hampshire Grants were threatened with penalties the most inhuman, for endeavoring to defend the homes that were dear to them. "Let it not be said," remarks a distinguished Vermonter,[*] "that the infliction of this barbarous punishment proves that the people of the Grants were less civilized than the people of other parts of New England; for long afterward this relic of barbarism was found in the criminal code of all the states; but a more advanced state of civilization has since broken up the habit by which it had been continued through generations of civilized man, and it has been exploded, never again to find a place in the code of any of the American states." Aside from the reasons heretofore given for retaliation on the part of the Green-Mountain Boys, it need not escape remembrance that as necessity drove them to resistance, so sound policy would naturally dictate that such resistance should be of a character to inspire a full and firm belief that it would be effectual. Every prospect of reconciliation or submission to the claims of New York had vanished. The New-Hampshire grantees, believing the action of the New-York authorities to originate in the avarice of a set of speculators who

[*] Hon. Daniel Chipman.

coveted their lands, and that the *people* of New York felt no disposition to aid in enforcing such claims—satisfied that the public sentiment was highly favorable to the rights of the settlers—and being aware, from past experience, that the militia of the colony could never be induced to contend against them—regarded with contempt every threat or legal enactment intended to inspire terror. The idea of submission seems never for a moment to have occupied the attention of the handful of brave men against whom these measures were directed. Educated in the school of adversity, and inured to hardships and dangers, they met and sustained the shock with a firm, unbroken spirit.

At the commencement of the controversy in regard to the jurisdiction of the New-Hampshire Grants, the population of that district is supposed not to have exceeded three hundred families; but in the year 1775 the number of inhabitants was estimated at twenty thousand. The smoke of the settlers' cabins curled up from almost all the numerous, beautiful and fertile valleys which nestle amid the Green Mountains; and the sound of the woodman's ax echoed from almost every hill-side. As is usually the case with the pioneers of a new country, the early settlers of Vermont were poor, and wholly dependent upon their efforts for obtaining homes for themselves and families. Their descendants can scarcely realize the privations and sufferings they endured in thus establishing themselves in the unbroken wilderness. In numerous instances, families proceeded to the farms they had purchased, miles from any other human habitation, and encamped in the forest until, by their own unaided efforts, they could erect log-cabins. Many of them traveled in canoes, or on foot, carrying their entire effects upon their backs. The heads of other families proceeded to their farms in the summer, erected cabins, cleared their lands, and in the winter brought their families to their rude and solitary homes. It was not uncommon for them to travel on foot, drawing their household utensils on "handsleds," and, frequently, when the wife was too feeble to endure these trials, the husband would draw her in this manner. A single family would thus move into a township, and reside months without seeing another human being. Mr. Amos Cutler, the first settler in the town of Brandon, spent an entire winter without seeing any other person; and Mr. Abijah Wheelock, an early pioneer of Calais, after a flourishing town had grown up around him, would allude pleasantly to the hermit-life he had formerly endured, by asserting there had been a time when he was the most respectable man in the town. The wife of Thomas Whitmore, the earliest settler in Marlborough, spent the most of one winter alone, her husband being absent on business. This lady lived to the advanced age of eighty-seven years, and saw a flourishing state grow up, where but a few scattered families resided when she entered the territory. Throughout her active years she performed the duties of a nurse; and so indispensable was her assistance considered in that vicinity, in cases where the census of the new state was affected, that the good old lady was enabled to boast, in her declining years, that she had assisted at the birth of over two thousand children!

The New-Hampshire grantees were by no means so engrossed by their own troubles as to be indifferent to the policy pursued by the mother country toward her colonies in America. As the settlers were chiefly emigrants from Connecticut and Massachusetts, they sympathized with the feelings of discontent which pervaded those colonies. Those residing on Connecticut river, who had surrendered their original charters, and taken out new grants under the broad seal of New York, and had submitted to the jurisdiction of that colony, were comparatively unconcerned spectators of that bitter controversy in which the grantees on the west side of the mountains were interested. But their freedom from participation in the angry contest between the settlers and the governor of New York, gave them a better opportunity to understand and resist the tyrannical measures which England was preparing for the more complete subjection of the colonies. An event took place in the spring of the year 1775, in their midst, which served still further to arouse their detestation of the policy of the mother country. When, at a former day, the line was established between Massachusetts and Connecticut, many inhabitants, who had received grants of land from the former province, in compensation for their services against the French and Indians, found themselves thrown into the latter, and were required to abandon their possessions. The state of Massachusetts, with a commendable sense of justice, made them, in compensation, a grant of what is now the towns of Putney, Dummerston and Brattleborough, Vermont,— hence called, in those days, "the Equivalent Land,"— and their title, it is believed, was respected by New Hampshire. These men were of the old Puritan stock, and when, upon the conquest of Canada, in which they had aided, the British parliament established the Roman Catholic faith as the religion of that province, by an act called "the Quebec Bill," it was extremely exasperating to their feelings; and one Lieutenant Spalding, of Dummerston, on one occasion, called the king "the Pope of Canada." This remark, which might have been wisely and judiciously passed over, was seized upon by the royal satellites, as a good opportunity to show their power, and Spalding was arrested for high treason, and imprisoned in the jail at Westminster. This was on the 28th of October, 1774, and on the 29th, a majority of the inhabitants of Dummerston assembled and chose a committee of correspondence, "to join," in their own language, "with other towns and respectable bodies of people, the better to secure and protect the rights and privileges of themselves and fellow-creatures from the ravages and embarrassments of the British tyrant and his New-York and other emissaries." This led to such concert that a large body of men from Dummerston, Putney, Guilford, Halifax and Draper, (now Wilmington,) proceeded to Westminster, opened the door of the jail, and released Spalding from imprisonment.

This brought the controversy to a point, and it now became manifest that, on the one side, if the royal authority was to be upheld, the whole apparatus of executive and judicial power must be brought into play, numerous criminal proceedings instituted, and civil ejectments must follow; and on the other, the abandonment of the proceedings must be compelled by the people, and the whole machinery of royal oppression resisted and stayed, at once and forever.

Both parties prepared for the crisis; and as the court was to hold its next session on the 14th of March, 1775, at Westminster, they had about four months to make preparations and arrangements. On the 13th of March, 1775, they assembled at Westminster, the loyal officers of the county being supported by their adherents. The whigs, as they were then called, came also in considerable numbers, and having learned that it was the private intention of the royal party to get the first possession of the court-house, they placed therein about one hundred men, commanded by a captain of the militia, and determined to keep possession until their grievances were laid before the judges and redressed. Near the setting of the sun, the sheriff came with his *posse*, part of whom were armed with muskets, and demanded admittance; which was refused, unless he would order his men to lay aside their arms. About ten o'clock at night, the chief justice came among them, and assuring their captain that no attempt should be made to molest them until morning, the latter withdrew the principal part of his force, leaving only a small body of men, armed with bludgeons; among whom was William French, a young farmer, not twenty-two years of age, who lived in Brattleborough. The people of that town, who lived in his immediate neighborhood, were of the opposite party, and, indeed, some of them were in the sheriff's band; that officer being himself an inhabitant of the town. French, who generally acted with his friends in Dummerston, appears, though holding no official station, to have been much esteemed for his honesty, bravery and patriotism; and the treatment he afterward received from his opponents, sufficiently attests how much they feared his influence. About eleven o'clock at night, the persons appointed to watch reported that the sheriff, with an armed force, was approaching, and means were taken to prevent his coming into the house.

When he came up, he again demanded entrance, and was refused as before. He then ordered his men to fire, which they did by aiming above the heads of the people within; but finding that this produced no effect, he repeated his order, and the muskets were leveled and discharged with such effect, that the defenders were driven back, and the assailants rushed into the house, and commenced a horrid butchery upon the defenseless men. William French, in facing them, received five bullet-wounds in different places: in his thigh, leg, mouth, face and forehead. Several others were severely wounded; and one, Daniel Houghton, was shot through the body, and after lingering a few days, expired. About twenty, who had not retreated, including the wounded, were seized and inhumanly thrust into prison; and the bleeding body of the dying French was dragged to the prison-door, and thrown in among them, with circumstances of the most cruel insult and brutality.

The court was opened at the usual hour on the next morning, with something like triumphal ceremony, and adjourned formally until three o'clock in the afternoon. But that court never reassembled. The news of the murder spread with great rapidity, and before the appointed hour, the people were rushing to the scene from all directions. The principal aggressors took the alarm, and fled precipitately. On the 15th of March, an inquest was held on the body of French, and on the same day it was committed to the ground, in the common burial-place at Westminster—the militia from the neighboring towns attending, and firing volleys over his grave. A tombstone was soon brought from Dummerston, bearing an inscription peculiarly illustrative of the times, and placed at the head, where it still remains. Being of slate, taken from the quarry near his residence, it is not of the most enduring character, but quite liable to injury and decay. For, while the face of the stone retains to this day the "rude but emphatic inscription," the rains and snows of nearly eighty winters, lodging on the top, have percolated between the layers, and partially separated them; so that, if they had not been retained together by a small rivet of lead, inserted by no one knows who or when, the whole must long since have crumbled and been lost.* With the burial

* In November, 1852, the legislature of Vermont appropriated the sum of twenty-five hundred dollars to defray the expenses of the erection of a durable marble monument to the memory of William French. The following is a literal copy of the inscription upon the old monument:

> In Memory of William French
> Son of Mr Nathaniel French Who
> Was shot at Westminster March ye 13th
> 1775 by the hands of Cruel Ministereal
> tools of George ye 3d in the Corthouse at
> a 11 a Clock at Night in the 22d year of
> his Age——
> Here William French his Body lies

of William French, were buried the hopes of subjugating the men who dwelt on the hills and in the valleys of the Green Mountains. The spirit of resisting oppression to the last extremity, awakened by his death, was never extinguished; and within two years from that time, there was proclaimed from the same building in which he was martyred, the declaration of the independence of Vermont.

Highly irritated by the massacre of William French, a committee of the larger portion of the people on the east side of the Green Mountains met at Westminster, April 11, 1775, and adopted the following resolution: "Voted, that it is the duty of said inhabitants, as predicated on the eternal and immutable law of self-preservation, to wholly renounce and resist the administration of the government of New York, till such time as the lives and property of those inhabitants may be secured by it; or till such time as they can have opportunity to lay their grievances before his most gracious Majesty in council, together with a proper remonstrance against the unjustifiable conduct of that government; with an humble petition to be taken out of so oppressive a jurisdiction, and either annexed to some other government, or erected and incorporated into a new one, as may appear best to the said inhabitants, to the royal wisdom and clemency, and till such time as his Majesty shall settle this controversy."

> For Murder his blood for Vengance cries
> King Georg the third his Tory crew
> tha with a bawl his head Shot threw
> For Liberty and his Countrys Good
> he Lost his Life his Dearest blood

What would have been the final result of the controversy with New York, had not the attention of the people been diverted from the subject by one of greater importance, can only be conjectured. But a higher and more momentous controversy, involving the independence of the whole American people, was brought before them, and they forgot their land difficulties, their "beech-seal" certificates, and their midnight riots.

CHAPTER III.

ETHAN ALLEN.

"The *mountains green* that witnessed first his fame,
From rocks to rocks resounded far his name.
As the tough horn-beam, (peering o'er those rocks,)
With gnarled grain the riving thunder mocks,
Indignant Allen, manacled in vain,
With soul revolting, bit the British chain."
HUMPHREYS.

THE American Revolution called forth the latent energies of many individuals, who would, in a more peaceable state of political affairs, have slumbered in obscurity, and gone down to the grave unhonored and unknown. The very nature of the policy of Great Britain toward this country—a policy every way tyrannical and oppressive—was calculated to call into action the efforts of every friend of liberty. It was an attempt to strip the people of their rights, and manacle them with the fetters of slavery. But, thanks to the spirit which prevailed among our fathers—thanks to the patriotism which then warmed the hearts of the people—the mercenaries of a foreign power were unequal to the task of accomplishing the designs of their masters. True-hearted volunteers rallied to the calls of the brave and wise men of our country, imbued with a spirit worthy of the little band which defended the pass of Thermopylæ. They fought and conquered; and their declining years were cheered with the knowledge that the country for which they had struggled so long and fearfully, was prosperous and happy, and that their deeds were gratefully remembered.

Perhaps no individual, of equal advantages, and in the station he occupied, contributed more toward establishing the independence of our country, than Ethan Allen. The mass of the people among whom he resided, were rude and uncultivated; yet bold in spirit, and zealous in action. It consequently followed, that no one but a man of strong natural endowments—of much decision, energy and bravery—could control their prejudices and inclinations. Habit had rendered them familiar with danger, and impatient of restraint: hence it followed, that no policy, unless proceeding from a source in which they had confidence, ever gained their approbation. Upon Allen, whose courage was undoubted, and whose zealous devotion to their interests was universally acknowledged, they implicitly relied. They had known him in adversity and prosperity—they had weighed him, and found nothing lacking. To friend or foe, he was ever the same unyielding advocate of the rights of man, and universal liberty. The policy, therefore, he upheld, as beneficial to the common cause of American liberty, ever found strong and efficient supporters in the friends with whom he associated, and by whom he was known.

From the commencement of our revolutionary struggle until its final close, Ethan Allen proved a zealous and strenuous supporter of the cause. Whether in the field or council—whether at home, a freeman among the mountains of Vermont, or loaded with the manacles of despotism in a foreign country, his spirit never quailed beneath the sneer of the tory, or the harsh threats of insolent authority. A stranger to fear, his opinions were ever given without disguise or hesitation; and, an enemy to oppression, he sought every opportunity to redress the wrongs of the oppressed. It is not to be supposed, however, that he was faultless. Like other men, he had his errors — like other men, his foibles : yet he was not willfully stubborn in either. When convinced of an erroneous position, he was ever willing to yield; but, in theory, as in practice, he contested every inch of ground; and only yielded, when he had no weapons left to meet his antagonist. This trait in his character serves, at least, to prove that he was honest in his conclusions, however erroneous the premises from which they were deduced.

The period at which we have now arrived in the life of Ethan Allen, places him in a more conspicuous and interesting position before the reader. Heretofore he has been seen only as the zealous friend of the section in which he resided — as the champion of the humble citizen, contending for the rights of individual property, and private justice. In these offices of friendship and duty, however, he had ever the confidence and the esteem of his neighbors. He had evinced a spirit of patriotism, and a love of freedom, which warmly recommended him to the notice and the admiration of the most determined and able advocates of American liberty. That he should have been selected, therefore, as the leader in an enterprise of the highest moment to the cause of liberty, was alike due to his principles, his services, and his position.

A hasty glance at the posture of affairs at this juncture, however well the reader may be acquainted with it, cannot be improper. During the seventy-one years from 1689 to 1760, the colonies were involved in four wars, occupying, in all, twenty-seven years; not to allude to the interminable hostilities which raged between them and the Indian tribes, along their frontier settlements. Yet, in this period, the population had increased from two hundred thousand to about three millions. The arts and manufactures, being opposed by the mother country, made but little progress; but there was a steady advancement in agriculture. Trade and commerce had gone on greatly increasing — so much that, in the ten years preceding the revolutionary war, the average annual exports, to Great Britain and elsewhere, amounted to four million pounds sterling, and the imports, to three and a half millions. In the mean time, colleges, and other superior institutions of learning, had been established in nearly all the colonies, and popular instruction provided for, especially in New England. The country was advancing in intellectual culture; and, more than all, the necessity of uniting for the common defense, and the intercourse of the colonies that grew out of it, had tended to create a national spirit, which the events of the twelve years succeeding the peace of 1760, still further developed and strengthened.

The colonists, from the first, always cherished a jealous sense of their rights. As early as the middle of the seventeenth century, it was a settled doctrine among them, that the authority of parliament was limited to the regulation of trade, and that taxes could not be imposed upon them without their own consent. Previous, indeed, to the peace of Paris, the home government had never attempted to interfere with internal taxation. For a century, however, before that event, a variety of restrictions had, from time to time, been imposed upon the trade of the colonies; the object of which was to oblige the colonists to buy and sell exclusively in the English markets. Colonial manufactures were also, in every possible way, discouraged. These restrictions produced much discontent. In 1764, the first act avowedly for the purpose of raising a revenue in America was passed in parliament. This was followed, the next year, by the famous "stamp act," making illegal all deeds, mortgages, bonds, notes, and other instruments of a like character, unless written upon stamped paper, upon which a duty to the crown was imposed, varying in amount with the transaction which they represented. These acts excited great displeasure throughout the colonies; and in October, 1765, a congress of delegates from Rhode Island, Massachusetts, Connecticut, New York, New Jersey, Maryland, and North and South Carolina, met at New York, and passed several resolutions, acknowledging the rightful authority of parliament, but denouncing the stamp act, and other enactments of the kind, as subversive of the just rights and liberties of the colonists, as natural-born English subjects. The proceedings of this body were sanctioned by all the colonies. The public indignation, inflamed by newspapers, pamphlets, and popular meetings, rose to the highest pitch. Combinations were everywhere formed, to abstain from using articles of British manufacture, and, in every way, to oppose the measures of the home government. The officers appointed under the stamp act were, in many places, insulted, abused, and forced to resign; and when the time arrived for the act to go into operation, neither stamps nor stamp-officers were to be found. Business of all kinds requiring stamps, was, for a time, suspended; law-proceedings were stayed, and the courts were closed. The next year the stamp act was repealed; although the repeal was accompanied by a declaration of the "right of parliament to bind the colonies in all cases whatsoever." In a few months from this time, a new ministry came into power, and a new plan for taxing America was introduced into parliament: that of levying a tax on glass, paper, pasteboard, painters' colors, and tea, imported into the colonies. To enforce this law, a body of troops was sent out, and quartered in Boston. These measures produced great exasperation in the colonies, and led to combinations against using the articles subjected to duty. In 1770, this act was repealed, with the exception of the duty on tea. The colonists were only the more decided in renouncing the use of that article. An act of parliament was passed in 1773, allowing the East-India company a remission of certain government charges on the tea they should send to America, which would enable them to sell tea to the colonists cheaper than they could sell it in England. This was done with the hope of inducing the colonists to return to the use of the article. In this submission to the tax upon tea, it was expected that the principle, that parliament had a right to tax the colonists, would be adopted; and the way would be open for indiscriminate and oppressive taxation. Large shipments of tea were accordingly made; but the Americans refused to pay the slight duty upon it. The cargoes sent to New York and Philadelphia, were not suffered to be landed; in Charleston, it was not allowed to be sold; and, at Boston, it was thrown into the harbor, by a party of men disguised as Indians. These proceedings excited the fierce displeasure of the British government, especially against Boston; and in March, 1774, "the Boston port bill," so called, was passed, prohibiting all commercial intercourse with that city. Another bill subverted the charter-government of Massachusetts, vesting the appointment of the council and judges in the crown; and a third, shortly after, empowered the governor to send persons indicted for capital offenses, to another colony, or to Great Britain, for trial. These violent proceedings awakened the greatest indignation throughout the colonies. All made common cause with Massachusetts. In the fall of 1774, a general congress met at Philadelphia, and adopted a declaration of rights and grievances, and agreed to an entire suspension of all commercial intercourse with Great Britain, until the repeal of the acts of which they complained. They likewise voted an address to the king; another to the people of Great Britain, and a third to the inhabitants of Canada. These peaceful measures for redress proving ineffectual, the feeling of the necessity of resisting by force became quite general in the colonies. Preparations began to be made; warlike stores were collected, and the people began to arm. In Massachusetts, Governor Gage had convoked the legislative assembly, but afterward judged it expedient to countermand the meeting. Notwithstanding this, the assembly convened, and, the governor not appearing, organized themselves, and adopted a plan for the defense of the province. They resolved to raise a force of twelve thousand men, and to request the other New-England states to increase the number to twenty thousand. Early the next year, (1775) parliament, in spite of the conciliatory counsels of the Earl of Chatham, proceeded to pass a bill restraining still further the trade of New England. Soon after, restrictions were imposed upon the middle and southern colonies, except New York, Delaware, and North Carolina. These exceptions were made with a view to produce dissensions among the colonies; but it failed of its object. This brings us to the commencement of actual hostilities. General Gage, the royal governor of Massachusetts, sent a detachment of eight hundred soldiers to destroy some military stores which were deposited at Concord. On their way, they arrived at Lexington, on the morning of the 19th of April, 1775, where they found a company of provincial militia assembled on parade. This company, not instantly obeying an order to throw down their arms and disperse, were fired upon, and eight of their number killed. The detachment proceeded to Concord, and destroyed the stores, though not without opposition and bloodshed. But the spirit of the people was up; and on their return to Boston, the British were harassed the whole way, and continually fired upon from behind walls, buildings and fences. The British loss, in killed, wounded and missing, amounted to nearly three hundred; the American, to less than one-third of that number.

The vigilant patriots of Massachusetts, then the very hot-bed of rebellion, early perceived the necessity of securing Ticonderoga the moment hostilities should commence. Early in March, 1775, Samuel Adams and Joseph Warren, members of the committee of correspondence of Boston, sent a secret agent into Canada, to ascertain the opinions and temper of the people of that province, concerning the great questions at issue, and the momentous events then pending. After a diligent but cautious performance of this delicate task, the agent sent word to them from Montreal, that the people were, at best, lukewarm; and advised that, the moment hostilities commenced, Ticonderoga and its garrison should be seized. This advice was coupled with the positive assertion, that the people of the New-Hampshire Grants were ready to undertake the bold enterprise. Within three weeks after this information was received by Adams and Warren, the battle of Lexington occurred. This event aroused the whole country, and the patriots flocked from all quarters to Boston. The provincial assembly of Connecticut was then in session, and a plan was there concerted for surprising Ticonderoga, and seizing the cannon in that fortress for the use of the army then gathering in the vicinity of Boston. The whole plan and proceedings were of a private character, without the public sanction of the assembly, but with its full knowledge and tacit approbation. A committee was appointed, with instructions to proceed to the frontier towns, inquire into the state of the garrison, and, should they deem it expedient, raise men and take possession of it. Eighteen hundred dollars were supplied by the provincial territory, to purchase arms and ammunition, and defray the other expenses of the expedition. On their way to Bennington, to lay their plans before Ethan Allen and secure his coöperation, they enlisted between forty and fifty volunteers, among whom was Colonel James Easton, of Pittsfield, Massachusetts. On arriving at Bennington, they found that Ethan Allen was already preparing to accomplish the proposed object. He was chosen the commander of the expedition; Colonel Easton was appointed second in command, and Seth Warren, the third. Colonel Allen's Green-Mountain Boys, to the number of two hundred and thirty, were speedily in readiness, and on the 7th of May the little army reached Castleton. It was there decided that Colonel Allen and the principal officers, with the main body of their forces, consisting of about one hundred and forty men, should march directly to Shoreham, opposite to Ticonderoga; that Captain Herrick, with thirty men, should keep on to Skenesborough, (now Whitehall,) at the head of Lake Champlain, seize the establishment of Major Skene, and hasten with the boats and stores they might capture, to join Allen at Shoreham; and that Captain Drylas should proceed to Panton, and secure every boat or bateau that should fall in his way. They were joined at Castleton by Colonel Benedict Arnold, who, in the French wars, had greatly distinguished himself, at the battles in the vicinity of Ticonderoga and Crown Point. Possessing great genius, a restless character, and an intrepidity bordering upon madness, he seems to have conceived the same plan. To this end, he had conferred with the committee of safety of Massachusetts, who appointed him colonel, with authority to enlist volunteers for the attempt to capture Ticonderoga. In pursuance of this arrangement he proceeded to Castleton, and his surprise was extreme at finding himself anticipated. But, as nothing could delight him more than to engage in this hazardous service, he consented, after being assured that the Green-Mountain Boys would serve only under their favorite leader, to put himself under the command of Colonel Allen. It was deemed essential to the success of the enterprise, that it should be conducted with profound secrecy, and sentinels were posted upon all the roads, to prevent any rumor of their approach from reaching the menaced point. Allen, with his little army, reached Shoreham, opposite Ticonderoga, on the night of May 9th, 1775. It was important to have a guide who was acquainted with the grounds around the fortress, and the places of access. Allen made inquiries as to those points, of Mr. Beman, a farmer residing on the shore of the lake. He replied that he seldom crossed to Ticonderoga, and had no special knowledge in regard to the internal arrangement of the fortress; but that his son Nathan, a young lad, passed much of his time there in company with the boys of the garrison. Nathan was called, and appeared by his answers to be familiar with every part of the fort, and every passage by which it could be approached. In the opinion of Ethan Allen, he was the very person to guide him in the enterprise; and by the consent of his father, and a little persuasion, Nathan Beman was engaged for that purpose. But a serious difficulty now occurred. They had but a few boats, and none had been sent from Skenesborough or Panton. The day began to dawn, and only the officers and eighty-three men had crossed the lake. Delay was hazardous, for the garrison, if aroused, would make stout resistance. Allen, therefore, resolved not to wait for the rear division to cross, but to attack the fort at once. He drew up his men in three ranks upon the shore, and in low but distinct tones, briefly harangued them; and then, placing himself at their head, with Arnold by his side, they marched quickly but stealthily up the height to the sally-port. The sentinel snapped his fusee at the commander, but it missed fire, and he retreated within the fort under a covered way. The Americans followed close upon his heels, and were thus guided by the alarmed fugitive directly to the parade within the barracks. There another sentinel made a thrust at Colonel Easton, but a blow upon the head from Allen's sword made him beg for quarter, and the patriots met with no further resistance. As they rushed into the parade, they gave a tremendous shout, and filing off into two divisions, formed a line of forty men along each of the two ranges of barracks. The aroused garrison leaped from their pallets, seized their arms and rushed for the parade, but only to be made prisoners by the intrepid New-Englanders. Allen demanded to be shown to the apartment of Captain Delaplace, the commandant of the garrison. It was pointed out, and Colonel Allen, with Nathan Beman at his elbow, who knew the way, hastily ascended the stairs, which were attached to the outside of the barracks, and called out with a voice of thunder at the door, ordering the astonished captain instantly to appear, or the whole garrison should be sacrificed! Startled at so strange and unexpected a summons, he sprung from his bed and opened the door, when the first salutation of his boisterous and unseasonable visitor was an order immediately to surrender the fort. Rubbing his eyes and trying to collect his scattered senses, the captain asked by what authority he presumed to make such a demand. "In the name of the Great Jehovah and the Continental Congress!" replied Allen.* The commandant began to remonstrate, but Colonel Allen cut short the thread of his discourse by lifting his sword over his head, and reiterating the demand for an immediate surrender. Having neither permission to argue nor power to resist, Captain Delaplace submitted, ordering his men to parade without arms, and the garrison was given up to

* This is the language of Allen as given by himself in his narrative. But it was asserted by those who stood near him, that his demand was enforced by an emphatic oath. Lossing [see "Field-Book of the Revolution,"] was told by the surviving brother of a man named Rice, who stood at Allen's side, that he exclaimed, " In the name of the Great Jehovah and the Continental Congress, *by* ——." " Delaplace," says Lossing, " had about as much respect for the 'Continental Congress' as Allen had for 'Jehovah,' and they respectively relied upon and feared powder and ball more than either."

the victors. It is a singular fact that the "Continental Congress," instead of authorizing Allen to take Ticonderoga, were entirely ignorant of the enterprise, and did not meet for organization until six hours after the surrender of the fortress. This achievement, besides being the first on the part of the patriots, was of the utmost importance. Ticonderoga and Crown Point commanded the great avenue between Canada and the other colonies, and its possession gave the Americans facilities for the subsequent brilliant campaign in Canada, and the military spoils taken by Allen were of incalculable benefit to the army near Boston. These spoils consisted of one hundred and twenty pieces of iron cannon, fifty swivels, ten tons of musket-balls, three cart-loads of flints, thirty new carriages, a considerable quantity of shells, a warehouse full of material for boat-building, and a large quantity of other stores.

Warner crossed the lake with the rear division, and marched up to the fort just after the surrender was made. He was immediately dispatched against Crown Point, but a strong head-wind drove his boats back, and he returned to Ticonderoga. He renewed the attempt on the 12th of May, and succeeded in obtaining possession of the fortress without bloodshed. Thus another strong position was secured, and a great addition was made to the munitions of war acquired at Ticonderoga. Previous to this affair, Colonel Allen had sent a messenger to Captain Remember Baker, who was at Winooski River, requesting him to join the army at Ticonderoga with as large a number of men as he could assemble. Baker obeyed the summons; and when he was coming up the lake with his party, he met two small boats, which had been dispatched from Crown Point to carry intelligence of the reduction of Ticonderoga to St. John's and Montreal, and solicit reinforcements. The boats were seized by Baker, and he arrived at Crown Point just in time to unite with Warner in taking possession of that post. Thus the main object of the expedition was attained; but the troubles of the leaders were not at an end. No sooner had the fort surrendered, than Arnold assumed the command, affirming that he was the only officer invested with legal authority. His pretensions were not heeded, and although he was vehement and positive, yet it was in vain to issue orders which nobody would obey; and finally he consented to a sort of divided control between Colonel Allen and himself, he acting as a subordinate, but not wholly without official consideration.

But the plan of the captors of Ticonderoga would not have been complete had they not secured to themselves the exclusive control of the lake, to accomplish which it was necessary to take a corvette the English kept stationed near St. John's at the north end of Lake Champlain. They resolved, therefore, to arm a schooner, (taken at Skenesborough) for the purpose, the command of which was given to Arnold, while Allen was to follow him in flat-boats with a reinforcement. The wind blowing fresh from the south, the vessel of Arnold left the flat-boats far in the rear. He approached the corvette unexpectedly, the captain of which was far from apprehending the danger that menaced him, and took possession of it without resistance; and, as if Heaven was pleased to distinguish with evident tokens of its favor these first achievements of the Americans, the wind suddenly changed from south to north, so that, in a few hours, Colonel Arnold returned safely to Ticonderoga.

Colonel Allen exhibited great discretion in his new position. An account of his expedition was sent to the Massachusetts, Connecticut and New-York committees of safety, with an urgent solicitation for a reinforcement of his brave little army, and a supply of provisions. These were accordingly sent, and measures were taken to organize an army at the north for the defense of Lake Champlain. In the accomplishment of this object, and in the hope of having an expedition sent against Montreal and Quebec, Allen visited the provincial Congress at New York, as well as the general Congress at Philadelphia. Some opposition was made to his appearance before the former of these bodies, on account of the troubles existing between New York and the New-Hampshire Grants, and the prominent part taken by Allen in the hostilities resulting from them. But the majority felt the importance of forgetting local controversies in the impending contest with the mother country, and Ethan Allen was treated with the cordiality due to one engaged with them in a great cause, and with the distinction merited by one whose services had been of the most important character. Allen's representation had immense influence, not only in favor of his projects for the conquest of the British army in Canada, but in fixing the determination of Congress and the country to resist, by force of arms, the tyrannical measures of the British government. While on his way to lay his schemes before the Continental Congress, he visited Bennington, where the Rev. Mr. Dewey preached, before him and other officers, a sermon on the capture of Ticonderoga. In his prayer, Mr. Dewey, with much fervor, poured forth his thanks to the Lord for having given the possession of this important fortress into the hands of a people struggling for the defense of their dearest rights. Allen was displeased, and as the preacher continued in this strain of thanksgiving, the bluff old hero cried out, "Parson Dewey!" The reverend gentleman gave no heed to the interruption. Allen exclaimed still louder, "Parson Dewey!" But as the minister pursued his prayer, Allen sprung to his feet and roared out in a voice of thunder, "Parson Dewey!" The clergyman opened his eyes and gazed with astonishment at Allen. The latter then said with great energy, "Parson Dewey, please make mention of *my* being there!"*

But Ethan Allen, who has the imperishable honor of achieving the first momentous enterprise in the history of the American Revolution, had the misfortune, soon afterward, to fall into the hands of the British, and to be carried a prisoner to England. The narrative of this captivity, written by Allen after his return to Vermont, will form the remainder of the present chapter, in order that the subsequent history of the part taken by the Green-Mountain Heroes in the Revolution, may be given without interruption. The

* This anecdote is given on the authority of Aaron Robinson, Esq., son of Moses Robinson, the second governor of Vermont, and is undoubtedly authentic.

"Narrative" was first published in 1779. "The critic," he says in the original Preface, "will be pleased to excuse any inaccuracies in the performance itself, as the author has unfortunately missed of a liberal education." The Narrative, the faults of which the author so happily excuses, is here republished, without alteration, from the original edition:

NARRATIVE.

Ever since I arrived at the state of manhood, and acquainted myself with the general history of mankind, I have felt a sincere passion for liberty. The history of nations, doomed to perpetual slavery, in consequence of yielding up to tyrants their natural-born liberties, I read with a sort of philosophical horror; so that the first systematical and bloody attempt, at Lexington, to enslave America, thoroughly electrified my mind, and fully determined me to take part with my country. And, while I was wishing for an opportunity to signalize myself in its behalf, directions were privately sent to me from the then colony, (now state) of Connecticut, to raise the Green-Mountain Boys, and, if possible, with them to surprise and take the fortress of Ticonderoga. This enterprise I cheerfully undertook; and, after first guarding all the several passes that led thither, to cut off all intelligence between the garrison and the country, made a forced march from Bennington, and arrived at the lake opposite to Ticonderoga, on the evening of the ninth day of May, 1775, with two hundred and thirty valiant Green-Mountain Boys; and it was with the utmost difficulty that I procured boats to cross the lake. However, I landed eighty-three men near the garrison, and sent the boats back for the rear guard, commanded by Col. Seth Warner, but the day began to dawn, and I found myself under the necessity to attack the fort, before the rear could cross the lake; and, as it was viewed hazardous, I harangued the officers and soldiers in the manner following:—

"Friends and fellow soldiers, You have, for a number of years past been a scourge and terror to arbitrary power. Your valor has been famed abroad, and acknowledged, as appears by the advice and orders to me, from the General Assembly of Connecticut, to surprise and take the garrison now before us. I now propose to advance before you, and, in person, conduct you through the wicket-gate; for we must this morning either quit our pretensions to valor, or possess ourselves of this fortress in a few minutes; and, inasmuch as it is a desperate attempt, which none but the bravest of men dare undertake, I do not urge it on any contrary to his will. You that will undertake voluntarily, poise your firelocks."

The men being, at this time, drawn up in three ranks, each poised his firelock. I ordered them to face to the right, and at the head of the centre-file, marched them immediately to the wicket-gate aforesaid, where I found a sentry posted, who instantly snapped his fusee at me; I ran immediately towards him, and he retreated through the covered way into the parade within the garrison, gave a halloo, and ran under a bomb-proof. My party, who followed me into the fort, I formed on the parade in such a manner as to face the two barracks which faced each other.

The garrison being asleep, except the sentries, we gave three huzzas which greatly surprised them. One of the sentries made a pass at one of my officers with a charged bayonet, and slightly wounded him: My first thought was to kill him with my sword; but, in an instant, I altered the design and fury of the blow to a slight cut on the side of the head, upon which he dropped his gun, and asked quarter, which I readily granted him, and demanded of him the place where the commanding officer kept; he shewed me a pair of stairs in the front of a barrack, on the west part of the garrison, which led up to a second story in said barrack, to which I immediately repaired, and ordered the commander, Capt. De la Place, to come forth instantly, or I would sacrifice the whole garrison; at which the Capt. came immediately to the door, with

OLD TICONDEROGA.

his breeches in his hand; when I ordered him to deliver me the fort instantly; he asked me by what authority I demanded it: I answered him, "*In the name of the great Jehovah, and the Continental Congress.*" The authority of the Congress being very litle known at that time, he began to speak again; but I interrupted him, and with my drawn sword over his head, again demanded an immediate surrender of the garrison; with which he then complied, and ordered his men to be forthwith paraded without arms, as he had given up the garrison. In the mean time some of my officers had given orders, and in consequence thereof, sundry of the barrack doors were beat down, and about one third of the garrison imprisoned, which consisted of the said commander, a Lieut. Feltham, a conductor of artillery, a gunner, two serjeants, and forty-four rank and file; about one hundred pieces of cannon, one thirteen inch mortar, and a number of swivels. This surprise was carried into execution in the grey of the morning of the tenth of May, 1775. The sun seemed to rise that morning with a superior lustre; and Ticonderoga and its dependencies smiled to its conquerors, who tossed about the flowing bowl, and wished success to Congress, and the liberty and freedom of America. Happy it was for me, at that time, that the then future pages of the book of fate, which afterwards unfolded a miserable scene of two years and eight months imprisonment were hid from my view.

But to return to my narrative: Col. Warner, with the rear guard, crossed the lake, and joined me early in the morning, whom I sent off, without loss of time, with about one hundred men, to take possession of Crown Point, which was garrisoned with a serjeant and twelve men; which he took possession of the same day, as also of upwards of one hundred pieces of cannon. But one thing now remained to be done, to make ourselves complete masters of lake Champlain; this was to possess ourselves of a sloop of war, which was then lying at St. Johns; to effect which, it was agreed in a council of war, to arm and man out a certain schooner, which lay at South Bay, and that Capt. (now general) Arnold should command her, and that I should command the batteaux. The necessary preparations being made, we set sail from Ticonderoga, in quest of the sloop, which was much larger, and carried more guns and heavier metal than the schooner. General Arnold, with the schooner, sailing faster than the batteaux, arrived at St. Johns; and by surprise, possessed himself of the sloop, before I could arrive with the batteaux: He also made prisoners of a serjeant and twelve men, who were garrisoned at that place. It is worthy of remark that as soon as General Arnold had secured the prisoners on board, and had made preparation for sailing, the wind, which but a few hours before was fresh in the south, and well served to carry us to St. Johns, now shifted, and came fresh from the north; and in about one hour's time, General Arnold sailed with the prize and schooner for Ticonderoga. When I met him with my party, within a few miles of St. Johns, he saluted me with a discharge of cannon, which I returned with a volley of small arms. This being repeated three times, I went on board the sloop with my party, where several loyal Congress healths were drank.

We were now masters of lake Champlain, and the garrison depending thereon. This success I viewed of consequence in the scale of American politics; for, if a settlement between the then colonies and Great Britain, had soon taken place, it would have been easy to have restored these acquisitions; but viewing the then future consequences of a cruel war, as it has really proved to be, and the command of that lake, garrisons, artillery, &c., it must be viewed to be of signal importance to the American cause, and it is marvellous to me that we ever lost the command of it. Nothing but taking a Burgoyne with a whole British army, could, in my opinion, atone for it; and notwithstanding such an extraordinary victory, we must be obliged to regain the command of that lake again, be the cost what it will; by doing this Canada will easily be brought into union and confederacy with the United States of America. Such an event would put it out of the power of the western tribes of Indians to carry on a war with us, and be a solid and durable bar against any further inhuman barbarities committed on our frontier inhabitants, by cruel and blood-thirsty savages; for it is impossible to carry on a war, except they are supported by the trade and commerce of some civilized nation; which to them would be impracticable, did Canada compose a part of the American empire.

Early in the fall of the year, the little army under the command of the Generals Schuyler and Montgomery, were ordered to advance into Canada. I was at Ticonderoga, when this order arrived; and the Generals, with most of the field officers, requested me to attend them in the expedition; and, though at that time I had no commission from Congress, yet they engaged me, that I should be considered as an officer, the same as though I had a commission; and should, as occasion might require, command certain detachments of the army. This I considered as an honorable offer, and did not hesitate to comply with it, and advanced with the army to the Isle-aux-Noix; from whence I was ordered by the General, to go in company with Major Brown, and certain interpreters, through the woods into Canada, with letters to the Canadians, and to let them know that the design of the army was only against the English garrisons, and not the country, their liberties, or religion; and having, through much danger, negotiated this business, I returned to the Isle-aux-Noix in the fore part of September, when General Schuyler returned to Albany; and in consequence the command devolved upon General Montgomery, whom I assisted in laying a line of circumvallation round the fortress of St. Johns. After which I was ordered, by the General, to make a second tour into Canada, upon nearly the same design as before; and withal to observe the disposition, designs and movements of the inhabitants of the country. This reconnoiter I undertook reluctantly, choosing rather to assist at the seige of St. Johns, which was then closely invested; but my esteem for the general's person, and opinion of him as a politician and brave officer, induced me to proceed.

I passed through all the parishes on the river Sorel, to a parish at the mouth of the same, which is called by the same name, preaching politics; and went from thence across the Sorel to the river St. Lawrence, and up the river through the parishes to Longueuil, and so far met with good success as an itinerant. In this round my guard were Canadians, my interpreter, and some few attendants excepted. On the morning of the 24th day of September, I set out with my guard of about eighty men, from Longueuil, to go to Laprairie; from whence I determined to go to General Montgomery's camp; but had not advanced two miles before I met with Major Brown, who has since been advanced to the rank of a Colonel, who desired me to halt, saying that he had something of importance to communicate to me and my confidants; upon which I halted the party, and went into a house, and took a private room with him and several of my associates, where Col. Brown proposed that, "provided I would return to Longueuil, and procure some canoes, so as to cross the the river St. Lawrence a little north of Montreal, he would cross it a little to the south of the town, with near two hundred men, as he had boats sufficient; and that we could make ourselves masters of Montreal." This plan was readily approved by me and those in council; and in consequence of which I returned to Longueuil, collected a few canoes, and added about thirty English-Americans to my party, and crossed the river in the night of the 24th, agreeably to the before proposed plan.

My whole party at this time, consisted of about one hundred and ten men, near eighty of whom were Canadians. We were most of the night crossing the river, as we had so few canoes that they had to pass and repass three times, to cary my party across. Soon after day-break, I set a guard between me and the town, with special orders to let no person pass or repass them, another guard on the other end of the road, with like directions; in the mean time, I reconnoitered the best ground to make a defence, expecting Col. Brown's party was landed on the other side of the town, he having, the day before, agreed to give three huzzas with his men early in the morning, which signal I was to return, that we might each know that both parties were landed; but the sun, by this time, being nearly two hours high, and the sign failing, I began to conclude myself to be in a premunire, and would have crossed the river back again, but I knew the enemy would have discovered such an attempt; and as there could not more than one third part of my troops cross at a time, the other two-thirds would of course fall into their hands. This I could not reconcile to my own feelings as a man, much less as an officer: I therefore concluded to maintain the ground, if possible, and all to fare alike. In consequence of this resolution, I despatched two messengers, one to Laprairie, to Col. Brown, and the other to l'Assomption, a French settlement, to Mr. Walker, who was in our interest, requesting their speedy assistance, giving them, at the same time to understand my critical situation. In the mean time sundry persons came to my guards, pretending to be friends, but were by them taken prisoners and brought to me. These I ordered to confinement, until their friendship could be further confirmed; for I was jealous they were spies, as they proved to be afterwards. One of the principal of them making his escape, exposed the weakness of my party, which was the final cause of my misfortune; for I have been since informed that Mr. Walker, agreeably to my desire, exerted himself, and had raised a considerable number of men for my assistance, which brought him into difficulty afterwards, but upon hearing of my misfortune, he disbanded them again.

The town of Montreal was in a great tumult. General Carleton and the royal party, made every preparation to go on board their vessels of force, as I was afterwards informed, but the spy escaped from my guard to the town, occasioned an alteration in their policy, and emboldened Gen. Carleton to send the force which he had there collected, out against me. I had previously chosen my ground, but when I saw the number of the enemy as they sallied out of the town, I perceived it would be a day of trouble, if not of rebuke; but I had no chance to flee, as Montreal was situated on an island, and the St. Lawrence cut off my communication to General Montgomery's camp. I encouraged my soldiery to bravely defend themselves, that we should soon have help, and that we should be able to keep the ground, if no more. This, and much more, I affirmed with the greatest seeming assurance, and which in reality I thought to be in some degree probable.

The enemy consisted of not more than forty regular troops, together with a mixed multitude, chiefly Canadians, with a number of English who lived in town, and some Indians; in all to the number of five hundred.

The reader will notice that most of my party were Canadians; indeed it was a motely parcel of soldiery which composed both parties. However, the enemy began to attack from wood-piles, ditches, buildings, and such like places, at a considerable distance, and I returned the fire from a situation more than equally advantageous. The attack began between two and three o'clock in the afternoon, just before which I ordered a volunteer by the name of Richard Young, with a detachment of nine men as a flank guard, which, under the cover of the bank of the river, could not only annoy the enemy, but at the same time, serve as a flank guard to the left of the main body.

The fire continued for sometime on both sides; and I was confident that such a remote method of attack could not carry the ground, provided it should be continued till night: but near half the body of the enemy began to flank round to my right; upon which I ordered a volunteer by the name of John Dugan, who had lived many years in Canada, and understood the French language, to detach about fifty Canadians, and post himself at an advantageous ditch, which was on my right, to prevent my being surrounded: He advanced with the detachment, but instead of occupying the post, made his escape, as did likewise Mr. Young upon the left, with their detachments. I soon perceived that the enemy was in possession of the ground, which Dugan should have occupied. At this time I had but about forty five men with me; some of whom were wounded; the enemy kept closing round me, nor was it in my power to prevent it; by which means, my situation, which was advantageous in the first part of the attack, ceased to be so in the last; and being entirely surrounded with such vast, unequal numbers, I ordered a retreat, but found that those of the enemy, who were of the country, and their Indians, could run as fast as my men, though the regulars could not. Thus I retreated near a mile, and some of the enemy, with the savages, kept flanking me, and others crowded hard in the rear. In fine, I expected, in a very short time, to try the world of spirits; for I was apprehensive that no quarter would be given to me, and therefore had determined to sell my life as dear as I could. One of the enemy's officers, boldly pressing in the rear, discharged his fusee at me; the ball whistled near me, as did many others that day. I returned the salute, and missed him, as running had put us both out of breath; for I conclude we were not frightened: I then saluted him with my tongue in a harsh manner, and told him that, inasmuch as his numbers were so far superior to mine, I would surrender provided I could be treated with honor, and be assured of good quarter for myself and the men who were with me; and he answered I should; another officer, coming up directly after, confirmed the treaty; upon which I agreed to surrender with my party, which then consisted of thirty-one effective men, and seven wounded. I ordered them to ground their arms, which they did.

The officer I capitulated with, then directed me and my party to advance towards him, which was done; I handed him my sword, and in half a minute after, a savage, part of whose head was shaved, being almost naked and painted, with feathers intermixed with the hair of the other side of his head, came running to me with an incredible swiftness; he seemed to advance with more than mortal speed; as he approached near me, his hellish visage was beyond all description; snake's eyes appear innocent in comparison to his; his features extorted; malice, death, murder, and the wrath of devils and damned spirits are the emblems of his countenance; and in less than twelve feet of me, presented his firelock; at the instant of his present, I twitched the officer, to whom I gave my sword, between me and the savage; but he flew round with great fury, trying to single me out to shoot me without killing the officer; but by this time I was nearly as nimble as he, keeping the officer in such a position that his danger was my defence; but, in less than half a minute, I was attacked by just such another imp of hell: Then I made the officer fly around with incredible velocity, for a few seconds of time, when I perceived a Canadian, who had lost one eye, as appeared afterwards, taking my part against the savages; and in an instant an Irishman came to my assistance with a fixed bayonet, and drove away the fiends, swearing by —— he would kill them. This tragic scene composed my mind. The escaping from so awful a death, made even imprisonment happy; the more so as my conquerors on the field treated me with great civility and politeness.

The regular officers said that they were very happy to see Colonel Allen: I answered them, that I should rather choose to have seen them at General Montgomery's camp. The gentlemen replied, that they gave full credit to what I said, and as I walked to the town, which was, as I should guess, more than two miles, a British officer walking at my right hand, and one of the French noblesse at my left; the latter of which, in the action, had his eyebrow carried away by a glancing shot, but was nevertheless very merry and facetious, and no abuse was offered me till I came to the barrack yard at Montreal, where I met general Prescott, who asked me my name, which I told him: He then asked me whether I was that Col. Allen, who took Ticonderoga. I told him that I was the very man: Then he shook his cane over my head, calling many hard names, among which he frequently used the word rebel, and put himself in a great rage. I told him he would do well not to cane me, for I was not accustomed to it, and shook my fist at him, telling him that was the beetle of mortality for him if he offered to strike;

upon which Capt. M'Cloud of the British, pulled him by the skirt, and whispered to him, as he afterwards told me, to this import; that it was inconsistent with his honor to strike a prisoner. He then ordered a serjeant's command with fixed bayonets, to come forward, and kill thirteen Canadians who were included in the treaty aforesaid.

It cut me to the heart to see the Canadians in so hard a case, in consequence of their having been true to me; they were wringing their hands, saying their prayers, as I concluded, and expected immediate death. I therefore stepped between the executioners and the Canadians, opened my clothes, and told Gen. Prescott to thrust his bayonet into my breast, for I was the sole cause of the Canadians taking up arms.

The guard, in the mean time, rolling their eyeballs from the General to me, as though impatiently waiting his dread command to sheath their bayonets in my heart; I could, however, plainly discern, that he was in a suspense and quandary about the matter: This gave me additional hopes of succeeding; for my design was not to die, but to save the Canadians by a finesse. The general stood a minute, when he made me the following reply; "I will not execute you now; but you shall grace a halter at Tyburn, —— —— you."

I remember I disdained his mentioning such a place; I was, notwithstanding, a little pleased with the expression, as it significantly conveyed to me the idea of postponing the present appearance of death; besides his sentence was by no means final, as to "gracing a halter," although I had anxiety about it, after I landed in England, as the reader will find in the course of this history. Gen. Prescott then ordered one of his officers to take me on board the Gaspee schooner of war, and confine me, hands and feet, in irons, which was done the same afternoon I was taken.

The action continued an hour and three quarters, by the watch, and I know not to this day how many of my men were killed, though I am certain there were but few. If I remember right, 7 were wounded; one of them, Wm. Stewart, by name, was wounded by a savage with a tomahawk, after he was taken prisoner and disarmed, but was rescued by some of the generous enemy; and so far recovered of his wounds, that he afterwards went with the other prisoners to England.

Of the enemy, were killed a major Carden, who had been wounded in eleven different battles, and an eminent merchant, Patterson, of Montreal, and some others, but I never knew their whole loss, as their accounts were different. I am apprehensive that it is rare, that so much ammunition was expended, and so little execution done by it; though such of my party as stood the ground, behaved with great fortitude, much exceeding that of the enemy, but were not the best of marksmen, and, I am apprehensive, were all killed or taken; the wounded were all put into the hospital at Montreal, and those that were not, were put on board of different vessels in the river, and shackled together by pairs, viz. two men fastened together by one hand-cuff, being closely fixed to one wrist of each of them, and treated with the greatest severity, nay as criminals.

I now come to the description of the irons, which were put on me: The hand-cuff was of common size and form, but my leg irons, I should imagine would weigh thirty pounds; the bar was eight feet long, and very substantial; the shackles, which encompassed my ancles, were very tight. I was told by the officer, who put them on, that it was the king's plate, and I heard other of their officers say, that it would weigh forty weight. The irons were so close upon my ancles, that I could not lay down in any other manner than on my back. I was put into the lowest and most wretched part of the vessel, where I got the favor of a chest to sit on; the same answered for my bed at night; and having procured some little blocks of the guard, who day and night, with fixed bayonets, watched over me, to lie under each end of the large bar of my leg irons, to preserve my ancles from galling, while I sat on the chest, or lay back on the same, though most of the time, night and day, I sat on it; but at length, having a desire to lie down on my side, which the closeness of my irons forbid, I desired the captain to loosen them for that purpose ; but was denied the favor. The captain's name was Royal, who did not seem to be an ill-natured man; but oftentimes said, that his express orders were to treat me with such severity, which was disagreeable to his own feelings ; nor did he ever insult me, though many others, who came on board did. One of the officers, by the name of Bradley, was very generous to me ; he would often send me victuals from his own table; nor did a day fail, but he sent me a good drink of grog.

The reader is now invited back to the time I was put into irons. I requested the privilege to write to General Prescott, which was granted. I reminded him of the kind and generous manner of my treatment of the prisoners I took at Ticonderoga ; the injustice and ungentleman-like usage I had met with from him, and demanded better usage, but received no answer from him. I soon after wrote to Gen. Carlton, which met the same success. In the mean while, many of those who were permitted to see me, were very insulting.

I was confined in the manner I have related, on board the Gaspee schooner, about six weeks ; during which time I was obliged to throw out plenty of extravagant language, which answered certain purposes, at that time, better than to grace a history.

To give an instance ; upon being insulted, in a fit of anger, I twisted off a nail with my teeth, which I took to be a ten-penny nail ; it went through the mortise of the bar of my hand-cuff, and at the same time I swaggered over those who abused me; particularly a Doctor Dace, who told me that I was outlawed by New-York, and deserved death for several years past ; was at last fully ripened for the halter, and in a fair way to obtain it. When I challenged him, he excused himself, in consequence, as he said, of my being a criminal ; but I flung such a flood of language at him that it shocked him and the spectators, for my anger was very great. I heard one say, —— him, can he eat iron ? After that, a small padlock was fixed to the hand-cuff, instead of the nail; and as they were mean-spirited in their treatment to me, so it appeared to me, that they were equally timorous and cowardly.

I was after sent, with the prisoners taken with me, to an armed vessel in the river, which lay off against Quebec, under the command of Capt. M'Cloud, of the British, who treated me in a very generous and obliging manner, and according to my rank; in about twenty-four hours I bid him farewell with regret; but my good fortune still continued. The name of the Captain of the vessel I was put on board, was Littlejohn; who, with his officers, behaved in a polite, generous, and friendly manner. I lived with them in the cabin, and fared on the best, my irons being taken off, contrary to the order he had received from the commanding officer; but Capt. Littlejohn swore, that a brave man should not be used as a rascal, on board his ship.

That I found myself in possession of happiness once more, and the evils I had lately suffered, gave me an uncommon relish for it.

Capt. Littlejohn used to go to Quebec almost every day, in order to pay his respects to certain gentlemen and ladies; being there on a certain day, he happened to meet with some disagreeable treatment, as he imagined, from a Lieutenant of a man of war, and one word brought on another, until the Lieutenant challenged him to a duel on the plains of Abraham. Capt. Littlejohn was a gentleman, who entertained a high sense of honor, and could do no less than accept the challenge.

At nine o'clock the next morning they were to fight. The Captain returned in the evening, and acquainted his Lieutenant and me with the affair. His Lieutenant was a high blooded Scotchman, as well as himself, who replied to his Captain that he should not want for a second. With this I interrupted him and gave the Captain to understand, that since an opportunity had presented, I would be glad to testify my gratitude to him, by acting the part of a faithful second; on which he gave me his hand, and said that he wanted no better man. Says he, I am a King's officer, and you a prisoner under my care; you must, therefore, go with me, to the place appointed in disguise, and added further; 'you must engage me, upon the honor of a gentleman, that whether I die or live, or whatever happens, provided you live, that you will return to my Lieutenant on board this ship.' All this I solemnly engaged him. The combatants were to discharge each a pocket pistol, and then to fall on with their iron-hilted muckle whangers; and one of that sort was allotted for me; but some British officers, who interposed early in the morning, settled the controversy without fighting.

Now having enjoyed eight or nine days' happiness, from the polite and generous treatment of Captain Littlejohn and his officers, I was obliged to bid them farewell, parting with them in as friendly a manner as we had lived together, which, to the best of my memory, was the eleventh of November: when a detachment of General Arnold's little army appeared on Point Levi, opposite Quebec, who had performed an extraordinary march through a wilderness country, with design to have surprised the capital of Canada; I was then taken on board a vessel called the Adamant, together with the prisoners taken with me, and put under the power of an English Merchant from London, whose name was Brook Watson: a man of malicious and cruel disposition, and who was probably excited, in the exercise of his malevolence, by a junto of tories, who sailed with him to England; among whom were Col. Guy Johnson, Col. Closs, and their attendants and associates, to the number of about 30.

All the ship's crew, Col. Closs, in his personal behavior excepted, behaved towards the prisoners with that spirit of bitterness, which is the peculiar characteristic of tories, when they have the friends of America in their power, measuring their loyalty to the English King by the barbarity, fraud and deceit which they exercise towards the whigs.

A small place in the vessel, enclosed with white oak plank, was assigned for the prisoners, and for me among the rest. I should imagine that it was not more than twenty feet one way, and twenty-two the other.

Into this place we were all, to the number of thirty-four, thrust and hand-cuffed, two prisoners more being added to our number, and were provided with two excrement tubs; in this circumference we were obliged to eat and perform the offices of evacuation, during the voyage to England; and were insulted by every black-guard sailor and tory on board, in the cruelest manner; but what is the most surprising thing is, that not one of us died in the passage. When I was first ordered to go into the filthy inclosure, through a small sort of door, I positively refused, and endeavored to reason the before named Brook Watson out of a conduct so derogatory to every sentiment of honor and humanity, but all to no purpose, my men being forced in the den already; and the rascal who had the charge of the prisoners commanded me to go immediately in among the rest. He further added that the place was good enough for a rebel; that it was impertinent for a capital offender to talk of honor or humanity; that any thing short of a halter was too good for me; and that that would be my portion soon after I landed in England; for which purpose only I was sent thither. About the same time a lieutenant among the tories, insulted me in a grievous manner, saying I ought to have been executed for my rebellion against New-York, and spit in my face; upon which, though I was hand-cuffed, I sprang at him with both hands, and knocked him partly down, but he scrambled along into the cabin, and I after him; there he got under the protection of some men with fixed bayonets, who were ordered to make ready to drive me into the place aforementioned. I challenged him to fight, notwithstanding the impediments that were on my hands, and had the exalted pleasure to see the rascal tremble for fear; his name I have forgot, but Watson ordered his guard to get me into the place with the other prisoners, dead or alive; and I had almost as lieve die as to do it, standing it out till they environed me round with bayonets; and brutish, prejudiced, abandoned wretches they were, from whom I could expect nothing but death or wounds; however, I told them, that they were good honest fellows; that I could not blame them; that I was only in dispute with a calico merchant, who knew not how to behave towards a gentleman of the military establishment. This was spoken rather to appease them for my own preservation, as well as to treat Watson with contempt; but still I found they were determined to force me into the wretched circumstances, which their prejudiced and depraved minds had prepared for me; therefore, rather than die, I submitted to their indignities, being drove with bayonets into the filthy dungeon with the other prisoners, where we were denied fresh water, except a small allowance, which was very inadequate to our wants: and in consequence of the stench of the place, each of us was soon followed with a diarrhœa and fever, which occasioned intolerable thirst. When we asked for water, we were, most commonly, instead of obtaining it, insulted and derided; and to add to all the horrors of the place, it was so dark that we could not see each other, and were overspread with body lice. We had, notwithstanding these severities, full allowance of salt provisions, and a gill of rum per day; the latter of which was of the utmost service to us, and, probably, was the means of saving several of our lives. About forty days we existed in this manner, when the land's end of England was discovered from the mast head; soon after which, the prisoners were taken from their gloomy abode, being permitted to see the light of the sun, and breathe fresh air, which to us was very refreshing. The day following we landed at Falmouth.

A few days before I was taken prisoner, I shifted my clothes, by which I happened to be taken in a Canadian dress, viz: a short fawn-skin jacket, double-breasted, an undervest and breeches of sagathy, worsted stockings, a decent pair of shoes, two plain shirts, and a red worsted cap; this was all the clothing I had, in which I made my appearance in England.

When the prisoners were landed, multitudes of the citizens of Falmouth, excited by curiosity, crowded to see us, which was equally gratifying to us. I saw numbers on the tops of houses, and the rising adjacent grounds were covered with them, of both sexes. The throng was so great, that the king's officers were obliged to draw their swords, and force a passage to Pendennis castle, which was near a mile from the town, where we were closely confined, in consequence of orders from General Carleton, who then commanded in Canada.

The rascally Brook Watson then set out for London in great haste, expecting the reward of his zeal; but the ministry received him, as I have been since informed, rather coolly; for the minority in parliament took advantage, arguing that the opposition of America to Great Britain, was not a rebellion : If it is, say they, why do you not execute Col. Allen according to law? But the majority argued that I ought to be executed, and that the opposition was really a rebellion, but that policy obliged them not to do it, inasmuch as the Congress had then most prisoners in their power; so that my being sent to England, for the purpose of being executed, and necessity restraining them, was rather a foil on their laws and authority, and they consequently disapproved of my being sent thither. But I had never heard the least hint of those debates, in parliament, or of the working of their policy, until sometime after I left England.

Consequently the reader will readily conceive I was anxious about my preservation, knowing that I was in the power of a haughty and cruel nation, considered as such. Therefore, the first proposition which I determined in my own mind was, that humanity and moral suasion would not be consulted in the determining of my fate; and those that daily came in great numbers out of curiosity to see me, both gentle and simple, united in this, that I would be hanged. A gentleman from America, by the name of Temple, and who was friendly to me, just whispered me in the ear, and told me that bets were laid in London, that I would be executed; he likewise privately gave me a guinea, but durst say but little to me.

However, agreeably to my first negative proposition, that moral virtue would not influence my destiny, I had recourse to stratagem, which I was in hopes would move in the circle of their policy. I requested of the commander of the castle, the privilege of writing to Congress, who, after consulting with an officer that lived in town, of a superior rank, permitted me to write. I wrote, in the fore part of the letter, a short narrative of my ill-treatment; but withal let them know that, though I was treated as a criminal in England, and continued in irons, together with those taken with me, yet it was in consequence of the orders which the commander of the castle received from Gen. Carleton, and therefore desired Congress to desist from matters of retaliation, until they should know the result of the government in England, respecting their treatment towards me, and the prisoners with me, and govern themselves accordingly, with a particular request, that if retaliation should be found necessary, it might be exercised not according to the smallness of my character in America, but in proportion to the importance of the cause for which I suffered. This is, according to my present recollection, the substance of the letter inscribed,—" *To the illustrious Continental Congress.*" This letter was written with the view that it should be sent to the ministry at London, rather than to Congress, with a design to intimidate the haughty English government, and screen my neck from the halter.

The next day the officer, from whom I obtained license to write, came to see me, and frowned on me on account of the impudence of the letter, as he phrased it, and further added, 'Do you think that we are fools in England, and would send your letter to Congress, with instructions to retaliate on our own people? I have sent your letter to Lord North.' This gave me inward satisfaction, though I carefully concealed it with a pretended resentment, for I found that I had come Yankee over him, and that the letter had gone to the identical person I designed it for. Nor do I know to this day, but that it had the desired effect, though I have not heard any thing of the letter since.

My personal treatment by Lieutenant Hamilton, who commanded the castle, was very generous. He sent me every day a fine breakfast and dinner from his own table, and a bottle of good wine. Another aged gentleman, whose name I cannot recollect, sent me a good supper. But there was no distinction between me and the privates; we all lodged on a sort of Dutch bunks, in one common apartment, and were allowed straw. The privates were well supplied with provisions, and with me, took effectual measures to rid ourselves of lice.

I could not but feel, inwardly, extremely anxious for my fate. This, I however, concealed from the prisoners, as well as from the enemy, who were perpetually shaking the halter at me. I nevertheless treated them with scorn and contempt; and having sent my letter to the ministry, could conceive of nothing more in my power but to keep up my spirits, behave in a daring, soldier-like manner, that I might exhibit a good sample of American fortitude. Such a conduct, I judged would have a more probable tendency to my preservation than concession and timidity. This therefore, was my deportment; and I had lastly determined in my mind, that if a cruel death must inevitably be my portion, I would face it undaunted; and, though I greatly rejoice that I returned to my country and friends, and to see the power and pride of Great Britain humbled; yet I am confident I could then have died without the least appearance of dismay.

I now clearly recollect that my mind was so resolved, that I would not have trembled or shewn the least fear, as I was sensible that it could not alter my fate, nor do more than reproach my memory, make my last act despicable to my enemies, and eclipse the other actions of my life. For I reasoned thus, that nothing was more common than for men to die with their friends around them, weeping and lamenting over them, but not able to help them, which was in reality not different in the consequence of it from such a death as I was apprehensive of; and, as death was the natural consequence of animal life to which the laws of nature subject mankind, to be timorous and uneasy as to the event and manner of it, was inconsistent with the character of a philosopher and soldier.

The cause I was engaged in, I ever viewed worthy hazarding my life for, nor was I, in the most critical moments of trouble, sorry that I engaged in it; and, as to the world of spirits, though I knew nothing of the mode or manner of it, I expected nevertheless, when I should arrive at such a world, that I should be as well treated as other gentlemen of my merit.

Among the great numbers of people, who came to the castle to see the prisoners, some gentlemen told me that they had come fifty miles on purpose to see me, and desired to ask me a number of questions, and to make free with me in conversation. I gave for answer that I chose freedom in every sense of the word. Then one of them asked me what my occupation in life had been? I answered him, that in my younger days I had studied divinity, but was a conjuror by profession. He replied that I conjured wrong at the time I was taken; and I was obliged to own, that I mistook a figure at that time, but that I had conjured them out of Ticonderoga. This was a place of great notoriety in England, so that the joke seemed to go in my favor.

It was a common thing for me to be taken out of close confinement, into a spacious green in the castle, or rather parade, where numbers of gentlemen and ladies were ready to see and hear me. I often entertained such audiences with harangues on the impracticability of Great Britain's conquering the then colonies of America. At one of these times I asked a gentleman for a bowl of punch, and he ordered his servant to bring it, which he did, and offered it to me, but I refused to take it from the hand of his servant; he then gave it to me with his own hand, refusing to drink with me in consequence of my being a state criminal: However, I took the punch and drank it all down at one draught, and handed the gentleman the bowl; this made the spectators as well as myself merry.

I expatiated on American freedom. This gained the resentment of a young beardless gentleman of the company, who gave himself very great airs, and replied that he 'knew the Americans very well, and was certain they could not bear the smell of powder.' I replied, that I accepted it as a challenge, and was ready to convince him on the spot, that an American could bear the smell of powder; at which he answered that he should not put himself on a par with me. I then demanded him to treat the character of the Americans with due respect. He answered that I was an Irishman; but I assured him that I was a full blooded Yankee, and in fine bantered him so much, that he left me in possession of the ground, and the laugh went against him. Two clergymen came to see me, and, inasmuch as they behaved with civility, I returned them the same. We discoursed on several parts of moral philosophy and Christianity; and they seemed to be surprised that I should be acquainted with such topics, or that I should understand a syllogism, or regular mode of argumentation. I am apprehensive my Canadian dress contributed not a little to the surprise, and excitement of curiosity: to see a gentleman in England regularly dressed and well behaved would be no sight at all; but such a rebel as they were pleased to call me, it is probable, was never before seen in England.

The prisoners were landed at Falmouth a few days before Christmas, and ordered on board of the Solebay frigate, Capt. Symonds, on the eighth day of January, 1776, when our hand irons were taken off. This remove was in consequence, as I have been since informed, of a writ of habeas corpus, which had been procured by some gentlemen in England, in order to obtain me my liberty.

The Solebay, with sundry other men-of-war, and about forty transports, rendezvoused at the cove of Cork, in Ireland, to take in provisions and water.

When we were first brought on board, captain Symonds ordered all the prisoners, and most of the hands on board to go on the deck, and caused to be read in their hearing, a certain code of laws or rules, for the regulation and ordering of their behavior; and then in a sovereign manner, ordered the prisoners, me in particular, off the deck, and never to come on it again: for, said he, this is a place for gentlemen to walk. So I went off, an officer following me, who told me he would shew me the place allotted to me, and took me down to the cable tier, saying to me this is your place.

Prior to this I had taken cold, by which I was in an ill state of health, and did not say much to the officer; but stayed there that night, consulted my policy, and I found I was in an evil case; that a captain of a man-of-war was more arbitrary than a king, as he could view his territory with a look of his eye, and a movement of his finger commanded obedience. I felt myself more desponding than I had done at any time before,; for I concluded it to be a government scheme, to do that clandestinely which policy forbid to be done under sanction of any public justice and law.

However, two days after, I shaved and cleansed myself as well as I could, and went on deck. The captain spoke to me in a great rage, and said : 'did I not order you not to come on deck?' I answered him, that at the same time he said, 'that it was the place for gentlemen to walk; that I was Colonel Allen, but had not been properly introduced to him.' He replied, —— —— you, sir, be careful not to walk the same side of the deck that I do. This gave me encouragement, and ever after that I walked in the manner he had directed, except when he, at certain times afterwards, had ordered me off in a passion, and I then would directly afterwards go on again, telling him to command his slaves; that I was a gentleman and had a right to walk the deck; yet when he expressly ordered me off, I obeyed, not out of obedience to him, but to set an example to the ship's crew, who ought to obey him.

To walk to the windward side of the deck is, according to custom, the prerogative of the captain of a man-of-war, though he, sometimes, nay commonly, walks with his lieutenants, when no strangers are by. When a captain from some other man-of-war comes on board, the captains walk to the windward side, and the other gentlemen to the leeward.

It was but a few nights I lodged in the cable tier, before I gained an acquaintance with the master of arms, his name was Gillegan, an Irishman, who was a generous and well disposed man, and in a friendly manner made me an offer of living with him in a little birth, which was allotted him between decks, and enclosed in canvass; his preferment on board was about equal to that of a sergeant in a regiment. I was comparatively happy in the acceptance of his clemency, and lived with him in friendship till the frigate anchored in the harbor of Cape Fear, North Carolina, in America.

Nothing of material consequence happened till the fleet rendezvoused at the cove of Cork, except a violent storm which brought old hardy sailors to their prayers. It was soon rumored in Cork that I was on board the Solebay, with a number of prisoners from America; upon which Messrs. Clark & Hays, merchants in company, and a number of other benevolently disposed gentlemen, contributed largely to the relief and support of the prisoners, who were thirty-four in number, and in very needy circumstances. A suit of clothes from head to foot, including an overcoat or surtout, and two shirts were bestowed upon each of them. My suit I received in superfine broadcloths, sufficient for two jackets and two pair of breeches, overplus of a suit throughout, eight fine Holland shirts and socks ready made, with a number of pairs of silk and worsted hose, two pair of shoes, two beaver hats, one of which was sent me richly laced with gold, by James Bonwell. The Irish gentlemen furthermore made a large gratuity of wines of the best sort, spirits, gin, loaf and brown sugar, tea and chocolate, with a large round of pickled beef, and a number of fat turkies, with many other articles, for my sea stores, too tedious to mention here. To the privates they bestowed on each man two pounds of tea, and six pounds of brown sugar. These articles were received on board at a time when the captain and first lieutenant were gone on shore, by the permission of the second lieutenant, a handsome young gentleman, who was then under twenty-one years of age; his name was Douglass, son of admiral Douglass, as I was informed.

As this munificence was so unexpected and plentiful, I may add needful, it impressed on my mind the highest sense of gratitude towards my benefactors ; for I was not only supplied with the necessaries and conveniences of life, but with the grandeurs and superfluities of it. Mr. Hays, one of the donators before-mentioned, came on board, and behaved in the most obliging manner, telling me that he hoped my troubles were past ; for that the gentlemen of Cork determined to make my sea stores equal to that of the captain of the Solebay ; he made an offer of live stock and wherewith to support them ; but I knew this would be denied. And to crown all, did send me by another person, fifty guineas, out I could not reconcile receiving the whole to my own feelings, as it might have the appearance of avarice ; and therefore received but seven guineas only, and am confident, not only from the exercise of the present well-timed generosity, but from a large acquaintance with gentlemen of this nation, that as a people they excel in liberality and bravery.

Two days after the receipt of the aforesaid donations, captain Symonds came on board full of envy towards the prisoners, and swore by all that is good, that the damned American rebels should not be feasted at this rate, by the damned rebels of Ireland ; he therefore took away all my liquors before-mentioned, except some of the wine which was secreted, and a two gallon jug of old spirits which was reserved for me per favor of lieutenant Douglass. The taking of my liquors was abominable in his sight; he therefore spoke in my behalf, till the captain was angry with him; and in consequence, proceeded and took away all the tea and sugar, which had been given to the prisoners, and confiscated it to the use of the ship's crew. Our clothing was not taken away, but the privates were forced to do duty on board. Soon after this there came a boat to the side of the ship, and captain Symonds asked a gentleman in it, in my hearing, what his business was? who answered that he was sent to deliver some sea stores to Col. Allen, which if I remember right, he said were sent from Dublin; but the captain damned him heartily, ordering him away from the ship, and would not suffer him to deliver the stores. I was furthermore informed that the gentlemen in Cork, requested of captain Symonds, that I might be allowed to come into the city, and that they would be responsible I should return to the frigate at a given time, which was denied them.

We sailed from England on the 8th day of January, and from the cove of Cork on the 12th day of February. Just before we sailed, the prisoners with me were divided, and put on board three different ships of war. This gave me some uneasiness, for they were to a man zealous in the cause of liberty, and behaved with a becoming fortitude in the various scenes of their captivity; but those, who were distributed on board other ships of war were much better used than those who tarried with me, as appeared afterwards. When the fleet, consisting of about forty-five sail, including five men of war, sailed from the cove with a fresh breeze, the appearance was beautiful, abstracted from the unjust and bloody designs they had in view. We had not sailed many days, before a mighty storm arose, which lasted near twenty-four hours without intermission. The wind blew with relentless fury, and no man could remain on deck, except he was lashed fast, for the waves rolled over the deck by turns, with a forcible rapidity, and every soul on board was anxious for the preservation of the ship, alias, their lives. In this storm the Thunder-bomb man of war sprang a leak, and was afterwards floated to some part to the coast of England, and the crew saved. We were then said to be in the Bay of Biscay. After the storm abated, I could plainly discern the prisoners were better used for some considerable time.

Nothing of consequence happened after this, till we sailed to the island of Madeira, except a certain favor I had received of captain Symonds, in consequence of an application I made to him for the privilege of his tailor to make me a suit of clothes of the cloth bestowed on me in Ireland, which he generously granted. I could then walk the deck with a seeming better grace. When we had reached Madeira, and anchored, sundry gentlemen with the captain went on shore, who I conclude, gave the rumor that I was in the frigate; upon which I soon found that Irish generosity was again excited; for a gentleman of that nation sent his clerk on board, to know of me if I would accept a sea store from him, particularly wine. This matter I made known to the generous lieutenant Douglass, who readily granted me the favor, provided the articles could be brought on board, during the time of his command; adding that it would be a pleasure to him to serve me, notwithstanding the opposition he met with before. So I directed the gentleman's clerk to inform him that I was greatly in need of so signal a charity, and desired the young gentleman to make the utmost despatch, which he did; but in the meantime, captain Symonds and his officers came on board, and immediately made ready for sailing; the wind at the same time being fair, set sail when the young gentleman was in fair sight with the aforesaid store.

The reader will doubtless recollect the seven guineas I received at the cove of Cork. These enabled me to purchase of the purser what I wanted, had not the captain strictly forbidden it, though I made sundry applications to him for that purpose; but his answer to me, when I was sick, was, that it was no matter how soon I was dead, and that he was no ways anxious to preserve the lives of rebels, but wished them all dead; and indeed that was the language of most of the ship's crew. I expostulated not only with the captain, but with other gentlemen on board, on the unreasonableness of such usage; inferring that, inasmuch as the government in England did not proceed against me as a capital offender, they should not; for that they were by no means empowered by any authority, either civil or military, to do so; for the English government had acquitted me by sending me back a prisoner of war to America, and that they should treat me as such. I further drew an inference of impolicy on them, provided they should by hard usage destroy my life; inasmuch as I might, if living, redeem one of their officers; but the captain replied, that he needed no directions of mine how to treat a rebel; that the British would conquer the American rebels, hang the Congress, and such as promoted the rebellion, me in particular, and retake their own prisoners; so that my life was of no consequence in the scale of their policy. I gave him for answer that if they stayed till they conquered America, before they hanged me, *I should die of old age*, and desired that till such an event took place, he would at least allow me to purchase of the purser, for my own money, such articles as I greatly needed; but he would not permit it, and when I reminded him of the generous and civil usage that their prisoners in captivity in America met with, he said that it was not owing to their goodness, but to their timidity; for, said he, they expect to be conquered, and therefore dare not misuse our prisoners; and in fact this was the language of the British officers, till Burgoyne was taken; happy event! and not only of the officers but the whole British army. I appeal to all my brother prisoners, who have been with the British in the southern department, for a confirmation of what I have advanced on this subject. The surgeon of the Solebay, whose name was North, was a very humane, obliging man, and took the best care of the prisoners who were sick.

The third day of May we cast anchor in the harbor of Cape Fear, in North Carolina, as did Sir Peter Parker's ship, of 50 guns, a little back of the bar; for there was not depth of water for him to come into the harbor. These two men of war, and fourteen sail of transports and others, came after, so that most of the fleet rendezvoused at Cape Fear, for three weeks. The soldiers on board the transports were sickly, in consequence of so long a passage; add to this the small-pox carried off many of them. They landed on the main, and formed a camp; but the riflemen annoyed them, and caused them to move to an island in the harbor; but such cursing of riflemen I never heard.

A detachment of regulars was sent up Brunswick river; as they landed they were fired on by those marksmen, and they came back next day damning the rebels for their unmanly way of fighting, and swearing they would give no quarter, for they took sight at them, and were behind timber skulking about. One of the detachments said they lost one man; but a negro man who was with them, and heard what was said, soon after told me that he helped to bury thirty-one of them; this did me some good to find my countrymen giving them battle; for I never heard such swaggering as among Gen. Clinton's little army who commanded at that time; and I am apt to think there were four thousand men, though not two thirds of them fit for duty. I heard numbers of them say, that the trees in America should hang well with fruit that campaign for they would give no quarter. This was in the mouths of most who I heard speak on the subject, officer as well as soldier. I wished at that time my countrymen knew, as well as I did, what a murdering and cruel enemy they had to deal with; but experience has since taught this country what they are to expect at the hands of Britons when in their power.

The prisoners, who had been sent on board different men of war at the cove of Cork, were collected together, and the whole of them put on board the Mercury frigate, capt. James Montague, except one of the Canadians, who died on the passage from Ireland, and Peter Noble, who made his escape from the Sphynx man-of-war in this harbour, and, by extraordinary swimming, got safe home to New-England, and gave intelligence of the usage of his brother prisoners. The Mercury set sail from this port for Halifax, about the 20th of May, and Sir Peter Parker was about to sail with the land forces, under the command of Gen. Clinton, for the reduction of Charleston, the capitol of South-Carolina, and when I heard of his defeat in Halifax, it gave me inexpressible satisfaction.

I now found myself under a worse captain than Symonds; for Montague was loaded with prejudices against every body and every thing that was not stamped with royalty; and being by nature under-witted, his wrath was heavier than the others, or at least his mind was in no instance liable to be diverted by good sense, humour or bravery, of which Symonds was by turns susceptible. A Capt. Francis Proctor was added to our number of prisoners when we were first put on board this ship. This gentleman had formerly belonged to the English service. The captain, and in fine, all the gentlemen of the ship were very much incensed against him, and put him in irons without the least provocation, and he was continued in this miserable situation about three months. In this passage the prisoners were infected with the scurvy, some more and some less, but most of them severely. The ship's crew was to a great degree troubled with it, and I concluded it was catching. Several of the crew died with it on their passage. I was weak and feeble in consequence of so long and cruel a captivity, yet had but little of the scurvy.

The purser was again expressly forbid by the captain to let me have any thing out of his store; upon which I went upon deck, and in the handsomest manner requested the favor of purchasing a few necessaries of the purser, which was denied me; he further told me, that I should be hanged as soon as I arrived at Halifax. I tried to reason the matter with him, but found him proof against reason; I also held up his honor to view, and his behavior to me and the prisoners in general, as being derogatory to it, but found his honor impenetrable. I then endeavored to touch his humanity, but found he had none; for his prepossession of bigotry to his own party, had confirmed him in an opinion, that no humanity was due to unroyalists, but seemed to think that heaven and earth were made merely to gratify the King and his creatures; he uttered considerable unintelligible and grovelling ideas, a little tinctured with monarchy, but stood well to his text of hanging me. He afterwards forbade his surgeon to administer any help to the sick prisoners. I was every night shut down in the cable tier, with the rest of the prisoners, and we all lived miserably while under his power. But I received some generosity from several of the midshipmen, who in degree alleviated my misery; one of their names was Putrass, the names of the others I do not recollect; but they were obliged to be private in the bestowment of their favor, which was sometimes good wine bitters, and at others a generous drink of grog.

Sometime in the first week of June, we came to anchor at the Hook off New York, where we remained but three days; in which time Governor Tryon, Mr. Kemp, the old attorney general of New York, and several other perfidious and over grown tories and land-jobbers, came on board. Tryon viewed me with a stern countenance, as I was walking on the leeward side of the deck with the midshipmen; and he and his companions were walking with the captain and lieutenant, on the windward side of the same, but never spoke to me, though it is altogether probable that he thought of the old quarrel between him, the old government of New York, and the Green-Mountain Boys. Then they went with the captain into the cabin, and the same afternoon returned on board a vessel, where at that time they took sanctuary from the resentment of their injured country. What passed between the officers of the ship and these visitors I know not; but this I know that my treatment from the officers was more severe afterwards.

We arrived at Halifax not far from the middle of June, where the ship's crew, which was infested with the scurvy, were taken on shore and shallow trenches dug, into which they were put, and partly covered with earth. Indeed every proper measure was taken for their relief. The prisoners were not permitted any sort of medicine, but were put on board a sloop which lay in the harbor, near the town of Halifax, surrounded by several men-of-war and their tenders, and a guard constantly set over them, night and day. The sloop we had wholly to ourselves except the guard who occupied the forecastle: here we were cruelly pinched with hunger; it seemed to me that we had not more than one third of the common allowance. We were all seized with violent hunger and faintness; we divided our scanty allowance as exact as possible. I shared the same fate with the rest, and though they offered me more than an even share, I refused to accept it, as it was a time of substantial distress, which in my opinion I ought to partake equally with the rest, and set an example of virtue and fortitude to our little commonwealth.

I sent letter after letter to captain Montague, who still had the care of us, and also to his lieutenant, whose name I cannot call to mind, but could obtain no answer, much less a redress of grievances; and to add to the calamity, nearly a dozen of the prisoners were dangerously ill of the scurvy. I wrote private letters to the doctors, to procure, if possible, some remedy for the sick, but in vain. The chief physician came by in a boat, so close that the oars touched the sloop that we were in, and I uttered my complaint in the genteelest manner to him, but he never so much as turned his head, or made me any answer, though I continued speaking till he got out of hearing. Our cause then became deplorable. Still I kept writing to the captain, till he ordered the guards, as they told me, not to bring any more letters from me to him. In the mean time an event happened worth relating. One of the men almost dead with the scurvy, lay by the side of the sloop, and a canoe of Indians coming by, he purchased two quarts of strawberries, and ate them at once, and it almost cured him. The money he gave for them, was all the money he had in the world. After that we tried every way to procure more of that fruit, reasoning from analogy that they might have the same effect on others infested with the same disease, but could obtain none.

Meanwhile the doctor's mate of the Mercury came privately on board the prison sloop and presented me with a large vial of smart drops, which proved to be good for the scurvy, though vegetables and some other ingredients were requisite for a cure; but the drops gave at least a check to the disease. This was a well-timed exertion of humanity, but the doctor's name has slipped my mind, and in my opinion, it was the means of saving the lives of several men.

The guard, which was set over us, was by this time touched with feelings of compassion; and I finally trusted one of them with a letter of complaint to governor Arbuthnot, of Halifax, which he found means to communicate, and which had the desired effect; for the governor sent an officer and surgeon on board the prison sloop, to know the truth of the complaint. The officer's name was Russell, who held the rank of lieutenant, and treated me in a friendly and polite manner, and was really angry at the cruel and unmanly usage the prisoners met with; and with the surgeon made a true report of matters to governor Arbuthnot, who, either by his order or influence, took us next day from the prison sloop to Halifax jail, where I first became acquainted with the now Hon. James Lovel, one of the members of Congress for the state of Massachusetts. The sick were taken to the hospital, and the Canadians, who were effective, were employed in the King's works; and when their countrymen were recovered from the scurvy and joined them, they all deserted the king's employ, and were not heard of at Halifax, as long as the remainder of the prisoners continued there, which was till near the middle of October. We were on board the prison sloop about six weeks, and were landed at Halifax near the middle of August. Several of our English-American prisoners, who were cured of the scurvy at the hospital, made their escape from thence, and after a long time reached their old habitations.

I had now but thirteen with me, of those who were taken in Canada, and remained in jail with me at Halifax, who, in addition to those that were imprisoned before, made our number about thirty-four, who were all locked up in one common large room, without regard to rank, education or any other accomplishment, where we continued from the setting to the rising sun: and, as sundry of them were infected with the jail and other distempers, the furniture of this spacious room consisted principally of excrement tubs. We petitioned for a removal of the sick into the hospitals, but were denied. We remonstrated against the ungenerous usage of being confined with the privates, as being contrary to the laws and customs of nations. and particularly ungrateful in them in consequence of the gentleman-like usage which the British imprisoned officers met with in America; and thus we wearied ourselves, petitioning and remonstrating, but to no purpose at all; for general Massey, who commanded at Halifax, was as inflexible as the devil himself, a fine preparative this for Mr. Lovel, member of the Continental Congress.

Lieutenant Russell, whom I have mentioned before, came to visit me in prison, and assured me that he had done his utmost to procure my parole for enlargement; at which a British captain, who was then town-major, expressed compassion for the gentlemen confined in the filthy place, and assured me that he had used his influence to procure their enlargement; his name was near like Ramsey. Among the prisoners there were five in number, who had a legal claim to a parole, a Mr. Howland, master of a continental armed vessel, a Mr. Taylor, his mate, and myself.

As to the article of provision, we were well served, much better than in any part of my captivity; and since it was Mr. Lovel's misfortunes and mine to be prisoners, and in so wretched circumstances, I was happy that we were together as a mutual support to each other, and to the unfortunate prisoners with us. Our first attention was the preservation of ourselves and injured little republic; the rest of our time we devoted interchangeably to politics and philosophy, as patience was a needful exercise in so evil a situation, but contentment mean and impracticable.

I had not been in this jail many days, before a worthy and charitable woman, by the name of Mrs. Blacden, supplied me with a good dinner of fresh meats every day, with garden fruit, and sometimes with a bottle of wine: notwithstanding which I had not been more than three weeks in this place before I lost my appetite to the most delicious food, by the jail distemper, as also did sundry of the prisoners, particularly a sergeant Moore, a man of courage and fidelity. I have several times seen him hold the boatswain of the Solebay frigate, when he attempted to strike him, and laughed him out of conceit of using him as a slave.

A doctor visited the sick, and did the best, as I suppose, he could for them, to no apparent purpose. I grew weaker and weaker, as did the rest. Several of them could not help themselves. At last I reasoned in my own mind, that raw onion would be good. I made use of it, and found immediate relief by it, as did the sick in general, particularly sergeant Moore, whom it recovered almost from the shades; though I had met with a little revival, still I found the malignant hand of Britain had greatly reduced my constitution with stroke upon stroke. Esquire Lovel and myself used every argument and entreaty that could be well conceived of in order to obtain gentleman-like usage, to no purpose. I then wrote Gen. Massey as severe a letter as I possibly could with my friend Lovel's assistance. The contents of it was to give the British, as a nation, and him as an individual, their true character. This roused the rascal, for he could not bear to see his and the nation's deformity in that transparent letter, which I sent him; he therefore put himself in a great rage about it, and showed the letter to a number of British officers, particularly to captain Smith of the Lark frigate, who, instead of joining with him in disapprobation, commended the spirit of it; upon which general Massey said to him do you take the part of a rebel against me? Captain Smith answered that he rather spoke his sentiments and there was a dissention in opinion between them. Some officers took the part of the general, and others of the captain. This I was informed of by a gentleman who had it from captain Smith.

In a few days after this, the prisoners were ordered to go on board of a man-of-war, which was bound for New York; but two of them were not able to go on board, and were left at Halifax; one died; and the other recovered. This was about the 12th of October, and soon after we had got on board, the captain sent for me in particular to come on the quarter deck. I went, not knowing that it was captain Smith, or his ship, at that time, and expected to meet the same rigorous usage I had commonly met with, and prepared my mind accordingly; but when I came on deck, the captain met me with his hand, welcomed me to his ship, invited me to dine with him that day, and assured me that I should be treated as a gentleman, and that he had given orders, that I should be treated with respect by the ship's crew. This was so unexpected and sudden a transition, that it drew tears from my eyes, which all the ill usage I had before met with, was not able to produce, nor could I at first hardly speak, but soon recovered myself and expressed my gratitude for so unexpected a favor; and let him know that I felt anxiety of mind in reflecting that his situation and mine was such, that it was not probable that it would ever be in my power to return the favor. Captain Smith replied, that he had no reward in view, but only treated me as a gentleman ought to be treated; he said this is a mutable world, and one gentleman never knows but it may be in his power to help another. Soon after I found this to be the same captain Smith who took my part against general Massey; out he never mentioned any thing of it to me, and I thought it impolite in me to interrogate him, as to any disputes which might have arisen between him and the general on my account, as I was a prisoner, and that it was at his option to make free with me on that subject, if he pleased; and if he did not, I might take it for granted that it would be unpleasing for me to query about it, though I had a strong propensity to converse with him on that subject.

I dined with the captain agreeable to his invitation, and oftentimes with the lieutenant, in the gun-room, but in general ate and drank with my friend Lovel and the other gentlemen who were prisoners with me, where I also slept.

We had a little birth enclosed with canvas, between

decks, where we enjoyed ourselves very well, in hopes of an exchange ; besides, our friends at Halifax had a little notice of our departure, and supplied us with spirituous liquor, and many articles of provisions for the cost. Captain Burk, having been taken prisoner, was added to our company, (he had commanded an American armed vessel,) and was generously treated by the captain and all the officers of the ship, as well as myself. We now had in all near thirty prisoners on board, and as we were sailing along the coast, if I recollect right, off Rhode-Island, captain Burk, with an under officer of the ship, whose name I do not recollect, came to our little berth, proposed to kill captain Smith and the principal officers of the frigate and take it ; adding that there were thirty-five thousand pounds sterling in the same. Captain Burk likewise averred that a strong party out of the ship's crew was in the conspiracy, and urged me, and the gentleman that was with me, to use our influence with the private prisoners, to execute the design, and take the ship with the cash into one of our own ports.

Upon which I replied, that we had been too well used on board to murder the officers ; that I could by no means reconcile it to my conscience, and that, in fact, it should not be done ; and while I was yet speaking, my friend Lovel confirmed what I had said, and farther pointed out the ungratefulness of such an act ; that it did not fall short of murder, and in fine all the gentlemen in the berth opposed captain Burk and his colleague. But they strenuously urged that the conspiracy would be found out, and that it would cost them their lives, provided they did not execute their design. I then interposed spiritedly, and put an end to further argument on the subject, and told them that they might depend upon it, upon my honor, that I would faithfully guard captain Smith's life. If they should attempt the assault, I would assist him, for they desired me to remain neuter, and that the same honor that guarded captain Smith's life, would also guard theirs ; and it was agreed by those present not to reveal the conspiracy, to the intent that no man should be put to death, in consequence of what had been projected; and captain Burk and his colleague went to stifle the matter among their associates. I could not help calling to mind what captain Smith said to me, when I first came on board: "This is a mutable world, and one gentleman never knows but that it may be in his power to help another." Captain Smith and his officers still behaved with their usual courtesy, and I never heard any more of the conspiracy.

We arrived before New-York, and cast anchor the latter part of October, where we remained several days, and where captain Smith informed me, that he had recommended me to admiral Howe and general Sir Wm. Howe, as a gentleman of honor and veracity, and desired that I might be treated as such. Captain Burk was then ordered on board a prison-ship in the harbor. I took my leave of captain Smith, and with the other prisoners, was sent on board a transport ship, which lay in the harbor, commanded by captain Craige, who took me into the cabin with him and his lieutenant. I fared as they did, and was in every respect well treated, in consequence of directions from captain Smith. In a few weeks after this I had the happiness to part with my friend Lovel, for his sake, whom the enemy affected to treat as a private; he was a gentleman of merit, and liberally educated, but had no commission; they maligned him on account of his unshaken attachment to the cause of his country. He was exchanged for a governor Philip Skene of the British. I was continued in this ship till the latter part of November, where I contracted an acquaintance with the captain of the British; his name has slipped my memory. He was what we may call a genteel, hearty fellow. I remember an expression of his over a bottle of wine, to this import: "That there is a greatness of soul for personal friendship to subsist between you and me, as we are upon opposite sides, and may at another day be obliged to face each other in the field." I am confident that he was as faithful as any officer in the British army. At another sitting he offered to bet a dozen of wine, that fort Washington would be in the hands of the British in three days. I stood the bet, and would, had I known that that would have been the case; and the third day afterwards we heard a heavy cannonade, and that day the fort was taken sure enough. Some months after, when I was on parole, he called upon me with his usual humor, and mentioned the bet. I acknowledged I had lost it, but he said he did not mean to take it then, as I was a prisoner; that he would another day call on me, when their army came to Bennington. I replied that he was quite too generous, as I had fairly lost it; besides, the Green-Mountain-Boys would not suffer them to come to Bennington. This was all in good humor. I should have been glad to have seen him after the defeat at Bennington, but did not. It was customary for a guard to attend the prisoners, which was often changed. One was composed of tories from Connecticut, in the vicinity of Fairfield and Green Farms. The sergeant's name was Hoit. They were very full of their invectives against the country, swaggered of their loyalty to their king, and exclaimed bitterly against the "cowardly yankees," as they were pleased to term them, but finally contented themselves with saying, that when the country was overcome, they should be well rewarded for their loyalty out of the estates of the whigs, which would be confiscated. This I found to be the general language of the tories, after I arrived from England on the American coast. I heard sundry of them relate, that the British generals had engaged them an ample reward for their losses, disappointments and expenditures, out of the forfeited rebels' estates. This language early taught me what to do with tories' estates, as far as my influence can go. For it is really a game of hazard between whig and tory. The whigs must inevitably have lost all, in consequence of the abilities of the tories, and their good friends the British; and it is no more than right the tories should run the same risk, in consequence of the abilities of the whigs. But of this more will be observed in the sequel of this narrative.

Some of the last days of November, the prisoners

were landed at New-York, and I was admitted to parole with the other officers, viz: Proctor, Howland, and Taylor. The privates were put into filthy churches in New-York, with the distressed prisoners that were taken at Fort Washington; and the second night, sergeant Roger Moore, who was bold and enterprising, found means to make his escape with every of the remaining prisoners that were taken with me, except three, who were soon after exchanged. So that out of thirty-one prisoners, who went with me the round exhibited in these sheets, two only died with the enemy, and three only were exchanged; one of whom died after he came within our lines; all the rest, at different times, made their escape from the enemy.

I now found myself on parole, and restricted to the limits of the city of New-York, where I soon projected means to live in some measure agreeably to my rank, though I was destitute of cash. My constitution was almost worn out by such a long and barbarous captivity. The enemy gave out that I was crazy, and wholly unmanned, but my vitals held sound, nor was I delirious any more than I had been from youth up; but my extreme circumstances, at certain times, rendered it politic to act in some measure the madman; and in consequence of a regular diet and exercise, my blood recruited, and my nerves in a great measure recovered their former tone, strength and usefulness, in the course of six months.

I next invite the reader to a retrospective sight and consideration of the doleful scene of inhumanity exercised by general Sir William Howe, and the army under his command, towards the prisoners taken on Long-Island, on the 27th of August, 1776; sundry of whom were, in an inhuman and barbarous manner, murdered after they had surrendered their arms; particularly a general Odel, or Woodhull, of the militia, who was hacked to pieces with cutlasses, when alive, by the light horsemen, and a captain Fellows, of the continental army, who was thrust through with a bayonet, of which wound he died instantly. Sundry others were hanged up by the neck till they were dead; five on the limb of a white oak tree, and without any reason assigned, except that they were fighting in defence of the only blessing worth preserving. And indeed those who had the misfortune to fall into their hands at Fort Washington, in the month of November following, met with very little better usage, except that they were reserved from immediate death to famish and die with hunger; in fine, the word rebel, applied to any vanquished persons, without regard to rank, who were in the continental service, on the 27th of August aforesaid, was thought, by the enemy, sufficient to sanctify whatever cruelties they were pleased to inflict, death itself not excepted; but to pass over particulars which would swell my narrative far beyond my design.

The private soldiers, who were brought to New York, were crowded into churches, and environed with slavish Hessian guards, a people of a strange language, who were sent to America for no other design but cruelty and desolation; and at others, by merciless Britons whose mode of communicating ideas being intelligible in this country, served only to tantalize and insult the helpless and perishing; but above all, the hellish delight and triumph of the tories over them, as they were dying by hundreds. This was too much for me to bear as a spectator; for I saw the tories exulting over the dead bodies of their murdered countrymen. I have gone into the churches, and seen sundry of the prisoners in the agonies of death, in consequence of very hunger, and others speechless, and very near death, biting pieces of chips; others pleading for God's sake, for something to eat, and at the same time, shivering with the cold. Hollow groans saluted my ears, and despair seemed to be imprinted on every of their countenances. The filth in these churches, in consequence of the fluxes, was almost beyond description. The floors were covered with excrements. I have carefully sought to direct my steps so as to avoid it, but could not. They would beg for God's sake for one copper, or morsel of bread. I have seen in one of these churches seven dead, at the same time, lying among the excrements of their bodies.

It was a common practice with the enemy, to convey the dead from these filthy places, in carts, to be slightly buried, and I have seen whole gangs of tories making derision, and exulting over the dead, saying, there goes another load of damned rebels. I have observed the British soldiers to be full of their blackguard jokes, and vaunting on those occasions, but they appeared to me less malignant than tories.

The provision dealt out to the prisoners was by no means sufficient for the support of life. It was deficient in quantity, and much more so in quality. The prisoners often presented me with a sample of their bread, which I certify was damaged to that degree, that it was loathsome and unfit to be eaten, and I am bold to aver it, as my opinion, that it had been condemned, and was of the very worst sort. I have seen and been fed upon damaged bread, in the course of my captivity, and observed the quality of such bread as has been condemned by the enemy, among which was very little so effectually spoiled as what was dealt out to these prisoners. Their allowance of meat (as they told me) was quite trifling, and of the basest sort. I never saw any of it, but was informed, that bad as it was, it was swallowed almost as quick as they got hold of it. I saw some of them sucking bones after they were speechless; others, who could yet speak, and had the use of their reason, urged me in the strongest and most pathetic manner, to use my interest in their behalf; for you plainly see, said they, that we are devoted to death and destruction; and after I had examined more particularly into their truly deplorable condition, and had become more fully apprized of the essential facts, I was persuaded that it was a premeditated and systematical plan of the British council, to destroy the youths of our land, with a view thereby to deter the country, and make it submit to their despotism; but that I could not do them any material service, and that, by any public attempt for that purpose, I might endanger myself by frequenting places the most nauseous and contagious that could be conceived of. I refrained going into churches, but frequently conversed with such of the prisoners as were admitted to come out into the yard, and found that the systematical usage still continued. The guard would often drive me away with their fixed bayonets. A Hessian one day followed me five or six rods, but by making use of my legs, I got rid of the lubber. Sometimes I could obtain a little conversation, notwithstanding their severities.

I was in one of the church yards, and it was rumored among those in the church, and sundry of the prisoners came with their usual complaints to me, and among the rest a large boned, tall young man, as he told me, from Pennsylvania, who was reduced to a mere skeleton; he said he was glad to see me before he died, which he expected to have done last night, but was a little revived; he furthermore informed me, that he and his brother had been urged to enlist into the British Army, but both had resolved to die first; that his brother had died last night, in consequence of that resolution, and that he expected shortly to follow him; but I made the other prisoners stand a little off, and told him with a low voice to enlist; he then asked, whether it was right in the sight of God! I assured him that it was, and that duty to himself obliged him to deceive the British by enlisting and deserting the first opportunity; upon which he answered with transport that he would enlist. I charged him not to mention my name as his adviser, lest it should get air, and I should be closely confined, in consequence of it. The integrity of these suffering prisoners is hardly credible. Many hundreds, I am confident, submitted to death, rather than to enlist in the British service, which, I am informed, they most generally were pressed to do. I was astonished at the resolution of the two brothers particularly; it seems that they could not be stimulated to such exertions of heroism from ambition, as they were but obscure soldiers; strong indeed must the internal principle of virtue be, which supported them to brave death, and one of them went through the operation, as did many hundred others. I readily grant that instances of public virtue are no excitement to the sordid and vicious, nor, on the other hand, will all the barbarity of Britain and Heshland awaken them to a sense of their duty to the public; but these things will have their proper effect on the generous and brave. The officers on parole were most of them zealous, if possible, to afford the miserable soldiery relief, and often consulted with one another on the subject, but to no effect, being destitute of the means of subsistence, which they needed; nor could the officers project any measure, which they thought would alter their fate, or so much as be a means of getting them out of those filthy places to the privilege of fresh air. Some projected that all the officers should go in procession to General Howe, and plead the cause of the perishing soldiers; but this proposal was negatived for the following reasons, viz: because that general Howe must needs be well acquainted, and have a thorough knowledge of the state and condition of the prisoners in every of their wretched apartments, and that much more particular and exact than any officer on parole could be supposed to have, as the general had a return of the circumstances of the prisoners, by his own officers, every morning, of the number which were alive, as also the number which died every twenty-four hours; and consequently the bill of mortality, as collected from the daily returns, lay before him with all the material situations and circumstances of the prisoners; and provided the officers should go in procession to general Howe, according to the projection, it would give him the greatest affront, and that he would either retort upon them, that it was no part of their parole to instruct him in his conduct to prisoners; that they were mutining against his authority, and by affronting him, had forfeited their parole; or that, more probably, instead of saying one word to them, would order them all into as wretched confinement as the soldiers whom they sought to relieve; for, at that time, the British, from the general to the private sentinel, were in full confidence, nor did they so much as hesitate, but that they should conquer the country. Thus the consultation of the officers was confounded and broken to pieces, in consequence of the dread, which at that time lay on their minds, of offending Gen. Howe; for they conceived so murderous a tyrant would not be too good to destroy even the officers, on the least pretence of an affront, as they were equally in his power with the soldiers; and, as Gen. Howe perfectly understood the condition of the private soldiers, it was argued that it was exactly such as he and his council had devised, and as he meant to destroy them, it would be to no purpose for them to try to dissuade him from it, as they were helpless and liable to the same fate, on giving the least affront; indeed anxious apprehensions disturbed them in their then circumstances.

Mean time mortality raged to such an intolerable degree among the prisoners, that the very school boys in the streets knew the mental design of it in some measure; at least, they knew that they were starved to death. Some poor women contributed to their necessity, till their children were almost starved, and all persons of common understanding knew that they were devoted to the cruelest and worst of deaths. It was also proposed by some to make a written representation of the condition of the soldiery, and the officers to sign it, and that it should be couched in such terms, as though they were apprehensive that the General was imposed upon by his officers, in their daily returns to him of the state and condition of the prisoners; and that therefore the officers, moved with compassion, were constrained to communicate to him the facts relative to them, nothing doubting but that they would meet with a speedy redress; but this proposal was most generally negatived also, and for much the same reason offered in the other case; for it was conjectured that Gen. Howe's indignation would be moved against such officers as should attempt to whip him over his officers' backs; that he would discern that himself was really struck at, and not the officers who made the daily returns; and therefore self-preservation deterred the officers from either petitioning or remonstrating to Gen. Howe, either verbally or in writing; as also the consideration that no valuable purpose to the distressed would be obtained.

I made several rough drafts on the subject, one of which I exhibited to the colonels Magaw, Miles and Atlee, and they said that they would consider the matter; soon after I called on them, and some of the gentlemen informed me that they had written to the general on the subject, and I concluded that the gentlemen thought it best that they should write without me, as there was such spirited aversion subsisting between the British and me.

In the mean time a colonel Hussecker, of the continental army, as he then reported, was taken prisoner, and brought to New-York, who gave out that the country was almost universally submitting to the English king's authority, and that there would be little or no more opposition to Great-Britain. This at first gave the officers a little shock, but in a few days they recovered themselves; for this colonel Hussecker, being a German, was feasting with general De Heister, his countryman, and from his conduct they were apprehensive that he was a knave; at least he was esteemed so by most of the officers; it was nevertheless a day of trouble. The enemy blasphemed. Our little army was retreating in New-Jersey, and our young men murdered by hundreds in New-York. The army of Britain and Heshland prevailed for a little season, as though it was ordered by Heaven to shew, to the latest posterity, what the British would have done if they could, and what the general calamity must have been, in consequence of their conquering the country, and to excite every honest man to stand forth in the defence of liberty, and to establish the independency of the United States of America forever. But this scene of adverse fortune did not discourage a Washington. The illustrious American hero remained immoveable. In liberty's cause he took up his sword. This reflection was his support and consolation in the day of his humiliation, when he retreated before the enemy, through New-Jersey into Pennsylvania. Their triumph only roused his indignation; and the important cause of his country, which lay near his heart, moved him to cross the Delaware again, and take ample satisfaction on his pursuers. No sooner had he circumvallated his haughty foes, and appeared in terrible array, but the host of Heshland fell. This taught America the intrinsic worth of perseverance, and the generous sons of freedom flew to the standard of their common safeguard and defence; from which time the arm of American liberty hath prevailed.

This surprise and capture of the Hessians enraged the enemy, who were still vastly more numerous than the continental troops. They therefore collected, and marched from Princetown to attack general Washington, who was then at Trenton, having previously left a detachment from their main body at Princeton, for the support of that place. This was a trying time, for our worthy general, though in possession of a late most astonishing victory, was by no means able to withstand the collective forces of the enemy; but his sagacity soon suggested a stratagem to effect that which, by force, to him was at that time impracticable. He therefore amused the enemy with a number of fires, and in the night made a forced march, undiscovered by them, and next morning fell in with their rear-guard at Princetown, and killed and took most of them prisoners. The main body too late perceived their rear was attacked, hurried back with all speed, but to their mortification, found that they were out-generalled and baffled by general Washington, who was retired with his little army towards Morristown, and was out of their power. These repeated successes, one on the back of the other, chagrined the enemy prodigiously, and had an amazing operation in the scale of American politics, and undoubtedly was one of the corner stones, on which their fair structure of Independency has been fabricated, for the country at no other time has ever been so much dispirited as just before the morning of this glorious success, which in part dispelled the gloomy clouds of oppression and slavery, which lay pending over America, big with the ruin of this and future generations, and enlightened and spirited her sons to redouble their blows on a merciless, and haughty, and I may add perfidious enemy.

Farthermore, this success had a mighty effect on general Howe and his council, and roused them to a sense of their own weakness, and convinced them that they were neither omniscient nor omnipotent. Their obduracy and death-designing malevolence, in some measure, abated, or was suspended. The prisoners, who were condemned to the most wretched and cruelest of deaths, and who survived to this period, though most of them died before, were immediately ordered to be sent within general Washington's lines for an exchange, and, in consequence of it, were taken out of their filthy and poisonous places of confinement, and sent from New-York to their friends in haste; several of them fell dead in the streets of New-York, as they attempted to walk to the vessels in the harbor, for their intended embarkation. What numbers lived to reach the lines I cannot ascertain, but, from concurrent representations which I have since received from numbers of people who lived in and adjacent to such parts of the country, where they were received from the enemy, I apprehend that most of them died in consequence of the vile usage of the enemy. Some who were eye witnesses of that scene of mortality, more especially in that part which continued after the exchange took place, are of opinion, that it was partly in consequence of a slow poison; but this I refer to the doctors who attended them, who are certainly the best judges.

Upon the best calculation I have been able to make from personal knowledge, and the many evidences I have collected in support of the facts, I learn that, of the prisoners taken on Long-Island, Fort Washington, and some few others, at different times and places, about two thousand perished with hunger, cold and sickness, occasioned by the filth of their prisons, at New-York, and a number more on their passage to the continental lines. Most of the residue, who reached their friends, having received their death wound, could not be restored by the assistance of physicians and friends; but like their brother prisoners, fell a sacrifice to the relentless and scientific barbarity of Britain. I took as much pains as my circumstances would admit of, to inform myself not only of matters of fact, but likewise of the very design and aims of general Howe and his council. The latter of which I predicated on the former, and submit it to the candid public.

And lastly, the aforesaid success of the American arms had a happy effect on the continental officers, who were on parole at New-York. A number of us assembled, but not in a public manner, and with full bowls and glasses, drank general Washington's health, and were not unmindful of Congress and our worthy friends on the continent, and almost forgot that we were prisoners.

A few days after this recreation, a British officer of rank and importance in their army, whose name I shall not mention in this narrative, for certain reasons, though I have mentioned it to some of my close friends and confidants, sent for me to his lodgings, and told me "That faithfulness, though in a wrong cause, had nevertheless recommended me to general Sir William Howe, who was minded to make me a colonel of a regiment of new levies, alias tories, in the British service; and proposed that I should go with him, and some other officers, to England, who would embark for that purpose in a few days, and there be introduced to Lord G. Germaine, and probably to the King; and that previously I should be clothed equal to such an introduction, and, instead of paper rags, be paid in hard guineas; after this, should embark with general Burgoyne, and assist in the reduction of the country, which infallibly would be conquered, and, when that should be done, I should have a large tract of land, either in the New-Hampshire grants, or in Connecticut, it would make no odds, as the country would be forfeited to the crown." I then replied, "That, if by faithfulness I had recommended myself to general Howe, I should be loth, by unfaithfulness, to lose the general's good opinion; besides, that I viewed the offer of land to be similar to that which the devil offered Jesus Christ, 'To give him all the kingdoms of the world, if he would fall down and worship him; when at the same time, the damned soul had not one foot of land upon earth.'" This closed the conversation, and the gentleman turned from me with an air of dislike, saying, that I was a bigot; upon which I retired to my lodgings.*

* An anecdote of a different character is told of Allen's sojourn in New York. Rivington, the "king's printer," a forcible and venomous writer, had incurred Allen's enmity by his caustic allusions to him, and the hero of Ticonderoga swore "he would lick Rivington the very first opportunity he had!" How the printer escaped the threatened castigation shall be narrated in his own words: I was sitting, [says Rivington,] after a good dinner, alone, with my bottle of Madeira before me, when I heard an unusual noise in the street, and a huzza from the boys. I was in the second story, and, stepping to the window, saw a tall figure in tarnished regimentals, with a large cocked hat and an enormous long sword, followed by a crowd of boys, who occasionally cheered him with huzzas, of which he seemed insensible. He came up to my door and stopped. I could see no more. My heart told me it was Ethan Allen. I shut my window and retired behind my table and my bottle. I was certain the hour of reckoning had come. There was no retreat. Mr. Staples, my clerk, came in paler than ever, and, clasping his hands, said, "Master, he has come!" "I know it." "He entered the store and asked 'if James Rivington lived there?' I answered, 'Yes, sir.' 'Is he at home?' 'I will go and see, sir,' I said; and now, master, what is to be done? There he is in the store, and the boys peeping at him from the street." I had made up my mind. I looked at the Madeira — possibly took a glass. "Show him up," said I; "and if such Madeira can not mollify him, he must be harder than adamant." There was a fearful moment of suspense. I heard him on the stairs, his long sword clanking at every step. In he stalked. "Is your name James Rivington?" "It is, sir, and no man could be more happy than I am to see Colonel Ethan Allen." "Sir, I have come ——" "Not another word, my dear colonel, until you have taken a seat and a glass of old Madeira." "But, sir, I do n't think it proper ——" "Not another word, colonel. Taste this wine. I have had it in glass for ten years. Old

Near the last of November, I was admitted to parole in New-York, with many other American officers, and on the 22d day of January, 1777, was with them directed by the British commissary of prisoners to be quartered on the westerly part of Long-Island, and our parole continued. During my imprisonment there, no occurrence worth observation happened. I obtained the means of living as well as I desired, which in a great measure repaired my constitution, which had been greatly injured by the severities of an inhuman captivity. I now began to feel myself composed, expecting either an exchange, or continuance in good and honorable treatment; but alas! my visionary expectations soon vanished. The news of the conquest of Ticonderoga by general Burgoyne, and the advance of his army into the country, made the haughty Britons again feel their importance, and with that, their insatiable thirst for cruelty.

The private prisoners at New-York, and some of the officers on parole, felt the severity of it. Burgoyne was to them a demi-god. To him they paid adoration; in him the tories placed their confidence, "and forgot the Lord their God," and served Howe, Burgoyne and Knyphausen, "and became vile in their own imagination, and their foolish hearts were darkened," professing to be great politicians, and relying on foreign and merciless invaders, and with them seeking the ruin, bloodshed and destruction of their country; "became fools," expecting with them to share a dividend in the confiscated estates of their neighbors and countrymen who fought for the whole country, and the religion and liberty thereof. "Therefore, God gave them over to strong delusion, to believe a lie, that they all might be damned."

wine, you know, unless it is originally sound, never improves by age." He took the glass, swallowed the wine, smacked his lips, and shook his head approvingly. "Sir, I come ———." "Not another word until you have taken another glass, and then, my dear colonel, we will talk of old affairs, and I have some queer events to detail." In short, we finished two bottles of Madeira, and parted as good friends as if we had never had cause to be otherwise.

The 25th day of August, I was apprehended, and under pretext of artful, mean and pitiful pretences, that I had infringed on my parole, taken from a tavern, where there were more than a dozen officers present, and, in the very place where those officers and myself were directed to be quartered, put under a strong guard and taken to New-York, where I expected to make my defence before the commanding officer; but, contrary to my expectations, and without the least solid pretence of justice or trial, was again encircled with a strong guard with fixed bayonets, and conducted to the provost-gaol in a lonely apartment, next above the dungeon, and was denied all manner of subsistence either by purchase or allowance. The second day I offered a guinea for a meal of victuals, but was denied it, and the third day I offered eight Spanish milled dollars for a like favor, but was denied, and all I could get out of the sergeant's mouth, was that by —— he would obey his orders. I now perceived myself to be again in substantial trouble. In this condition I formed an oblique acquaintance with a Capt. Travis, of Virginia, who was in the dungeon below me, through a little hole which was cut with a pen-knife, through the floor of my apartment which communicated with the dungeon; it was a small crevice, through which I could discern but a very small part of his face at once, when he applied it to the hole; but from the discovery of him in the situation which we were both then in, I could not have known him, which I found to be true by an after acquaintance. I could nevertheless hold a conversation with him, and soon perceived him to be a gentleman of high spirits, who had a high sense of honor, and felt as big, as though he had been in a palace, and had treasures of wrath in store against the British. In fine I was charmed with the spirit of the man; he had been near or quite four months in that dungeon, with murderers, thieves, and every species of criminals, and all for the sole crime of unshaken fidelity to his country; but his spirits were above dejection, and his mind unconquerable. I engaged to do him every service in my power, and in a few weeks afterwards, with the united petitions of the officers in the provost, procured his dismission from the dark mansion of fiends to the apartments of his petitioners.

And it came to pass on the 3d day, at the going down of the sun, that I was presented with a piece of boiled pork, and some biscuit, which the sergeant gave me to understand, was my allowance, and I fed sweetly on the same ; but I indulged my appetite by degrees, and in a few days was taken from that apartment, and conducted to the next loft or story, where there were above twenty continental, and some militia officers, who had been taken, and imprisoned there, besides some private gentlemen, who had been dragged from their own homes to that filthy place by tories. Several of every denomination mentioned, died there, some before, and others after I was put there.

The history of the proceedings relative to the provost only, were I particular, would swell a volume larger than this whole narrative. I shall therefore only notice such of the occurrences which are mostly extraordinary.

Capt. Vandyke bore, with an uncommon fortitude, near twenty months' confinement in this place, and in the mean time was very serviceable to others who were confined with him. The allegation against him, as the cause of his confinement, was very extraordinary. He was accused of setting fire to the city of New-York, at the time the west part of it was consumed, when it was a known fact, that he had been in the provost a week before the fire broke out ; and in like manner, frivolous were the ostensible accusations against most of those who were there confined ; the case of two militia officers excepted, who were taken in their attempting to escape from their parole ; and probably there may be some other instances which might justify such a confinement.

Mr. William Miller, a committee man, from West Chester county, and state of New-York, was taken from his bed in the dead of the night by his tory neighbors, and was starved for three days and nights in an apartment of the same gaol ; add to this the denial of fire, and that in a cold season of the year, in which time he walked day and night, to defend himself against the frost, and when he complained of such a reprehensible conduct, the word rebel or committee man was deemed by the enemy a sufficient atonement for any inhumanity that they could invent or inflict. He was a man of good natural understanding, a close and sincere friend to the liberties of America, and endured fourteen months' cruel imprisonment with that magnanimity of soul, which reflects honor on himself and country.

Major Levi Wells, and Capt. Ozias Bissel were apprehended and taken under guard from their parole on Long-Island, to the provost, on as fallacious pretences as the former, and were there continued till their exchange took place which was near five months. Their fidelity and zealous attachment to their country's cause, which was more than commonly conspicuous was undoubtedly the real cause of their confinement.

Major Brinton Payne, Capt. Flahaven, and Capt. Randolph, who had at different times distinguished themselves by their bravery, especially at the several actions, in which they were taken, were all the provocation they gave, for which they suffered about a year's confinement, each in the same filthy gaol.

A few weeks after my confinement, on the like fallacious and wicked pretences, was brought to the same place, from his parole on Long-Island, Major Otho Holland Williams now a full Col. in the continental army. In his character are united the gentleman, officer, soldier, and friend; he walked through the prison with an air of great disdain; said he, "Is this the treatment which gentlemen of the continental army are to expect from the rascally British, when in their power? Heavens forbid it!" He was continued there about five months, and then exchanged for a British Major.

John Fell, Esq. now a member of Congress for the state of New-Jersey, was taken from his own house by a gang of infamous tories, and by order of a British General, was sent to the provost, where he was continued near one year. The stench of the gaol, which was very loathsome and unhealthy, occasioned a hoarseness of the lungs, which proved fatal to many who were there confined, and reduced this gentleman near to the point of death; he was indeed given over by his friends who were about him, and himself concluded that he must die. I could not endure the thought that so worthy a friend to America should have his life stolen from him in such a mean, base, and scandalous manner, and that his family and friends should be bereaved of so great and desirable a blessing, as his further care, usefulness and example, might prove to them. I therefore wrote a letter to George Robertson, who commanded in town, and being touched with the most sensible feelings of humanity, which dictated my pen to paint dying distress in such lively colors that it wrought conviction even on the obduracy of a British General, and produced his order to remove the now honorable John Fell, Esq. out of a gaol, to private lodgings in town; in consequence of which he slowly recovered his health. There is so extraordinary a circumstance which intervened concerning this letter, that it is worth noticing.

Previous to sending it, I exhibited the same to the gentleman in whose behalf it was written, for his approbation, and he forbid me to send it in the most positive and explicit terms; his reason was, "That the enemy knew, by every morning's report, the condition of all the prisoners, mine in particular, as I have been gradually coming to my end for a considerable time, and they very well knew it, and likewise determined it should be accomplished, as they had served many others; that, to ask a favor, would give the merciless enemy occasion to triumph over me in my last moments, and therefore I will ask no favors from them, but resign myself to my supposed fate." But the letter I sent without his knowledge, and I confess I had but little expectations from it, yet could not be easy till I had sent it. It may be worth a remark, that this gentleman was an Englishman born, and from the beginning of the revolution has invariably asserted and maintained the cause of liberty.

The British have made so extensive an improvement of the provost during the present revolution till of late, that a very short definition will be sufficient for the dullest apprehensions. It may be with propriety called the British inquisition, and calculated to support their oppressive measures and designs, by suppressing the spirit of liberty; as also a place to confine the criminals, and most infamous wretches of their own army, where many gentlemen of the American army, and citizens thereof, were promiscuously confined, with every species of criminals; but they divided into different apartments, and kept at as great a remove as circumstances permitted; but it was nevertheless at the option of a villainous sergeant, who had the charge of the provost, to take any gentleman from their room, and put them into the dungeon, which was often the case. At two different times I was taken down stairs for that purpose, by a file of soldiers with fixed bayonets, and the sergeant brandishing his sword at the same time, and having been brought to the door of the dungeon, I there flattered the vanity of the sergeant, whose name was Keef, by which means I procured the surprizing favor to return to my companions; but some of the high mettled young gentlemen could not bear his insolence, and determined to keep at a distance, and neither please nor displease the villain, but none could keep clear of his abuse; however, mild measures were the best; he did not hesitate to call us damned rebels, and use us with the coarsest language. The Capts. Flahaven, Randolph and Mercer, were the objects of his most flagrant and repeated abuses, who were many times taken to the dungeon, and there continued at his pleasure. Capt. Flahaven took cold in the dungeon, and was in a declining state of health, but an exchange delivered him, and in all probability saved his life. It was very mortifying to bear with the insolence of such a vicious and ill-bred, imperious rascal. Remonstrances were preferred to the commander of the town, but no relief could be obtained, for his superiors were undoubtedly well pleased with his abusive conduct to the gentlemen, under the severities of his power; and remonstrating against his infernal conduct, only served to confirm him in authority; and for this reason I never made any remonstrances on the subject, but only stroked him, for I knew that he was but a cat's paw in the hands of the British officers, and that, if he should use us well, he would immediately be put out of that trust, and a worse man appointed to succeed him; but there was no need of making any new appointment; for Cunningham, their provost marshall, and Keef, his deputy, were as great rascals as their army could boast of, except one Joshua Loring, an infamous tory, who was commissary of prisoners; nor can any of these be supposed to be equally criminal with Gen. Sir William Howe and his associates, who prescribed and directed the murders and cruelties, which were by them perpetrated. This Loring is a monster!—There is not his like in human shape. He exhibits a smiling countenance, seems to wear a phiz of humanity, but has been instrumentally capable of the most consumate acts of wickedness, which were first projected by an abandoned British council clothed with the authority of a Howe, murdering premeditatedly, in cold blood, near or quite two thousand helpless prisoners and that in the most clandestine, mean and shameful manner, at New-York. He is the most mean spirited, cowardly, deceitful, and destructive animal in God's creation below, and legions of infernal devils, with all their tremendous horrors, are impatiently ready to receive Howe and him, with all their detestable accomplices, into the most exquisite agonies of the hottest region of hell fire.

The 6th day of July, 1777, Gen. St. Clair, and the army under his command, evacuated Ticonderoga, and retreated with the main body through Hubbarton into Castleton, which was but six miles distant, when his rear guard, commanded by Col. Seth Warner, was attacked at Hubbarton by a body of the enemy of about two thousand, commanded by General Fraser. Warner's command consisted of his own and other two regiments, viz. Francis's and Hale's, and some scattering and enfeebled soldiers. His whole number, according to information, was near or quite one thousand; part of which were Green Mountain Boys, about seven hundred of the whole he brought into action. The enemy advanced boldly, and the two bodies formed within about sixty yards of each other. Col. Warner having formed his own regiment, and that of Col. Francis's did not wait for the enemy, but gave them a heavy fire from his whole line, and they returned it with great bravery. It was by this time, dangerous for those of both parties, who were not prepared for the world to come; but Colonel Hale being apprised of the danger, never brought his regiment to the charge, but left Warner and Francis to stand the blowing of it, and fled, but luckily fell in with an inconsiderable number of the enemy, and to his eternal shame, surrendered himself a prisoner.

The conflict was very bloody. Col. Francis fell in the same, but Col. Warner, and the officers under his command, as also the soldiery, behaved with great resolution. The enemy broke, and gave way on the right and left, but formed again, and renewed the attack; in the mean time the British granadiers, in the center of the enemy's line maintained the ground, and finally carried it with the point of the bayonet, and Warner retreated with reluctance. Our loss was about thirty men killed, and that of the enemy amounting to three hundred killed, including a Major Grant. The enemy's loss I learnt from the confession of their own officers, when a prisoner with them. I heard them likewise complain, that the Green Mountain Boys took sight. The next movement of the enemy, of any material consequence, was their investing Bennington, with a design to demolish it, and subject its Mountaineers, to which they had a great aversion, with one hundred and fifty chosen men, including tories, with the highest expectation of success, and having chosen an eminence of strong ground, fortified it with slight breast works, and two pieces of cannon; but the government of the young state of Vermont, being previously jealous of such an attempt of the enemy, and in due time had procured a number of brave militia from the government of the state of New-Hampshire, who, together with the militia of the north part of Berkshire county, and state of Massachusetts, and the Green Mountain Boys, constituted a body of desperadoes, under the command of the intrepid general Stark, who in number were about equal to the enemy. Colonel Herrick, who commanded the Green Mountain Rangers, and who was second in command, being thoroughly acquainted with the ground where the enemy had fortified, proposed to attack them in their works upon all parts, at the same time. This plan being adopted by the general and his council of war, the little militia brigade of undisciplined heroes, with their long brown firelocks, the best security of a free people, without either cannon or bayonets, was, on the 16th day of August, led on to the attack by their bold commanders, in the face of the enemy's dreadful fire, and to the astonishment of the world, and burlesque of discipline, carried every part of their lines in less than one quarter of an hour after the attack became general, took their cannon, killed and captivated more than two-thirds of their number, which immortalized general Stark, and made Bennington famous to posterity.

Among the enemy's slain was found colonel Baum, their commander, a colonel Pfester, who headed an infamous gang of tories, and a large part of his command; and among the prisoners was major Meibome, their second in command, a number of British and Hessian officers, surgeons, &c., and more than one hundred of the aforementioned Pfester's command. The prisoners being collected together, were sent to the meeting-house in the town, by a strong guard, and Gen. Stark not imagining any present danger, the militia scattered from him to rest and refresh themselves; in this situation he was on a sudden attacked by a reinforcement of one thousand and one hundred of the enemy, commanded by a governor Skene, with two field pieces. They advanced in regular order, and kept up an incessant fire, especially from their field pieces, and the remaining militia retreating slowly before them, disputed the ground inch by inch. The enemy were heard to halloo to them, saying, stop Yankees! In the meantime, Col. Warner, with about one hundred and thirty men of his regiment, who were not in the first action, arrived and attacked the enemy with great fury, being determined to have ample revenge on account of the quarrel at Hubbardton, which brought them to a stand, and soon after general Stark and colonel Herrick, brought on more of the scattered militia, and the action became general; in a few minutes the enemy were forced from their cannon, gave way on all parts and fled, and the shouts of victory were a second time proclaimed in favor of the militia. The enemy's loss in killed and prisoners, in these two actions, amounted to more than one thousand and two hundred men, and our loss did not exceed fifty men. This was a bitter stroke to the enemy, but their pride would not permit them to hesitate but that they could vanquish the country, and as a specimen of their arrogancy, I shall insert general Burgoyne's proclamation:

"By John Burgoyne, Esq., Lieutenant-General of his Majesty's armies in America, Colonel of the Queen's regiment of light dragoons, Governor of Fort William in North-Britain, one of the Representatives of the Commons of Great Britain, in Parliament, and commanding an army and fleet employed on an expedition from Canada, &c. &c. &c.

"The forces entrusted to my command are designed to act in concert and upon a common principle, with the numerous armies and fleets which already display in every quarter of America, the power, the justice, and, when properly sought, the mercy of the King.

"The cause, in which the British arms are thus exerted, applies to the most affecting interests of the human heart; and the military servants of the crown, at first called forth for the sole purpose of restoring the rights of the constitution, now combine with love of their country, and duty to their sovereign, the other extensive excitements which spring from a due sense of the general privileges of mankind. To the eyes and ears of the temperate part of the public, and to the breasts of suffering thousands in the provinces, be the melancholy appeal, whether the present unnatural rebellion has not been made a foundation for the completest system of tyranny that ever God, in his displeasure, suffered for a time to be exercised over a froward and stubborn generation.

"Arbitrary imprisonment, confiscation of property, persecution and torture, unprecedented in the inquisitions of the Romish Church, are among the palpable enormities that verify the affirmative. These are inflicted by assemblies and committees, who dare to profess themselves friends to liberty, upon the most quiet subjects, without distinction of age or sex, for the sole crime, often for the sole suspicion, of having adhered in principle to the government under which they were born, and to which, by every tie, divine and human, they owe allegiance. To consummate these shocking proceedings, the profanation of religion is added to the most profligate prostitution of common reason; the consciences of men are set at nought; and multitudes are compelled not only to bear arms, but also to swear subjection to an usurpation they abhor.

"Animated by these considerations, at the head of troops in the full powers of health, discipline and valor; determined to strike where necessary, and anxious to spare where possible, I by these presents invite and exhort all persons, in all places where the progress of this army may point; and by the blessing of God I will extend it far to maintain such a conduct as may justify me in protecting their lands, habitations and families. The intention of this address is to hold forth security, not depredation to the country. To those whom spirit and principle may induce to partake of the glorious task of redeeming their countrymen from dungeons, and re-establishing the blessings of legal government, I offer encouragement and employment; and upon the first intelligence of their associations, I will find means to assist their undertakings. The domestic, the industrious, the infirm, and even the timid inhabitants I am desirous to protect, provided they remain quietly at their houses; that they do not suffer their cattle to be removed, nor their corn or forage to be secreted or destroyed; that they do not break up their bridges or roads: nor by any other act, directly or indirectly, endeavour to obstruct the operations of the king's troops, or supply or assist those of the enemy. Every species of provision brought to my camp, will be paid for at an equitable rate, and in solid coin.

"In consciousness of christianity, my royal master's clemency, and the honor of soldiership, I have dwelt upon this invitation, and wished for more persuasive terms to give it impression. And let not people be led to disregard it by considering their distance from the immediate situation of my camp. I have but to give stretch to the Indian forces under my direction, and they amount to thousands, to overtake the hardened enemies of Great Britain and America: I consider them the same wherever they may lurk.

"If, notwithstanding these endeavours, and sincere inclinations to effect them, the phrensy of hostility should remain, I trust I shall stand acquitted in the eyes of God and man, in denouncing and executing the vengeance of the state against the wilful outcasts. The messengers of justice and of wrath await them in the field; and devastation, famine, and every concomitant horror that a reluctant but indispensible prosecution of military duty must occasion, will bear the way to their return.

J. BURGOYNE.
"By order of his Excellency the Lieut. General,
ROBERT KINGSTON, *Sec.*
"Camp near Ticonderoga, 4th July, 1777."

Gen. Burgoyne was still the toast, and the severities towards the prisoners were in great measure increased or diminished, in proportion to the expectation of conquest. His very ostentatious Proclamation was in the hand and mouth of most of the soldiery, especially the tories, and from it, their faith was raised to assurrance. I wish my countrymen in general could have an idea of the assuming tyranny, and haughty, malevolent, and insolent behavior of the enemy at that time; and from thence discern the intolerable calamities which this country have extricated themselves from by their public spiritedness and bravery. The downfall of Gen. Burgoyne, and surrender of his whole army, dashed the aspiring hopes and expectations of the enemy, and brought low the imperious spirit of an opulent, puissant and haughty nation, and made the tories bite the ground with anguish, exalting the valor of the free-born sons of America, and raised their fame and that of their brave commanders to the clouds, and immortalized Gen. Gates with laurels of eternal duration.* No sooner had the knowledge of this inter-

---

* The defeat of Burgoyne gave Ethan Allen a welcome opportunity to return the ridicule with which the British officers had been accustomed to speak of the continental troops, and he was not the man to shut his teeth against the many biting sarcasms which pressed to his mouth for utterance. Nor was he the man to speak depreciatingly of his own merits; and on one occasion, while boasting of the success of the revolutionary army, he spoke of himself and his brothers, and said there was

esting and mighty event reached His most Christian Majesty, who in Europe shines with a superior lustre in goodness, policy and arms, but the illustrious potentate, auspiciously influenced by Heaven to promote the reciprocal interest and happiness of the ancient kingdom of France, and the new and rising states of America, passed the great and decisive decree that the United States of America, should be free and independent. Vaunt no more, Old England! consider you are but an island! and that your power has been continued longer than the exercise of your humanity. Order your broken vanquished battalions to retire from America, the scene of your cruelties. Go home and repent in dust and sackcloth for your aggravated crimes. The cries of bereaved parents, widows and orphans, reach the heavens, and you are abominated by every friend to America. Take your friends the tories with you, and be gone, and drink deep of the cup of humiliation. Make peace with the princes of the house of Bourbon, for you are in no condition to wage war with them. Your veteran soldiers are fallen in America, and your glory is departed. Be quiet and pay your debts, especially for the hire of the Hessians. There is no other way for you to get into credit again, but by reformation and plain honesty, which you have despised; for your power is by no means sufficient to support your vanity. I have had opportunity to see a great deal of it, and felt its severe effects, and learned lessons of wisdom and policy, when I wore your heavy irons, and bore your bitter revilings and reproaches. I have something of a smattering of philosophy, and understand human nature in all its stages tolerably well; am thoroughly acquainted with your national crimes, and assure you that they not only cry aloud for Heaven's vengeance, but excite mankind to rise up against you. Virtue, wisdom and policy are in a national sense, always

---

never a woman who had seven sons that could equal those of his mother. A British officer tartly insisted that Allen ought to except Mary Magdalen, who also was delivered of seven devils.

connected with power, or in other words, power is their offspring, and such power as is not directed by virtue, wisdom and policy never fails finally to destroy itself as yours has done. It is so in the nature of things, and unfit that it would be otherwise; for if it was not so, vanity, injustice, and oppression, might reign triumphant forever. I know you have individuals, who still retain their virtue, and consequently their honor and humanity. Those I really pity, as they must more or less suffer in the calamity, in which the nation is plunged headlong; but as a nation I hate and despise you.

My affections are Frenchified. I glory in Louis the sixteenth, the generous and powerful ally of these states; am fond of a connection with so enterprising, learned, polite, courteous and commercial a nation, and am sure that I express the sentiments and feelings of all the friends to the present revolution. I begin to learn the French tongue, and recommend it to my countrymen, before Hebrew, Greek or Latin, (provided that one of them only are to be attended to) for the trade and commerce of these states in future must inevitably shift its channel from England to France, Spain and Portugal; and therefore the statesman, politician and merchant, need be acquainted with their several languages, particularly the French, which is much in vogue in most parts of Europe. Nothing could have served so effectually to illuminate, polish and enrich these states as the present revolution, as well as preserve their liberty. Mankind are naturally too national, even to a degree of bigotry, and commercial intercourse with foreign nations, has a great and necessary tendency to improve mankind, and erase the superstition of the mind by acquainting them that human nature, policy and instinct, are the same in all nations, and at the same time they are bartering commodities for the conveniences and happiness of each nation, they may reciprocally exchange such part of their customs and manners as may be beneficial, and learn to extend charity and good will to the whole world of mankind. I was confined in the provost-gaol

at New-York, the 26th day of August, and continued
there to the 3d day of May, 1778, when I was taken
out under guard, and conducted to a sloop in the harbor of New-York, in which I was guarded to Staten-
Island, to general Campbell's quarters, where I was
permitted to eat and drink with the general and several other of the British field officers, and treated for
two days in a polite manner. As I was drinking wine
with them one evening, I made an observation on my
transition from the provost criminals to the company
of gentlemen, adding that I was the same man still,
and should give the British credit, by him (speaking
to the general) for two days good usage.

The next day colonel Archibald Campbell, who was
exchanged for me, came to this place, conducted by
Mr. Boudinot, the then American commissary of prisoners, and saluted me in a handsome manner, saying
that he never was more glad to see a gentleman in his
life, and I gave him to understand that I was equally
glad to see him, and was apprehensive that it was from
the same motive. The gentlemen present laughed at
the fancy, and conjectured that sweet liberty was the
foundation of our gladness: so we took a glass of
wine together, and then I was accompanied by general
Campbell, colonel Campbell, Mr. Boudinot, and a
number of British officers, to the boat which was ready
to sail to Elizabethtown-point. Meanwhile I entertained them with a rehearsal of the cruelties exercised
towards our prisoners; and assured them that I should
use my influence, that their prisoners should be treated,
in future, in the same manner, as they should in future
treat ours; that I thought it was right in such extreme
cases, that their example should be applied to their
own prisoners; then exchanged the decent ceremonies
of compliment, and parted. I sailed to the point
aforesaid, and, in a transport of joy, landed on liberty
ground, and as I advanced into the country, received
the acclamations of a grateful people.

I soon fell into company with colonel Shelden, of the
light horse, who in a polite and obliging manner accompanied me to head quarters, Valley Forge, where I

was courteously received by Gen. Washington, with peculiar marks of his approbation and esteem, and was introduced to most of the generals, and many of the principal officers of the army, who treated me with respect, and after having offered Gen. Washington my further services in behalf of my country, as soon as my health, which was very much impaired, would admit, and obtain his license to return home, I took my leave of his excellency, and set out from Valley Forge with general Gates and his suit for Fishkill, where we arrived the latter end of May. In this tour the general was pleased to treat me with the familiarity of a companion, and generosity of a lord, and to him I made known some striking circumstances which occurred in the course of my captivity. I then bid farewell to my noble general and the gentlemen of his retinue, and set out for Bennington, the capital of the Green Mountain Boys, where I arrived the evening of the last day of May, to their great surprise; for I was thought to be dead, and now both their joy and mine was complete. Three cannon were fired that evening, and next morning colonel Herrick gave orders and fourteen more were discharged, welcoming me to Bennington, my usual place of abode; thirteen for the United States, and one for Young Vermont.

After this ceremony was ended we moved the flowing bowl, and rural felicity, sweetened with friendship, glowed in each countenance, and with loyal healths to the rising States of America, concluded that evening, and, with the same loyal spirit, I now conclude my narrative.

CHAPTER IV.

THE GREEN-MOUNTAIN HEROES.

"Oh, few and weak their numbers were,
  A handful of brave men;
But to their God they gave their prayer,
  And rushed to battle then.
They left the plowshare in the mold,
Their flocks and herds without a fold,
The sickle in the unshorn grain,
The corn half-garnered on the plain,
And mustered in their simple dress,
For wrongs to seek a stern redress —
To right those wrongs, come weal, come woe,
To perish or o'ercome their foe."
                      M'Lellan.

In communities established after the manner of the United States, history does not begin with obscure or fabulous legends. The origin of the nation, and the rise and progress of all its institutions, may be distinctly known. The people may obtain accurate and familiar acquaintance with the character of their earliest national ancestors, and of every succeeding generation through which the inheritance of the national name and fortune has devolved upon themselves. When this interesting knowledge is blended with the information that their existence as a people originated in the noblest efforts of wisdom, fortitude, and magnanimity, and that every successive acquisition by which their liberty and happiness have been extended and secured, has arisen from the exercise of the same qualities, and evinced their faithful preservation and unimpaired efficacy,— respect for former times becomes the motive and pledge of virtue; the whole nation feels itself ennobled by ancestors whose renown will continue till the end of time the honor or reproach of their successors; and the love of virtue is so interwoven with patriotism and national glory, as to prevent the one from becoming a selfish principle, and the other a splendid or mischievous illusion. If an inspired apostle might with complacency proclaim himself a citizen of no mean city, an American may feel grateful exultation in avowing himself the native of no ignoble land,— but of a land that has yielded as great an increase of glory to God and of happiness to man, as any other portion of the world, since "the first syllable of recorded time," has ever had the honor of producing. A nobler model of human character could hardly be proposed to the inhabitants of New England, Pennsylvania, and others of the United States, than that which their own history supplies. It is at once their interest and their glory to preserve with sacred care a model so richly fraught with the instructions of wisdom and the incitements of duty. The memory of those whom they claim as their natural or national ancestors, will bless all those who account it blessed; and the ashes of their fathers will give forth a nobler influence than the bones of the prophet of Israel, in reviving piety and invigorating virtue. So much, at the same time, of human weakness and imperfection is discernible in the conduct, or is attested by the avowals of these eminent men, and so steady and explicit was their reference to heavenly aid, of all the good they were capable to perform or attain, that the admiration they so strongly deserve, enforces the scriptural testimony to the riches of divine grace, and the reflected luster of human virtue.

The history of man never exhibited an effort of more vigorous and enterprising virtue, than the original migration of the colonists of this then distant and desolate region; and the annals of colonization do not supply a single instance of the foundation of a commonwealth, and its advancement through a period of weakness and danger to strength and security, in which the principal actors have left behind them a reputation at once so illustrious and unsullied, with fewer memorials calculated to pervert the moral sense, or awaken the regret ot mankind. The relation of their achievements has a powerful tendency to excite hope, and animate perseverance — to impart courage to the good, and to fortify the virtues of the brave. The Puritans could not, indeed, boast, like the founders of Pennsylvania, that by a resolute profession of non-resistance of injuries, and as faithful adherence to that profession, they had so realized the divine protection by an exclusive reliance on it, as to disarm the ferocity of savages, and conduct the establishment of their commonwealth without violence and bloodshed. But if they were involved in numerous wars, it was the singular and honorable characteristic of them all, that they were invariably the offspring of self-defense against the unprovoked malignity of their adversaries, and that not one of them was undertaken from motives of conquest or plunder. Though they considered these wars as necessary and justifiable, they deeply deplored them; and, more than once, the most distressing doubts were expressed, at the close of their hostilities, if it were lawful for Christians to carry even the rights of self-defense to such fatal extremity. They behaved to the Indian tribes with as much good-faith and justice as they could have shown to a powerful and civilized people,* and were incited by their inferiority to no other acts than a series of the most magnanimous and laudable endeavors to instruct their ignorance, and elevate their condition.† If they fell short of the colonists of Pennsylvania in the exhibition of Christian meekness, they unquestionably excelled them in the extent and activity of Christian labor. If the Quakers succeeded in disarming the Indians, the Puritans labored to convert them.

* Not only were all the lands occupied by the colonists fairly purchased from their Indian owners, but in some parts of the country, the lands were subject to quit-rents to the Indians, " which," says Belknap, in 1784, " are annually paid to their posterity." From the many deeds and other documents still in existence, especially in the New-England states and New York, it is certain that regular purchases were invariably made of the Indians. The consideration given was usually small; but there is no reason to suppose that it was not all the lands were worth at the time. A curious example of the opinions prevalent in early times, and the change which has since occurred, is afforded by the manner in which their payments were made, a portion of the consideration usually being spirituous liquors. Two townships in the western part of Massachusetts, for instance, were purchased, according to a deed which is still preserved, for " £460, *three barrels of cider, and thirty quarts of rum.*"

† The accounts of the first conversations which the missionaries had with these heathen, abound with curious questions and observations that proceeded from the Indians in relation to the tidings that were brought to their ears. The account which Elliott, the " Apostle of the Indians,"

The history of the colonization of this continent, clearly indicates the destiny for which it was ultimately designed. This great republic is but the natural development of the little community that first landed on Plymouth rock. The American Revolution was no sudden outburst of popular fury. It had its origin in the first landing of the pilgrims. Tyranny had become so strong in the eastern world, that there seemed no possibility that the people would ever succeed in the attainment of their just rights. The fires of freedom were quenched by the blood of the scaffold, or, if a tyrant was overthrown by an indignant people, anarchy in its most appalling form succeeded, from which there was no escape, but submission to the yoke of another oppressor. But Columbus, ignorant of the boon he was

gave of one interview with the savages, will illustrate this. One Indian asked, Whether Englishmen were ever as ignorant of Jesus Christ as the Indians ? A second, Whether Jesus Christ could understand prayers in the Indian language ? A third, How there could be an image of God, since it was forbidden in the second commandment ? On another occasion, an old Indian, with tears in his eyes, asked, Whether it was not too late for such an old man as he, who was near death, to repent and seek after God ? A second asked, How the English came to differ so much from the Indian in their knowledge of Jesus Christ, since they had all at first but one father ? Several inquired, How Judas could deserve blame for facilitating the end which it was the purpose of God to effect ? One woman asked, Whether she was entitled to consider herself as having prayed, when she merely joined in her mind with her husband, who prayed by her side ? Another, *If her husband's prayer signified any thing while he continued to beat his wife ?* Many of the converts continued to believe that the gods whom they had formerly served, had in reality great power, but were spirits subordinate to the true and only God. One sachem sent for an Indian convert, and desired to know how many Gods the English had ? When he heard they had but one, he replied scornfully : "Is that all ? I have *thirty-seven!* Do they suppose I would exchange so many for one ?"

conferring on mankind, discovered a new world. The seeds of freedom, which were not permitted to germinate in the old world, were brought in the Mayflower to the new. Wise and good men, disheartened by their warfare against wrong, fled to it for an asylum. Neglected by the government under whose control they nominally remained, they were compelled to govern themselves — to make and administer their own laws. They were a small community — all mutually known, — all mutually loved, — all intelligent, conscientious, and animated by an ardent piety. It was not difficult for them to do justice to each other, and in doing this, they were unconsciously evolving the great principles upon which all just government must be founded. Had they known the importance of the work in which they were engaged, it is doubtful whether they would have done it so well. They gradually grew in strength. Other colonies were at intervals established along the Atlantic coast. All were greatly influenced by the example of New England and Pennsylvania. For a century they increased in power, their condition being but little known and little cared for in Europe, and their future greatness in no degree anticipated by themselves. In their wars with the Indians and the French colony of Canada, they were thrown almost entirely upon their own resources, for the parent country gave them but a feeble and reluctant support. They were compelled to unite for their common defense, and in 1754, delegates from the several colonies met at Albany, and with the illustrious Franklin at their head, devised a "plan of union," which, although it was not adopted then, aided powerfully in creating a unity of feeling among the colonies, and prepared them for combined resistance to the tyranny of the British king, and for a lasting confederation. And thus a spirit of freedom had been nurtured on this continent; republican institutions had become firmly rooted, and when the English government was at last conscious of the importance of the colonies, the day had passed in which it had the power to tyrannize over them. A series of oppressive measures was rapidly prepared by the minions of George III., but they were resisted promptly, perseveringly, and, after a bloody struggle of seven years, effectually.

The war had already commenced, when the congress which ultimately announced the final separation of the colonies from the parent country, assembled at Philadelphia. The most eminent men of the various colonies had met together. The meeting was awfully solemn. The object which had brought them there was of incalculable magnitude. The liberties of no less than three millions of people, with that of all their posterity, were staked on the wisdom and energy of their councils. No wonder, then, at the long and deep silence which is said to have followed upon their organization; at the anxiety with which the members looked round upon each other; and the reluctance which every individual felt to open a business so fearfully momentous. The embarrassing silence was broken by the eloquent Patrick Henry, in a speech of wonderful power. An ardent love of liberty pervaded every breast, and this speech produced a unanimity as advantageous to the cause they had determined to maintain, as it was appalling to their adversaries.

The proceedings of this celebrated congress, the tone and temper of their various resolutions, the style of their addresses, the composition of the several papers that were drawn up by them, were in every particular calculated to excite the admiration of the world. That an assembly of fifty-two men, nearly all educated in the wilds of a new world, unpracticed in the arts of polity and diplomacy, most of them inexperienced in the arduous duties of legislation, coming from distant and distinct governments, differing in religion, manners, customs, and habits, as they did in their views with regard to the nature of their connection with Great Britain — that such an assembly, so constituted, should display so much wisdom, sagacity, foresight and knowledge of the world, such skill in argument, such force of reasoning, such firmness and soundness of judgment, so profound an acquaintance with the rights of man, such elevation of sentiment, such genuine patriotism, and, above all, such unexampled unity of opinion upon the measures brought before them, was indeed a political phenomenon, to which history has yet furnished no parallel. Nor is it less wonderful, that the whole people of the colonies represented, should have regarded the simple recommendations of this congress with the reverence and obedience due to the strongest ties of law. Even in those colonies where law and authority had been set at defiance, the injunctions of the congress were scrupulously obeyed. The whole country was in that awful calm of expectation, which precedes the bursting storm. They were yet willing to be reconciled with the British government, but ready to enforce their rights at the risk of life.

Who can consider, without deep and affecting sympathy, that little body of men, who, in the name of a young and unskilled people, then set at defiance the power of a mighty empire — not rashly and ignorantly, but advisedly and calmly,— having weighed their own weakness, as well as their adversaries' strength,— feeling the heavy responsibility that rested on their decision,— calculating the consequences of attempt and failure, and then, with a full conviction of all the mighty odds against them, "having counted the cost of the contest, and finding nothing so dreadful as voluntary slavery," solemnly "appealing to the supreme Judge of the world for the rectitude of their intentions," and pledging to each other their lives, their fortunes, and their sacred honor; ranging themselves and their infant nation under the banners of liberty, denouncing their oppressors "enemies in war, in peace, friends." There is not, in the whole page of human history, any thing more truly grand and morally sublime than the conduct of the American congress throughout the unequaled contest that followed, upon which hung not the liberties of our people only, but those of mankind. How admirable was the moderation which marked their earlier deliberation; the calmness with which they met ministerial haughtiness; the firmness which they opposed to parliamentary obstinacy, tempering vigor with prudence, and inflexible principle with forbearance! How majestic their dignity when called upon finally to decide between unconditional submission and resistance by force! With what undaunted courage they made the noble choice, and, having made it, with what unshrinking fortitude they met all the vicissitudes of fortune; the ebb and flow of the tide of war; the discontent of the factious; the fears of the timid; the despondency of the high-minded;—never cast down by repeated misfortunes, nor too much elated by momentary success. When the houseless people were scattered before their invaders; when the army, unpaid, unclothed, vainly sought assistance from the commander, and he vainly sought it in the exhausted treasury; when the sword fell from their fainting hands, and the blank of despair seemed falling on their hearts; still did these patriots struggle on—still did they find confidence in their just cause, and, with their eyes upon the polestar of liberty, did they steady the helm of the reeling vessel of the infant state, ride out triumphantly the storm of war and revolution, and gain the glorious haven from which their thoughts had never swerved.

The annals of every nation can supply us with some brilliant characters, who stand superior to the sordid passions which sway the minds of ordinary men and but too often dictate the feelings of national communities. But rarely, if ever, has there been an entire assembly of men, uniting all the qualities of sages and heroes,—cautious in their deliberations, firm and united in their measures, pure in their motives, and beyond suspicion in their conduct. To the unbending spirit and perfect rectitude of the continental congress was mainly owing the preservation of the American people, not only from foreign conquest, but from intestine broils. To their little senate-room, amid all the changes of war, did the eyes of the people ever turn in hope and confidence. Were their little armies defeated; were their heroic generals fighting in retreat; were their cities taken; were their houses in flames; was their commerce destroyed; were their fields devastated; were their gold and their credit gone; they still looked to that high-minded assembly, whose counsels, they were satisfied, were ever patriotic and wise, and whose energies were ever employed to relieve the sufferings they could not prevent. It is interesting to imagine what must have been the earnest thoughts of this noble body of men throughout that trying contest; what their anxieties; and, finally, what the flood of joy that must have poured on their hearts when the tidings reached them that the last great victory was achieved. The old door-keeper of the congress, when the news suddenly reached him of the surrender of Cornwallis, dropped instantly dead! The feelings of the veteran, too intense for his feeble age, seem to image well those of the members of that assembly upon which he had been so faithful an attendant.

In the history of the American Revolution, the integrity of the congress and the confidence of the people in their integrity equally challenge admiration. The first was so pure, that throughout that distracted period, which might so well have furnished temptation to the selfish or the ambitious,* we do not find one member

* "Tell the king of England," said one of them, when a heavy bribe was offered him to desert the cause of his country, " I am not worth buying; but that such as I am, he is not rich enough to do it!" And another, while a prisoner in England, was threatened with death unless he would persuade his son to abandon the cause of freedom. "My son is of age," said the heroic father of a heroic son, "and has a will of his own. I know him to be a man of honor. He loves me dearly, and

of that magnanimous body even suspected of peculation, or of a desire for personal aggrandizement; and the latter was so entire, that, during the worst days of that stormy period, the public suffering was never charged to any willful mismanagement on the part of the government — not even when its faith was violated, by the gradual depreciation and final extinction of a paper currency, which had been issued without funds, and which ceased to circulate, with scarce the shadow of a prospect being held out for its future redemption. The people saw the necessity of the measure, and being well convinced that the good of their country had been promoted, quietly submitted to measures which, under other circumstances, would scarcely have been expiated by the lives and fortunes of their authors.

That a government framed in all the distraction of revolution — with a powerful enemy in the very heart of the country, the Indians on one side as their allies, and the ocean on the other, possessed by their fleets, — that, at such a time, a government so hastily organized, with armies untrained, unfed, unclothed, and without a treasury to meet the demands that assailed them on every side, should have preserved the public confidence, argues a degree of moderation on the part of congress, and of good sense and devoted feeling on that of the people, which, perhaps, in the history of ancient or modern times was never equaled, and certainly has never been surpassed.

would lay down his life to save mine, but I am sure that he would not sacrifice his honor to save my life, and I applaud him." This prisoner, not long afterward, had the gratification of assisting in negotiating a peace between Great Britain and the free Republic of the United States

In the history of the dispute which involved the liberty of the colonies, the congress was equally distinguished for its prudence, and its intrepidity. Like a cautious general, they advanced slowly, but never yielding an inch of the ground they had once assumed. At first called together by the voice of their fellow-citizens, without the consent, or rather in very despite of existing authorities, the legality of whose title remained unquestioned, they calmly took in review the colonial grievances, and petitioned for redress upon those constitutional grounds, acknowledged by the distant monarchy which claimed their allegiance. Without assuming the power to enact laws, they passed resolutions, to the sacred observance of which, until the redress of their enumerated grievances should be obtained, they bound themselves by the ties of honor, and of patriotism. That these simple ties should have proved sufficient to hold together the people of distant provinces, who had heretofore often been divided by jealousies and clashing interests, and to give an effect to the recommendations of private individuals, as absolute as could have followed upon the fiat of an established despot, affords a beautiful evidence of the readiness with which national obedience is yielded, when the hearts of the people are with their rulers. These recommendations were sufficient at once to supersede the authority of existing law, and to triumph over the strongest passions of humanity. From whatever cause it proceeded, it is certain that a disposition to do, to suffer, and to accommodate, spread from breast to breast, and from colony to colony, beyond the expectations of human opinions. It seemed as though one mind inspired the whole. The merchants put far behind them the gains of trade, and cheerfully submitted to a total suspension of business, in obedience to the recommendations of men claiming no legislative authority. The cultivators of the soil, with unanimity assented to the determination that the hard-earned produce of their farms should remain unshipped, although, in case of a free exportation, many would have been eager to purchase it from them at advanced prices. The sons and daughters of ease renounced imported conveniences, and voluntarily engaged to eat, drink, and wear only such articles as their country produced. These sacrifices were made, not from the pressure of present distress, but on the generous principle of sympathy with an invaded sister colony : and the prudent policy of guarding against a precedent which might, on a future day, operate against their liberties.

This season of universal distress exhibited a striking proof how practicable it is for mankind to sacrifice ease, pleasure, and interest, when the mind is strongly excited by its passions. In the midst of their sufferings, cheerfulness appeared in the face of the people. They counted every thing cheap in comparison with liberty, and readily gave up whatever tended to endanger it. A noble strain of generosity and mutual support was generally excited. The animation of the times raised the actors in these scenes above themselves, and incited them to deeds of self-denial, which the interested prudence of calm reason can scarcely credit.

But, though empowered by **their** fellow citizens to think and act for them, at a time, too, when the public feeling was wrought to the highest pitch of enthusiasm, the delegates in congress never exceeded the necessity of the occasion. They kept in view the interest and honor of the community, but held their passions in check. So long as the most distant prospect remained to them of obtaining the acknowledgment of their country's rights, they preserved the language and character of British subjects. When all hope of reconciliation had expired, the Declaration of Independence followed. The wishes of the people had preceded the act of their representatives, and the style of that act yet affixed a new seal of confirmation to their wishes. The simple exposition of moral and political truths with which it opens, elevated still higher the already sublime character of the public sentiment; the energetic enumeration of the national wrongs, opposed as in contrast to these great laws of nature, kindled anew the national indignation; the solemn appeal to the Creator, and the sacred pledge of life, fortune and honor, with which it closes, roused all the devotion of human hearts and manly minds — and, assuredly, never was it aroused in a better or nobler cause. It was not the cause of the Americans only; it was the cause of the very people whose injustice they opposed; it was the cause of every people on earth. Well might that high-minded patriot and statesman, the Earl of Chatham, exclaim in the British parliament, in the face of the British minister, "I rejoice that America has resisted!" Well might he observe, that "three millions of fellow-creatures, so lost to every sense of virtue as tamely to give up their liberties, would be fit instruments to make slaves of the rest." Had America basely submitted to the encroachments of ministerial parliaments, soon would that same parliament have tried encroachments upon the liberties of England; or had the infant America been overwhelmed by the armies poured upon her shores, with the buried liberties of the people, her victors would have buried forever their own national virtue, and honor, and character. Then, indeed, upon England's faded brow would have been stamped the moral, that

> "Nations, like men, who others' rights invade,
> Shall doubly rue the havoc they have made;
> And, in a brother's liberty o'erthrown,
> Shall weep to find that they have wrecked their own."

Hostilities had been continued between the parent country and the colonies for upward of a year before the Declaration of Independence was promulgated. The affair of Lexington had, of course, been the signal for war, throughout the colonies. The forts, magazines, and arsenals were everywhere seized. Troops were raised, and money for their support; and it was not many weeks before an army of thirty thousand men appeared in the environs of Boston, under the command of General Putnam, a veteran of the French war, in whom the people had great confidence. Allen had succeeded in the capture of Ticonderoga and Quebec. The next act in the grand drama then unfolding was the battle of Bunker Hill. Toward the close of May, 1775, reinforcements of British troops had arrived at Boston, with Generals Howe, Burgoyne and Clinton, all of whom were officers of reputation. The provincial congress of Massachusetts had, early in that month, renounced General Gage, as governor of the colony, declared him an enemy of the country, and forbidden obedience to his orders. On the other hand, Gage had issued his proclamation, promising a gracious pardon to all who would lay down their arms and return to the duties of peaceable subjects, excepting only Samuel Adams and John Hancock, whose offenses were declared of " too flagitious a nature to admit of any other consideration than that of condign punishment." By the same instrument, Massachusetts was declared to be under martial law. General Gage was also preparing, in other respects, for more energetic action ; but every measure he took, and every moment that passed, served only to unite and embolden the patriots, and increase the audacity with which they now, by their conduct as well as by their words, contemned the royal authority. The provincial troops had assembled in force around Boston, and were throwing up defenses, when the battle of Bunker Hill at once and forever severed the tie that bound the colonies to Great Britain. The fighting on this occasion was of such a determined character, as to show the enemy that it was no pastime upon which they had entered. One of the British officers, in writing home to a friend, declared that " the rebels fought more like devils than men." The loss of the British in killed and wounded was upward of a thousand, while that of the provincials fell short of half that number. The great calamity of the day was the fall of the brave and accomplished Warren, who was shot through the head early in the action.

The inhabitants of the New-Hampshire Grants, with but few exceptions, partook largely of the feelings which pervaded the country during the progress of the events which led to the Revolution. Having been successfully engaged in subduing a forest, and in laying a foundation for the happiness of themselves and families, and in defending their homes against the encroachments of a neighboring government, they had acquired a high sense of their personal rights, and a fixed determination to maintain them. They had become inured to privation and hardship, and were familiar with enterprise and adventure. Although their isolated position had shielded them from the actual effects of the oppressive measures of the British ministry, and they were engaged in the protection of their property from determined aggression, they sympathized cordially with the sufferings of their brethren along the Atlantic coast, and at once concurred in the earliest measures for securing a redress of their grievances. The first bloodshed at Lexington, was the signal for them to act, and under their heroic leaders they achieved the first important conquest of the Revolution. The battle of Lexington was a defensive one on the part of the colonies — the taking of Ticonderoga was a carefully planned, aggressive measure. It was truly the commencement of the war on the part of the colonies. And the military stores there acquired were taken to Boston by the Green-Mountain Boys, many of whom participated in the battle of Bunker Hill.

The capture of Ticonderoga prepared the way for the invasion of Canada, which closed the first campaign. This measure had been earnestly recommended to congress by Ethan Allen and Seth Warner. The British ministry had sent, as governor of this province,

Sir Guy Carleton, a man of resolute character, vast genius, and a brilliant reputation for military achievements. He was invested with extraordinary powers. It was known that he exerted all his efforts to arouse the Canadians and Indians, and stimulate them to arms against the colonies. Though, at the commencement, he had found great repugnance among the former, it was to be feared that, by employing address and authority, he might succeed, at length, in drawing them to his standard. The character of the people of Canada was not unknown: they were ever French at heart, and were considered fickle. It was known, also, that they cherished a sullen discontent on account of the "Quebec act," which, though favorable to their religion, was unsatisfactory in its provisions regarding their civil rights. It was therefore essential to take advantage of their discontent, before Carleton should win their favor. It was hoped that when the Americans should have penetrated into Canada, the inhabitants would not hesitate to espouse their cause, excited on the one hand by their hatred to their rulers, and reassured on the other by the moderation which the colonists had generally manifested in matters touching religion. The province of Canada was unsupplied with troops of the regular army, these having been called to Boston. In addition to these considerations, congress had been informed that in the following spring, the government was to make a grand effort in Canada; that numerous forces, arms, and munitions would be poured into it, in order to attack the colonies by way of Lake Champlain, an operation which, if not seasonably prevented, might lead to fatal consequences. The colonists, assailed at the same time in front and rear, could not have expected to resist.

Lake Champlain was in possession of the Americans, which opened to them the most eligible route to Canada. A more propitious occasion could never occur. The British troops, shut up in Boston, and occupied with their own defense, were not in a condition to carry succors into a part so remote from the position they then occupied. But it was to be feared that longer delays would afford time for the British ministry to make the necessary preparations to overpower the colonies by a single effort, and reduce them to their former dependence. Prudent men, however, could not shut their eyes upon the numerous difficulties it presented. But a resolution having been carried in favor of the expedition, congress was not tardy in taking all the measures proper to secure its success. Three thousand soldiers, partly of New England, and partly of New York, were selected for the enterprise. One regiment, under the command of Seth Warner, who had been elected their colonel, was composed of Green-Mountain Boys. It was determined to invade Canada by two routes — one portion of the army being destined to proceed by the way of Lake Champlain, against Forts Chambly and St. John, near the mouth of the lake, and then, after reducing Montreal, to march against Quebec : the other branch of the army was to be detached from the environs of Boston, and, going by the way of the Kennebec river, move directly toward Quebec, with design of reaching that fortress cotemporaneously with the other. Major-general Schuyler was appointed commander-in-chief of the expedition, while Brigadier-general Montgomery* was assigned to the command of the first division of the army, and Colonel Benedict Arnold to the other.

* Richard Montgomery was born in the north of Ireland, December 2d, 1736. Little is known of his early life. When quite young, he was placed in Dublin college, where he obtained a good education. At the age of twenty he joined the army. He was sent with the army against Louisbourg, afterward served under Amherst, at Ticonderoga, and was with Wolfe at the siege of Quebec. He thus became specially qualified, in the service of the King of England, to lead the continental troops against that monarch. At the close of the French war, Montgomery was permitted to return to Europe, where he remained until 1772. Toward the close of that year, he resigned the service, sailed for America, and arrived in New York in the following January. He purchased a farm in the neighborhood of that city, but soon afterward removed to Dutchess county, where for a long time he devoted himself to the pursuit of agriculture. While at the former place, he married the eldest daughter of R. R. Livingston, one of the judges of the supreme court of the province, and subsequently member of the continental congress. As the dispute between England and her colonies had now become serious, it was impossible for an individual circumstanced like Montgomery to remain neutral. Accordingly, he took a decided part for the cause of freedom, and in April, 1775, he was elected to represent Dutchess county in the delegation to the first New-York provincial convention. The labors of the convention seem to have been rather tedious and unsatisfactory, and finally resulted in little good to the cause to espouse which they had convened. Soon after the meeting of this body, Montgomery received a more highly important office than any that had hitherto fallen to his lot, and one, too, of which he had little expectation. In June, the continental congress appointed four major, and eight brigadier generals, naming, among the latter, Montgomery. His surprise at the news of this flattering distinction was equaled by his modest though heartfelt acknowledgment of it; and, with the acceptance of that commission, commenced his brief but glorious career in the cause of freedom. In a letter to a friend he says: "The Congress having done me the honor of electing me a brigadier-general in their service, is an event which must put an end for a while, perhaps forever, to the quiet scheme of life I had prescribed for myself; for, though entirely unexpected and undesired

General Montgomery repaired to Ticonderoga on the 17th of August. He here learned that Sir Guy Carleton, the military governor of Canada, was preparing a naval force destined to the defense of Lake Champlain. As immediate action was now of vital importance, Montgomery determined to take possession of the Isle Aux Noix in the lake, and wrote to General Schuyler, signifying his intention to that effect, and entreating his immediate presence. Without awaiting the arrival of this commander, he selected about one thousand men, and two pieces of cannon, and embarked on the lake, August 26th. The weather was so boisterous that he was not able to reach the island before the 5th of September, on which day he was joined by Major-general Schuyler, who determined upon a nearer approach to the enemy, both with a view of reconnoitering their position, and of enlisting the esteem and confidence of the population. This maneuver was signally successful, the army landing within about a mile and a half of St. John's without encountering opposition. The troops were soon formed and marched toward the fort. In this movement, while fording a creek, they met with a party of Indians, who fired upon their left, and threw it into disorder. But Montgomery hastened forward with the

by me, the will of an oppressed people, compelled to choose between liberty and slavery, must be obeyed." Under these noble and self-sacrificing views and feelings, Montgomery accepted the commission tendered to him; and from that hour to the moment of his death, the whole force of his mind and body was devoted to the honor and interest of his adopted country. The glory and fate of Wolfe, his former commander, were present to his thoughts; and to his young wife his parting words were, "You shall never blush for your Montgomery."

other troops, and speedily repulsed the assailants with some loss.

In this enterprise, Captain Remember Baker lost his life. He had been sent forward by Montgomery to reconnoiter the enemy's position. When within a few miles of St. John's, he secreted his boat, with the intention of marching through the woods. He had scarcely left the boat when a party of Indians took possession of it. He called to them to return it, and on their refusal to do so, attempted to fire at them, but as he drew up his gun, he received a shot through the head. His companions then fled, and made their way back to the army with the sad intelligence. Captain Baker fell at the early age of thirty-five. His life had been one of peculiar usefulness. At the age of eighteen he had served in an expedition against Canada. He became a resident of the New-Hampshire Grants in 1764, where he at once became one of the most influential and useful of the leaders of the Green-Mountain Boys. As an officer and soldier he was cool and temperate in council, but resolute and determined in the execution of his plans. As a neighbor he was distinguished for his kindness, and his memory was held dear by many families whose distresses he had generously relieved.

At Isle Aux Noix Schuyler's increasing ill health rendered him unfit for service, and he retired to Ticonderoga, leaving the command of the expedition with General Montgomery. In his report to congress he speaks thus of the latter officer: "I cannot estimate the obligations I lie under to General Montgomery for the many important services he has done and daily does, and in which he has had little assistance from me, as I have not enjoyed a moment's health since I left Fort George, and am now so low as not to be able to hold the pen. Should we not be able to do any thing decisively in Canada, I shall judge it best to move from this place, which is a very wet and unhealthy part of the country; unless I receive your orders to the contrary."

Colonel Allen, the hero of Ticonderoga, had a command under Montgomery. Having been dispatched, with Major Brown, into the interior of Canada, he was, on his return, persuaded by the latter to undertake the rash project of attacking Montreal. He divided his detachment, consisting of less than three hundred men, into two parties, intending to assail the city at opposite points. Major Brown was prevented from executing his part of the enterprise. Colonel Allen and his small party, opposed by the whole force of the enemy under Governor Carleton, fought with desperate valor. Many were killed; the survivors, overpowered by numbers, were compelled to surrender. The governor, viewing Allen, not as the intrepid soldier, but as a factious rebel, loaded him with irons and sent him to England for trial. Carleton afterward admitted that if Brown had not failed to join Allen, Montreal would have fallen into their hands.

Montgomery remained at Isle Aux Noix only long enough to receive a reinforcement of men and a few pieces of artillery. He then re-embarked, again landed at St. John's, and commenced operations for its investment. On the 18th of September, he marched with a party of five hundred men to the north of the fort, where he met a considerable portion of the garrison returning from the repulse of the party under Ethan Allen. A skirmish ensued, which in a few minutes terminated in the repulse of the enemy, who fled in disorder. But for a timidity among the Americans, the whole party might have been captured. In speaking of his men, General Montgomery says, "As soon as we saw the enemy, the old story of treachery spread among the men; and the cry was, we are trepanned and drawn under the guns of the fort. The woodsmen were less expert in forming than I had expected, and too many of them hung back. Had we kept more silence, we should have taken a field-piece or two."

Montgomery now determined to push the siege of St. John's with all possible vigor. In order to cut off supplies, he established a camp at the junction of the two roads leading to Chambly and Montreal, and defended it with a ditch, and a garrison of three hundred men. But he was surrounded with difficulties. His artillery was so light as to make little impression upon the walls, and the artillerists were raw and unskillful. Besides, his ammunition was almost exhausted, and the engineer was as ignorant of duty as were the artillerists. To all these was added another difficulty far greater than the rest,—his men, through constant exposure to a damp soil and unhealthy climate, and unused to the rules of war, had become insubordinate, and even mutinous; and the circumstances in which the commander was placed, effectually prevented him from enforcing discipline. This feeling was openly exhibited in an attempt of the general to remove the seat of his active operations to the north side of the town; and so palpable were its demonstrations, that he was forced to compromise with professional dignity, and submit his opinion to that of a board of officers. They refused to accede to his plan, and it was for a time abandoned. Subsequently, however, their consent was obtained, and a position taken to the north-west of the fort.

Meanwhile an event took place, as fortunate as it was unexpected, the success of which, decided the fate of the garrison. A gentleman from New York named James Livingston, had resided for a considerable time in Canada, and by a proper course of conduct had won the esteem of a large number of the inhabitants. As he was known to be favorable to the cause of liberty, Montgomery determined to employ his popularity in service to himself. Accordingly, at the instigation of the general, he organized a number of the inhabitants into an armed corps, promising the protection of congress to all their movements. In company with Major Brown, he speedily made himself master of Fort Chambly, including all the garrison, one hundred and twenty-six barrels of gunpowder, and a large amount of military and other stores.

Colonel Seth Warner and his regiment were with Montgomery at the siege of St. John's, although it is evident that both Warren and the officers of his regiment were without commissions, for we find by Montgomery's orderly book, that on the 16th of September he issued an order appointing Seth Warner colonel of a regiment of Green-Mountain Rangers, requiring that he should be obeyed as such. Probably the provincial congress of New York withheld the commissions on the same grounds on which, in the following year, they urged the continental congress to recall the commissions which they had given to Warner, and the officers of his regiment. But the regiment fought as bravely, and performed as important services, as any other regiment during the campaign, as will appear by the following brief account of it. Montgomery, having obtained a supply of ammunition and military stores, by the capture of Chambly, made his advances upon the fort at St. John's, with increased vigor. The garrison consisted of six or seven hundred men, who, in hopes of being soon relieved by General Carleton, made a resolute defense. Carleton exerted himself for this purpose, but such was the disaffection of the Canadians to the British cause, that he could not muster more than one thousand men, including the regulars, militia of Montreal, Canadians and Indians. With this force he proposed to cross the St. Lawrence, and join Colonel McLean, who had collected a few hundred Scotch emigrants, and taken post at the mouth of the Richelieu, hoping, with their united forces, to be able to raise the siege of St. John's, and relieve the garrison. In pursuance of this design, Carleton embarked his troops at Montreal, with the view of crossing the St. Lawrence, and landing at Longueil. Their embarkation was discovered by Colonel Warner from the opposite shore, who, with about three hundred Green-Mountain Boys, watched their motions, and prepared for their approach. Just before they reached the south shore, Warner opened upon them a well-directed fire of musketry and grape-shot, from a four-pounder, by which unexpected assault, the enemy were thrown into the utmost confusion, and retreated with precipitation and disorder.

When the news of Carleton's defeat reached McLean, he abandoned his position at the mouth of the Richelieu, and hastened to Quebec. By these events, the garrison at St. John's was left without the hope of relief, and Major Preston, the commander, was consequently obliged to surrender. The garrison laid down their arms on the 3d of November, and became prisoners of war, to the number of five hundred regulars, and more than one hundred Canadian volunteers. In the fort were found a number of cannon and a large quantity of military stores. Colonel Warner having repulsed General Carleton, and caused McLean to retire to Quebec, the Americans proceeded to erect a battery at the mouth of the Richelieu, to command the passage of the St. Lawrence, and blockade General Carleton in Montreal. In this situation of things, Montgomery arrived from St. John's, and took possession of Montreal without opposition, General Carleton having abandoned it to its fate, and escaped down the river in the night, in a small canoe with muffled oars. A large number of armed vessels, loaded with provisions and military stores, and General Prescott, with one hundred officers and privates, also attempted to pass down the river, but they were all captured at the mouth of the Richelieu, without the loss of a man. Warner's regiment having served as volunteers, and the men being too miserably clothed to endure a winter campaign in that severe climate, on the 20th of November Montgomery discharged them, with peculiar marks of respect, and his thanks for their meritorious services.

While Montgomery was engaged in the reduction of Chambly, St. John's, and Montreal, the army destined to meet him before Quebec was passing through the dreary wilderness lying between the province of Maine and the the St. Lawrence. This extraordinary and most arduous enterprise had been committed to Colonel Arnold, who, with one thousand one hundred men, consisting of New-England infantry, some volunteers, a company of artillery, and three companies of riflemen, commenced his march on the 13th September. It is almost impossible to conceive the labor, hardships, and difficulties which this detachment had to encounter in their progress up the rapid stream of the Kennebec, frequently interrupted by falls, where they were obliged to land and carry the boats upon their shoulders, until they surmounted them, through a country wholly uninhabited, with a scanty supply of provisions, the season cold and rainy, and the men daily dropping down with fatigue, sickness and hunger. Arnold was indefatigable in his endeavors to alleviate the distress of his men, but to procure provisions for them was out of his power. They were at one time reduced to so great an extremity of hunger, that the dogs belonging to the army were killed and eaten, and many of the soldiers devoured their leather cartouch-boxes! Arnold and his party at length arrived at Point Levi, opposite the town of Quebec; but in consequence of information the British had received, by the treachery of the Indian to whom Arnold intrusted a letter to General Schuyler, the boats which he expected to find there to transport his troops across the river had been removed, and the enemy were no longer in a state to be surprised. Arnold, however, was not to be deterred from attempting something against the town — he calculated strongly upon the defection of the inhabitants; and having supplied himself with canoes, he crossed the river in the night, and gained possession of the heights of Abraham. Here, though he had no artillery, and scarcely half the number of men that composed the garrison of the town, he made a bold experiment to try the loyalty of the enemy's troops, by sending a flag to summon them to surrender. But no message would be admitted, and Arnold found himself compelled to retire to more comfortable quarters, where he awaited the arrival of General Montgomery.

General Carleton, who, it has already been stated, arrived at Quebec, had taken the best measures for its defense, and was prepared to receive him. In a few days, the American general opened a six-gun battery within about seven hundred yards of the walls; but his artillery was too light to make a breach, and he could do nothing more than to amuse the enemy, and conceal his real purpose. After continuing the siege nearly a month, he resolved on a desperate attempt to carry the place by escalade. To distract the garrison, two feigned attacks were made on the upper town by two divisions of the army under Majors Brown and Livingston, while two real attacks on opposite sides of the lower town were made by two other divisions under Montgomery and Arnold. Early in the morning of the last day in the year, the signal was given, and the several divisions moved to the assault in the midst of a heavy fall of snow, which covered the assailants from the sight of the enemy. Montgomery, at the head of the New-York troops, advanced along the St.

Lawrence, by Aunce de Mere, under Cape Diamond. The first barrier to be surmounted on that side was defended by a battery, in which were mounted a few pieces of artillery, in front of which were a block-house and picket. The guard at the block-house, after giving a random fire, threw away their arms and fled to the barrier, and for a time the battery itself was deserted. Enormous piles of ice impeded the progress of the Americans, who, pressing forward in a narrow defile, reached at length the block-house and picket. Montgomery, who was in front, assisted in cutting down or pulling up the pickets, and advanced boldly and rapidly at the head of about two hundred men, to force the barrier. At this time one or two persons had ventured to return to the battery, and, seizing a slow match, discharged one of the guns. Casual as this fire appeared, it was fatal to General Montgomery and to two valuable young officers near his person, who, together with his orderly sergeant and a private, were killed on the spot. Colonel Campbell, on whom the command devolved, precipitately retired with the remainder of the division. Thus fell one of the bravest and most accomplished generals that ever led an army to the field. But he was not more illustrious for his skill and courage as an officer, than he was estimable for his private virtues. All enmity to him, on the part of the British, ceased with his life, and respect for his private character prevailed over all other considerations. When the corpse of Montgomery was shown to Carleton, the heart of that noble officer melted. They had served in the same regiment under Wolfe, and the most friendly relation existed between them, throughout the whole French war. The Lieutenant-governor of Quebec, Mr. Cramche, ordered him a coffin, and friends and enemies united in expressions of sorrow, as his remains were conducted to their final resting-place.

At his death, General Montgomery was in the first month of his thirty-ninth year. He was a man of great military talents, whose measures were taken with judgment and executed with vigor. He shared all the hardships of his troops, and though they had been unused to discipline, and many of them were jealous of their commander, he prevented their complaints by timely measures, and inspired them with his own enthusiasm. His industry could not be wearied, his vigilance imposed upon, nor his courage intimidated. Above the pride of opinion, when a measure was adopted by the majority, he gave it his full support, even though contrary to his own judgment.

Few men have ever fallen in battle so much regretted on both sides as General Montgomery. His many amiable qualities had procured him an uncommon share of private affection, and his great abilities an equal proportion of public esteem. Being a sincere lover of liberty, he had engaged in the American cause from principle, and quitted the enjoyment of an easy fortune, and the highest domestic felicity, to take an active share in the fatigues and dangers of a war instituted for the defense of the community of which he was an adopted member. His well-known character was almost equally esteemed by the friends and foes of the side which he had espoused. In America he was celebrated as a martyr to the liberties of mankind; in Great Britain, as a misguided man, sacrificing himself

CHARACTER OF MONTGOMERY. 311

to what he supposed to be the rights of his country. His name was mentioned in parliament with singular respect. Some of the most powerful speakers in that assembly displayed their eloquence in sounding his praise and lamenting his fate. Those in particular who had been his fellow-soldiers in the previous war, expatiated on his many virtues. The minister himself acknowledged his worth, while he reprobated the cause for which he fell. He concluded an involuntary panegyric by saying, "Curse on his virtues, they have undone his country."

"In this brief story of a short and useful life," says Mr. Armstrong, in his memoir of Montgomery, "we find all the elements which enter into the composition of a great man, and distinguished soldier; 'a happy physical organization, combining strength and activity, and enabling its possessor to encounter laborious days and sleepless nights, hunger and thirst, all changes of weather, and every variation of climate.' To these corporeal advantages was added a mind, cool, discriminating, energetic and fearless; thoroughly acquainted with mankind, not uninstructed in the literature and sciences of the day, and habitually directed by a high and unchangeable moral sense. That a man so constituted should have won 'the golden opinions' of friends and foes, is not extraordinary.* The most eloquent men of the British senate became his panegyrists; and the

---

* As soon as the news of Montgomery's death reached congress, they adopted resolutions of condolence with his family for their bereavement, and directed a monument to be erected to his memory, with an inscription expressive of their veneration for his character, and of their deep sense of his "many signal and important services; and to transmit to future

American congress hastened to testify for him 'their grateful remembrance, profound respect, and high veneration.'"

On the fall of Montgomery, Colonel Campbell, the second in command, ordered a retreat, although, if he had pushed bravely forward, the city would have inevitably fallen into his hands. In the mean time, ages, as an example worthy of imitation, his patriotism, conduct, boldness of enterprise, insuperable perseverance, and contempt of danger and death." A monument of white marble, with appropriate emblematic devices, was accordingly erected to his memory, in front of St. Paul's church in New York, with the following inscription:

THIS
monument is erected by order of Congress
25th January, 1776,
to transmit to posterity a grateful remembrance of the patriotic conduct, enterprise and perseverance
of *Major-general* RICHARD MONTGOMERY,
who, after a series of success amid the most discouraging difficulties, *Fell* in the attack on
QUEBEC, 31st December, 1775, aged 37 years.

The widow of Montgomery survived him more than half a century, maintaining the dignified position of a wife who carries with her to the tomb a name illustrious and venerated by an entire nation. Left a widow when still young, she wore for upward of forty years her mourning for her soldier,— (it was thus she always named him) — and threw off that attire of gloom only on the eve of the day on which, from the same abode from which she had last beheld him at his parting from her, full of life and hope, she saw passing before her on the Hudson, a steamer which bore on its deck, overshadowed by twenty star-spangled banners, the mortal remains of her husband. In 1818, De Witt Clinton, then governor of New York, believed that the moment had arrived to accomplish a great act of national gratitude. The British government sympathized generously with the noble idea. The remains of the glorious Montgomery, found undisturbed in the tomb where they had been laid forty-two years before by the English soldiers, were delivered over by the governor of Canada to the American veterans commissioned to receive them. Transported with a religious pomp to New York, they were deposited in the cenotaph that had been erected in St. Paul's church-yard to the warrior's memory.

Colonel Arnold, at the head of about three hundred and fifty men, made a desperate attack on the opposite side. Advancing with the utmost intrepidity through a narrow path, exposed to an incessant fire of grape-shot and musketry, as he approached the first barrier, he received a musket-ball in the leg, which shattered the bone, and he was carried off to the camp. Captain Morgan, who commanded a company of Virginia riflemen, rushed forward to the batteries at their head, and received a discharge of grape-shot, which killed one man only. A few rifles were immediately fired into the embrasures, and the barricade was mounted; the battery was instantly deserted, but the captain of the guard, with the greater part of his men, fell into the hands of the Americans. Morgan formed his men, but from the darkness of the night and total ignorance of the situation of the town, it was judged unadvisable to proceed. He was soon joined by Lieutenant-colonel Green and Majors Bigelow and Meigs, with several fragments of companies, amounting collectively to about two hundred men. At daylight this gallant party was again formed, and a most bloody and dangerous engagement ensued. Many of the enemy were killed, but more Americans, who were exposed to a destructive fire of musketry from the windows of the houses. Some of the most daring mounted the wall, but, seeing, on the other side, two ranks of soldiers, with their muskets on the ground, presenting hedges of bayonets to receive them should they leap forward, they recoiled and descended. Weary with exertion, and benumbed with cold; exposed to a deadly fire from every quarter; their arms rendered useless by the snow which continued to fall, the soldiers sought refuge in the houses. Perceiving that all further attempts would be vain, Morgan gave the signal to retreat. Some of the men fled, but most were unwilling to encounter another tempest of shot. They refused, however, to yield, until assured of the fate of Montgomery; when, losing all hope of success and escape, they surrendered themselves prisoners of war.

Some of the Americans, on their escape from Quebec, retreated precipitately to Montreal. Arnold, with difficulty, detained four hundred, who, breaking up their camp, retired three miles from the city. Here this heroic band, though much inferior in number to the garrison, kept it in continual awe, and, by preventing all communication with the country, reduced it to great distress for the want of provisions. Congress, on receiving information of the disaster of the 31st of December, directed reinforcements to be sent to Canada; and after the beginning of March, Arnold's party was almost daily augmented by the arrival of small bodies of troops. But its strength did not increase with its numbers. The small-pox still continued its ravages; fatigue, without hope, depressed the spirits of the soldiers; the difficulty of obtaining provisions became every day greater; and the harsh measures adopted by Arnold to procure them, exasperated the inhabitants around him.

On the first of May, General Thomas, who had been appointed to succeed Montgomery, arrived from the camp at Roxbury. On reviewing his army, he found it to consist of less than two thousand men, of whom half were not fit for duty. A council of war was held, who resolved that it was expedient to take a more defensible position higher up the St. Lawrence. To this decision they were led by the knowledge that the ice was leaving the river, and by the expectation that reinforcements from England would immediately come up. The next morning, in fact, while the Americans were engaged in removing the sick, several ships appeared in sight, and entered the harbor. A multitude of troops were immediately poured into the city. At one o'clock, Carleton made a sortie at the head of a thousand men. Against these General Thomas, at that moment, could oppose but three hundred. All the stores, and many of the sick, fell into the power of the enemy. The latter were treated, by the governor, with great tenderness; and when restored to health, were assisted to return to their homes. The Americans retreated to the mouth of the Sorel, where they were joined by several regiments, and where their worthy commander died of the small-pox, which yet prevailed in the camp.

After the capture of Montreal, Colonel Seth Warner had returned with his regiment to the New-Hampshire Grants; but instead of enjoying a respite from the fatigues and hardships of a campaign during the winter, he was called on to return to Canada. Although he was not in commission, and had no troops under his command, yet, General Wooster, who knew him well, did not scruple to write, requesting him to raise a body of men, and march into Canada, in the middle of winter. The letter is dated at Montreal, January 6th, 1776. After giving a general account of the defeat at Quebec, General Wooster says: "I have sent an express to General Schuyler, to Washington, and to congress, but you know how very long it will be before we can have relief from them. You, sir, and your valiant Green-Mountain Boys, are in our neighborhood; you all have arms, and I am confident ever stand ready to lend a helping hand to your brethren in distress; therefore, let me beg of you to raise as many men as you can, and have them in Canada, with the least possible delay, to remain till we can have relief from the Colonies. You will see that proper officers are appointed under you, and the officers and privates will have the same pay as the continental troops. It will be for your men to start as soon as they can be collected. No matter whether they all march together, but let them come on by tens, twenties, thirties, forties, or fifties, as fast as they can be prepared to march. It will have a good effect upon the minds of the Canadians, to see succor coming in. You will be good enough to send copies of this letter, or such parts of it as you shall judge proper, to the people below you. I can but hope the people will make a push to get into this country, and I am confident I shall see you here, with your men, in a very short time." And General Wooster was not disappointed. He did see Warner in Canada, with his men, in a very short time. Probably no revolutionary patriot, during the war, performed a service evincing more energy, resolution, and perseverance, or a more noble patriotism, than the raising of a regiment in eleven days, and marching to Quebec in the face of a Canadian winter.

Warner had advantages in the performance of this service which no other man possessed. The Green-

Mountain Boys had long been armed in their own defense against the government of New York, and he had been their chosen leader. They had become habituated to turn out at his call, and follow his lead. And as they had been successful in every enterprise, they had the most unlimited confidence in his judgment, his vigilance, his prudence and his unflinching courage. Besides, they loved him for his moral and social qualities. He sympathized with all classes, which rendered him affable and familiar with them, and as this did not arise from any mean or selfish motive, but from the interest which he felt in the welfare of his fellow-men, he ever maintained a self-respect and a dignified deportment. Add to this, that the Green-Mountain Boys were zealous and active whigs, and it is no longer incredible that they turned out with such alacrity at the call of Warner, in defense of their country. This winter campaign in Canada proved extremely distressing. The troops were in want of comfortable clothing, barracks, and provisions. The American army, in their distressed situation, were compelled to make a hasty retreat. Warner took a position exposed to the greatest danger, and requiring the utmost care and vigilance. He was always in the rear, picking up the wounded and diseased, assisting and encouraging those least able to take care of themselves, and generally kept but a few miles in advance of the British, who closely pursued the Americans from post to post. By calmly and steadily pursuing this course, with his habitual vigilance and care, Warner brought off most of the invalids, and with this corps of the diseased and infirm, arrived at Ticonderoga a few days after the main army had reached that fortress.* Thus terminated the expedition against Canada. In its conception it was singularly bold and romantic. In its progress were displayed fortitude and bravery seldom equaled in military annals. Its failure was a painful disappointment to the patriots of the day. It is now consoling to reflect, that successes would probably have proved injurious to the cause of independence. To protect the province, the military force of the confederacy must have been too much extended, and colonies more important have been left defenseless.

In June, 1776, General Gates† was appointed to the command of the army at Crown Point. He entered upon the service with great energy. In addition to the labor and expense of putting Ticonderoga into a proper situation for defense, another object of great importance engaged their attention at the same time: it was equally necessary to preserve the command of

---

* See Life of Warner, by Hon. Daniel Chipman.

† Horatio Gates was born in England, in 1728. He early embraced the career of arms, and rose to the rank of major by the force of merit alone. He was an officer under the unfortunate Braddock, in the expedition against Fort Du Quesne, in the year 1755, and was, with the illustrious Washington, among the few officers who escaped with life on the memorable occasion. In consequence of a severe wound which he received in the battle, he was for some time debarred from actual service; and at the conclusion of the peace, he retired to his native country. He soon, however, returned, and purchased an estate in Virginia, on which he resided until the commencement of the revolutionary war, when he was appointed adjutant-general, by congress, with the rank of brigadier. In July 1775, he accompanied Washington to Massachusetts, where he continued until he received the chief command of the army which had just returned from Canada.

Lake Champlain, by the construction of a considerable naval force. In the prosecution of this business, the Americans labored with uncommon diligence and perseverance, but under complicated and immense difficulties. Their timber was to be cut down in the woods, and dragged by men to the lake; much of their artillery, their ammunition, stores, and most of their materials for a naval equipment, were to be brought from great distances, and then must be transported by land-carriage, over roads almost impassable. Carpenters and ship-builders were fully employed in the seaports, in fitting out privateers. The distance and difficulty of the communication rendered the transportation of bulky articles very expensive and tedious; and several of the articles which were wanted were not to be procured, and the supply of others was greatly deficient in quantity and quality. But amidst all their difficulties, such was the resolution, industry and perseverance of the men, that by the middle of August, they had equipped a very considerable naval force. This armament was manned with three hundred and ninety-five men, and was completely fitted for action. Considering the state of the country at that time, the difficulties and disadvantages under which this naval force had been constructed, it is surprising how so much could have been effected.

Such, however, was the importance to the designs of the English of obtaining an absolute control of the lakes, that General Carleton set himself with all diligence to the equipment of a fleet. His plan was, according to the instructions of the ministry, to penetrate by way of the lake to the Hudson river, and thus to effect a junction with the army of New York, at Albany. By the execution of this plan, the provinces of New England would have found themselves separated from the others by a powerful and victorious army, and the cause of freedom would have been exposed to the most imminent perils. Long deliberated upon in the councils of the British ministers, it was their favorite scheme. And, in effect, the very nature of the places between Canada and New York, appeared to favor this enterprise. With the exception of the heights which are found between the upper extremity of Lake George and the left bank of the Hudson, and which only occupy a space of sixteen miles, the entire passage from one of these provinces to the other, could easily be made by water, first by ascending from the St. Lawrence into the Sorel, and then traversing the Lakes Champlain and George, or Wood creek, to the lands which separate it from the Hudson. The English having an immense superiority at sea, Canada being entirely in their power, and as the principal seat of resistance was found in the provinces of New England, while the coasts of New York were peculiarly accessible to maritime attacks, it cannot be denied that this plan of the campaign presented great advantages. But the difficulty of the enterprise was equal to its importance. It was requisite to construct, or at least to equip a fleet of thirty vessels of different dimensions, and to arm them with artillery; the want of materials rendered either of these objects difficult to accomplish. The transportation afterward in certain places by land and drawing up the rapids of Chambly, of thirty large long-boats, a number of flat-bottomed boats of considerable burthen, with above four hundred bateaux, was an operation which offered not only great obstacles, but even an appearance of impossibility. But the English seamen, from their skill and patience, were not intimidated by it. The soldiers seconded them, and the Canadians, taken from their rustic labors, were compelled to share the toil. The generals urged forward this laborious undertaking on account of the lateness of the season. They felt all the importance of the enterprise, and persuaded themselves that if they could reach Albany before winter, their ultimate success would be secured. They labored, therefore, with incredible activity ; but notwithstanding all their efforts, the preparations could not be completed, nor the armament equipped, till the middle of the month of October. The fleet would have made no contemptible figure even upon the European seas. The admiral's ship carried eighteen twelve pounders, and was followed by two stout schooners, the one mounting fourteen, the other, twelve six-pounders, with a large flat-bottomed boat having six twenty-four and six twelve-pounders. Twenty vessels of less size carried each a brass piece of ordnance, from nine to twenty-four pounders, or howitzers. Several long-boats were equipped in the same manner. Besides these, there was a great number of boats and tenders of various sizes, to serve as transports for the troops, baggage, warlike stores, provisions, and arms of every sort.

The whole fleet was commanded by Captain Pringle, a sea-officer of great experience ; it was manned by a select body of seamen, animated with an extreme desire of victory. The land-troops, encamped in the environs, prepared, as soon as the navigation of the lake should be secured, to fall upon the enemy. Three thousand men occupied Isle Aux Noix, and as many were stationed at St. John's: the remainder were distributed either in the vessels or in the neighboring garrisons.

The Americans united all their forces to resist such formidable preparations. General Gates was at their head, and Arnold showed himself everywhere, inspiring the soldiers with that ardent courage for which he was himself distinguished. As the event of the campaign upon this frontier depended wholly upon naval operations, the Americans had exerted themselves to the utmost of their power to arm and equip a fleet capable of opposing that of the enemy. But, notwithstanding the activity and perseverance of the American generals, their squadron amounted to no more than fifteen vessels of different sizes, two brigs, one corvette, one sloop, three galleys, and eight flat-boats. Their largest vessel mounted only twelve six and four-pounders. But that this armament might not want a chief whose intrepidity equaled the danger of the enterprise, the command of it was given to General Arnold. It was expected of him to maintain, upon this new element, the reputation he had acquired on land. The American army, notwithstanding all the obstacles it had encountered, and the ravages of the small-pox, still amounted to eight or nine thousand men.

All the dispositions being made on both sides, General Carleton, impatient to conquer, ordered all his naval forces to advance toward Crown Point, intending to attack Arnold there. He had already reached the middle of the lake without having been able to discover him, and was proceeding without any distrust, when all at once the English perceived the American squadron, which was drawn up with great skill, behind the island of Valcour, and occupied the passage between the island and the western shore of the lake. This unexpected interview caused a violent agitation on both sides. A fierce engagement immediately ensued. But the wind being unfavorable to the English, they could not display their whole line; the Inflexible, and their other vessels of the largest class, took no part in the action. The brig Carleton, accompanied by several gun-boats, assailed Arnold's fleet with singular courage and ability. The Americans supported the combat with equal bravery; it lasted above four hours. The wind continuing to be contrary for the English, Captain Pringle perceived that he could not hope to obtain advantages with a part of his forces against all those of the enemy, and accordingly gave the signal for retreat; ordering the fleet to be anchored in a line, in presence of the American squadron.

The Americans had lost in the action their largest brig, which took fire and was consumed, as also a flat-boat which went to the bottom. They considered it extremely dangerous to await a second engagement in the anchorage they occupied, and consequently determined to retire under the walls of Crown Point, hoping that the artillery of the fortress would counterbalance the superiority of the enemy's force. Fortune seemed inclined to favor this design of General Arnold; and already his vessels, having lost sight of those of the English, sailed rapidly toward their new station;

when suddenly the wind became favorable to the enemy, who pursued and came up with them before their arrival at Crown Point. The battle was immediately renewed with greater fury than at first; it continued upward of two hours. Those vessels, in the mean while, which were most ahead, crowded sail, and, passing Crown Point, ran for Ticonderoga. Only two galleys and five flat-boats, remained with General Arnold. With these he made a desperate defense; but his second in command, Brigadier-general Waterburgh, being taken with his vessel, and the others making but a faint resistance, he determined, in order to prevent his people and shipping from falling into the power of the enemy, to run these on shore and set them on fire. He executed his intention with great address. He remained on board the vessel he commanded, and kept her colors flying, till she was on fire. Though he had been unsuccessful on this occasion, the disparity of strength duly considered, he lost no reputation, but rose, on the contrary, in the estimation of his countrymen. He had, in their opinion, acquitted himself with no less ability in this naval encounter, than he had before done on land. The Americans, having destroyed whatever could not be carried off, evacuated Crown Point and withdrew to Ticonderoga. General Carleton occupied the former immediately, and the rest of the army came soon after to join him there.

Completely masters of Lake Champlain, the English had no other obstacle to surmount besides the fortress of Ticonderoga, in order to penetrate into Lake George. If Carleton, rapidly availing himself of his advantage, had pushed forward against the Americans thrown into confusion by defeat, perhaps he might have seized this important place. But he was prevented from doing it by a south wind, which prevailed for several days. The Americans made the best use of this time in preparing and increasing their means of defense. They mounted their cannon, constructed new works, and repaired the old, surrounding them with moats and palisades. The garrison was reinforced with extreme expedition; and conformably to the orders of Washington, the oxen and horses were removed into distant places, that the English might not seize them for provision or draught. Meanwhile, General Carleton had not neglected to detach scouting parties upon the two banks of the lake; and, when the wind permitted, some light vessels were also sent toward Ticonderoga, to reconnoiter the force of the enemy and the state of the fortress. All the reports agreed that the fortifications were formidable, and the garrison full of ardor. He reflected, therefore, that the siege must be long, difficult, and sanguinary, and concluded, accordingly, that the possession of this fortress would not indemnify him for all it might cost. The winter approached; the want of provisions, the difficulty of direct communication with Canada, and the little hope of success from an expedition in the cold and desert regions which separate the Hudson river from Lake George, rendered the wintering upon this lake extremely perilous. In consequence of these considerations, the English general deemed the reduction of Ticonderoga of little utility in his present circumstances, whereas the command of the lakes secured him a clear passage to return in the spring to the attack of this fortress, without exposing his troops to the hardships of a siege, undertaken in the midst of the rigors of the winter. After having taken the advice of a council of war, he renounced the project of an attack, and early in November conducted his army back toward Montreal, leaving his advanced posts in Isle Aux Noix. But prior to his retreat, with the singular courtesy and humanity of his character, he sent to their homes the American officers who had fallen into his power, administering generously to all their wants. He exercised the same liberality toward the common soldiers. The greater part were almost naked; he caused them to be completely clothed, and set them at liberty, after having taken their oath that they would not serve against the armies of the king. General Carleton was blamed for having taken winter-quarters; this resolution was considered as a mark of weakness, and as highly prejudicial to the success of ulterior operations; since, if he had immediately made himself master of Ticonderoga, his troops, after having passed the winter in its vicinity, would have been able to enter the field early the following spring. It is probable, in effect, that the war would, in that case, have had a very different result from what it actually had. But the conquest of a place so strong by nature and by art as Ticonderoga, depended on the resistance the Americans would have made; and certainly their number, the valor they had displayed in the naval actions, and the extreme confidence they had in their chiefs, all announced that their defense would have been long and obstinate. Nor should the considerations be omitted of the difficulty of subsistence, and of the communications with Canada. Be this as it may, the retreat of the English general, and his inaction during the winter, had the most happy results for the Americans.

The services of the regiment of Green-Mountain Boys, and the aid furnished to the army at Ticonderoga by the inhabitants of the New-Hampshire Grants, have not been sufficiently commemorated by historians. Warner, with his brave regiment, was at Ticonderoga during the whole campaign of 1776, and by his activity and energy, did much toward protecting that important post. The patriotic heroes of the Green Mountains were ever ready at the call of freedom and their country. Few in number, and without recognition as a separate province, they were without representatives in the congress, but they had ever been zealous champions of liberty. Six months before the commencement of the Revolution, when the rumor reached Bennington that the British had slain six men in Boston and seized a depot of powder, it was at once resolved that two thousand armed Green-Mountain Boys should march to the aid of the Bostonians whenever hostilities should commence. And four weeks before the battle of Lexington, they sent assurances to New Hampshire and Massachusetts that they would "always be ready for aid and assistance to those states, if, by the dispensations of Providence, they should be called thereto." But the Massachusetts committee of safety anticipated a long and arduous struggle, and one week after the massacre at Lexington, they thus wrote to the leading men at Bennington: "For heaven's sake, pay the closest attention to sowing and planting; do as much of it as is possible, not for your own families merely. Do not think of coming down country to fight." That committee little anticipated how soon a small band of Green-Mountain Boys, armed only with muskets, and without a single bayonet among them, would attack the fortress of Ticonderoga. On the 22d of May, 1775, at a public meeting of the inhabitants of Marlborough, (near old Fort Dummer,) the following pledges were unanimously made : "We will, each of us, at the expense of our lives and fortunes, to the last extremity, unite and oppose the late cruel, unjust and arbitrary acts of the British parliament. We will be contented and subject to the honorable continental congress in all things which they shall resolve for the peace, safety and welfare of the American colonies."

In 1776, while Carleton, with superior forces, was attempting to drive the Americans from Lake Champlain, the inhabitants of the New-Hampshire Grants gave the most important assistance to the army at Ticonderoga. While the troops in that fortress were expecting to be immediately blockaded, they had provisions for only sixteen days, and there was no hope of receiving timely succors from Albany. A call was made upon the committee at Bennington for assistance, and within an hour they purchased a thousand bushels of wheat, and returned word that they would send on the flour as fast as it could be manufactured. The committee, in their reply to General Gates, also said : "It is difficult to transport what we have already on hand; for our militia, even before we received your letter, asking assistance, left us, almost to a man, marched, and have doubtless joined you before this." And thus the Green-Mountain Boys hurried to the defense of their country. Scattered through a mountainous country, it might have been thought difficult to collect the scanty population; but the cry of invasion echoed from hill to hill, from village to village, and, leaving their herds and their fields, and hastily exchanging a parting blessing with their wives and their mothers, the hardy mountaineers rushed to the battle.

> "From the gray sire, whose trembling hand
> Could hardly buckle on his brand,
> To the raw boy, whose shaft and bow
> Were yet scarce terror to the crow,
> Each valley, each sequestered glen,
> Mustered its little horde of men,
> That met, as torrents from the height,
> In highland dale their streams unite;
> Still gathering, as they pour along,
> A voice more loud, a tide more strong."

A hasty glance at the transactions in other parts of the country will appropriately close the history of the campaign of 1776. In March, General Washington executed a plan for driving the British from Boston, by seizing and fortifying Dorchester Heights, and thus getting command of the harbor and British shipping. On the 17th, the British forces evacuated the town and sailed for Halifax. In June, General Clinton and Sir Peter Parker made an attack on Fort Moultrie, near Charleston, South Carolina; but were repulsed with considerable loss. Congress, meanwhile, continued in session, and on the 4th of July, adopted the memorable Declaration of Independence. It was received with demonstrations of joyous enthusiasm throughout the colonies. The royal authority had been everywhere entirely subverted the year before: the Revolution was now in a political sense completed; but the war for its establishment was yet to be waged.

Shortly after the evacuation of Boston by the British, General Washington removed to New York, making that city his head-quarters. The American forces in and around the city were about seventeen thousand, a part of whom were on Long Island, under command of Sullivan. In June following, General Howe, with the forces from Halifax, arrived near New York, and was shortly after joined by his brother, Admiral Lord Howe, with a reinforcement of troops, a strong naval force, and abundant military stores. The army under Howe now amounted to twenty-four thousand. He attacked and defeated the American army on Long Island. General Washington witnessed the defeat of his best troops with indescribable anguish. Withdrawing from New York, he gradually retreated before the British, adopting the policy of wearing out the enemy by keeping them in perpetual pursuit. Avoiding any general engagement, small parties were involved in skirmishes whenever it could be done with decided advantage. Pursued by the enemy, Washington retreated slowly through New Jersey and across the Delaware into Pennsylvania. So hot was the pursuit, that the rear of the American army was often in sight of the van of the enemy. Washington's forces were reduced to three thousand men, and they were destitute of tents, blankets, and even utensils for cooking their provisions. This retreat through New Jersey was the darkest hour of the revolutionary struggle. On the same day that Washington was driven across the Delaware, the British took possession of Rhode Island. They already held New York and New Jersey. The army of Washington was continually diminishing by the discharge of the militia, whose term of service had expired. A general gloom and despondency hung over the whole country. But nothing could shake the constancy of Washington. Feeling the absolute necessity of doing something to rouse the army and the country from the depression that was weighing down all minds, Washington recrossed the Delaware with a detachment of his army, surprised and took prisoners one thousand Hessians, with the loss of but nine men among his own troops. Soon after, evading by night the British, who were encamped at Trenton in the confident expectation of forcing him into a general engagement the next day, he marched upon Princeton, where a part of the British force had been left, routed and put to flight two regiments which he met on his way, and captured nearly the whole of another. These brilliant actions turned the tide. The British immediately evacuated Trenton, and retreated to New Brunswick; the inhabitants, eager to revenge the brutalities they had suffered, took courage, and the enemy were driven from every post in New Jersey, except Amboy and New Brunswick; and Washington went into secure winter quarters at Morristown.

During the darkest period of this campaign, the American congress showed no sign of dismay. They adopted articles of confederation for a perpetual union of the states; took measures for raising a new army, with a longer term of enlistment; and solemnly proclaimed that they would listen to no terms of peace short of independence. They sent commissioners to France to treat for their acknowledgment of their independence, and for aid in their struggle. The cause of America was popular at the French court; countenance and assistance was at once, in various ways, secretly given. Many French officers became desirous of enlisting in the struggle, among whom was the young Marquis de Lafayette, who arrived in season to take part in the next campaign.

The principal object of the British, in the campaign of 1777, was to open a free communication between Canada and New York. The British ministry were sanguine in their hopes, that, the New-England states, which they considered as the soul of the confederacy, might be severed from the neighboring states, and compelled to submission. In prosecution of this design, an army of British and German troops, amounting to upward of seven thousand men, exclusive of artillery, was put under command of Lieutenant-general Burgoyne,* an enterprising and able officer. The plan of operations consisted of two parts. General Burgoyne with the main body, was to advance by way of Lake Champlain, and force his way to Albany, or, at least, so far as to effect a junction with the royal army from New York; and Lieutenant-colonel St. Leger, with about two hundred British, a regiment of New-York loyalists, raised and commanded by Sir John Johnson,

*John Burgoyne was an illegitimate son of Lord Bingley. He entered the army at an early age, and his early education, and the influence of his father, placed him in the line of promotion. He first served in Portugal and Spain. After his return to England, he became a privy counselor, and was elected to parliament. He came over to America in 1775, and was at Boston at the battle of Bunker Hill. He was sent to Canada the same year, but early in 1776 returned to England, and through the partiality of the king, was appointed to the command of the British army in Canada.

and a large body of Indians, was to ascend the St. Lawrence to Lake Ontario, and from that quarter to penetrate toward Albany, by the way of the Mohawk river.

The main army, under General Burgoyne, embarked at St. John's, and proceeded up Lake Champlain without any interruption; and soon arrived and encamped at the river Boquet, on the west side of the lake, and a little to the northward of Crown Point, at the place now called Willsborough. There the Indians had also assembled, and General Burgoyne, in conformity to their customs, gave them a war-feast. He made a speech, addressed to their chiefs and warriors, designed to excite their savage ardor in the British cause, and to give a direction to their cruelty and barbarity. He urged them to impetuosity in battle, but enjoined them not to kill any but those who were opposed to them in arms; that old men, women, children and prisoners, should be spared from the knife and hatchet, even in the midst of action; and they should only scalp those who were killed by their fire in fair opposition; but that, under no pretense whatever, should they scalp the wounded, or even dying, and much less kill any in that condition. A handsome compensation was promised, for all prisoners they should bring in; but if, instead of this, they brought in their scalps, they were to be called to account. The British general could not be so unacquainted with the established customs and habits of the Indians, as to expect that an elegant speech would have any considerable effect upon them; still, it might be useful to the British, as it bore the appearance of humanity, and might tend to abate the reproaches with which their conduct was loaded in every part of Europe, for calling forth the savage barbarities at all into the contest.

The command of the Americans in the northern department, had been assigned to Major-general Schuyler.* It was foreseen that the contest would be carried on in the northern and western parts of the state of New York; and it was supposed that he was the only man who would have influence enough to keep the inhabitants, in those parts of the state, united against the enemy. Four days before Burgoyne made his speech to the Indians, Schuyler arrived at Ticonderoga, but did not find either the garrison or the works in so respectable a condition as he expected. Most of the recruits which had been ordered to the place, had not arrived; but little had been done to repair or strengthen the fortifications; and General St. Clair,† who had commanded, had not, and did not dare to

* Philip Schuyler was born at Albany, in 1731. He served as an officer in the French war. When quite young, he became a member of the New-York legislature, and was eminent for his intelligence and influence. To him and to Governor Clinton it was chiefly owing that the province made an early and decided resistance to those measures which terminated in the independence of the colonies. In 1775 he was appointed a major-general, and was directed to proceed immediately from New York to Ticonderoga, to secure the lakes and to make preparations for entering Canada. Being taken sick, the command devolved on Montgomery. On his recovery, he devoted himself zealously to the management of the affairs of the northern department.

† Arthur St. Clair was a soldier from his youth. At an early age, while the independent states were yet British colonies, he entered the royal American army, and was commissioned as an ensign. He was actively engaged, during the French war, in the army of general Wolfe, and was

call in large numbers of the militia, for fear his provisions should fail before the arrival of a supply. Having inspected the works, Schuyler left the command with St. Clair, and returned to Fort Edward, as a more central situation.

On the 4th of July, Burgoyne issued a proclamation, designed to spread terror among the Americans, and affright those who were active in the support of their cause. The number, power, and cruelty of the Indians, was represented as extremely formidable and threatening; and their eagerness to be let loose on their prey, was described with uncommon energy. The accumulation of British power, which was now displayed by land and by sea, was declared to be ready to embrace or to crush every part of America. The rebellion in the colonies, and the conduct of their present rulers, were painted in the most disgusting and awful colors; and their leaders were charged with repeated acts of the most unparalleled

carrying a pair of colors, in the battle in which that celebrated commander was slain, on the Plains of Abraham. He was highly esteemed by the distinguished commanders under whom he served, as a young officer of merit, capable of obtaining a high grade of military reputation. After the peace of '63, he sold out and entered into trade, for which the generosity of his nature utterly disqualified him; he, of course, soon became disgusted with a profitless pursuit, and having married, after several vicissitudes of fortune, he located himself in Ligonier valley, west of the Alleghany mountains, and near the old route from Philadelphia. In this situation the American Revolution found him, surrounded by a rising family, in the enjoyment of ease and independence, with the fairest prospects of affluent fortune, the foundation of which had been already established by his intelligence, industry and enterprise. From this peaceful abode, these sweet domestic enjoyments, and the flattering prospects which accompanied them, he was drawn by the claims of a troubled country.

15

injustice, persecution and tyranny! Encouragement and employment were offered to those who should assist the British king in redeeming the colonies from the oppressions of congress, and restoring them to the blessings of British liberty and government! Protection and security, but not very explicitly expressed, were held out to the peaceable and industrious, who should remain in their habitations. And all the calamities and horrors of war were denounced to those who should any longer dare to persevere in their hostility to the British king and army. Nothing had ever appeared in America, in a style so pompous, tumid and bombastic. Instead of producing the desired effect, and frightening the people into submission, the proclamation was everywhere the subject of derision and ridicule; and treated as the production of ostentatious vanity, insolence and folly, not at all calculated to operate on the hopes or the fears of the people of the United States.

Having finished his speeches and proclamations, the British general employed himself in more formidable operations. After a short stay at Crown Point, Burgoyne moved on with his army to Ticonderoga. The state of the American fort and garrison at that place did not promise a very long or vigorous defense. The old French lines had indeed been strengthened with additional works and a block-house. On the eastern shore of the lake, and opposite to Ticonderoga, the Americans had taken still more pains in fortifying a high circular hill, to which they had given the name of Mount Independence. On the summit of this hill they had erected a star fort, enclosing a large square of barracks, well fortified and surrounded with artillery. These two posts were joined by a bridge thrown across the lake. This bridge was supported by twenty-two piers of very large timber, placed at equal distances; the spaces between these were filled with separate floats, each about fifty feet long, and twelve wide, strongly fastened together with chains and rivets. The north side of the bridge was defended by a boom of very large pieces of timber, fastened together by riveted bolts and double chains, made of iron an inch and a half square.

But notwithstanding the apparent strength of Ticonderoga, it was effectually overlooked and commanded by a neighboring eminence called Sugar Hill, or Mount Defiance. This mountain, by its height and proximity, had such an entire command both of Ticonderoga and Mount Independence, that an enemy might from thence have counted the numbers, and enfiladed every part of the works, in either of those places. This circumstance was well known to the American officers, and they had a consultation about fortifying the mountain; but it was declined, because their works were already so extensive, that, with the addition of what would be proper on Sugar Hill, they would require ten or twelve thousand men for their defense — a greater number than could be spared for that purpose. Instead of a full complement of troops to man the extensive lines and defend the numerous works, the whole force which St. Clair had, consisted only of two thousand five hundred continental troops, aided by nine hundred militia, badly equipped, worse armed, and most of them without bayonets. St.

Clair was in hopes that Burgoyne's impetuosity would have led him to make a sudden assault upon the place, which he expected to repel with success; but as soon as he was informed of the numbers in his army, and that a regular siege was intended, he was convinced that an effectual defense could not be made by his troops.

The royal army advanced with great celerity, but with much caution and order, on both sides of the lake, the naval force keeping its station in the center. On the near approach of the right wing of the British army on the Ticonderoga side, on the 2d of July, the Americans abandoned and set fire to their works, block-houses and saw mills, toward Lake George; and without making any opposition, permitted General Phillips to take possession of Mount Hope. This post commanded the American lines in a great degree, and cut off their communication with Lake George. The Americans, on this occasion, were charged with supineness and want of vigor. Their inactivity arose not from want of courage, but from lack of men enough to make an effectual opposition to the powerful force with which they were surrounded.

In the mean time the royal army proceeded with such expedition in the construction of their works, the bringing up of artillery, stores, and provisions, and the establishment of posts and communications, that by the fifth, matters were so far advanced as to require but one or two days more to completely invest the posts on both sides of the lake. Sugar Hill had also been examined, and the advantages which it presented were so important that it had been resolved to take possession, and erect a battery there. This work, though attended with extreme labor and difficulty, had been carried on by General Phillips, with much expedition and success. A road had been made through a very rough ground, to the top of the mountain; and the British were at work in constructing a level for a battery, and transporting their artillery. As soon as this battery should be ready to play, the American works would have been completely invested on every side.

In these circumstances a council of war was called by St. Clair. He was convinced that it was absolutely necessary to evacuate the place. The council were informed that their whole effective number was not sufficient to man one half of the works; that as the whole must be constantly upon duty, it would be impossible for them to support the fatigue for any considerable length of time; that General Schuyler, who was at Fort Edward, had not sufficient force to relieve the garrison; and that as the enemy's batteries were nearly ready to open, and the place would be completely invested in twenty-four hours, nothing could save the troops but an immediate evacuation of the posts. The general's representation was admitted to be correct, and it was unanimously agreed by the council to abandon the fortress that night. It was proposed that the baggage of the army, with such artillery, stores and provisions as the necessity of the occasion would admit, should be embarked with a strong detachment, on board two hundred bateaux, and dispatched under convoy of five armed galleys, up the south river to Skenesborough; and that the main body of the army should proceed by land, taking its route on the road to Castleton, which was about thirty miles to the south of Ticonderoga, and join the boats and galleys at Skenesborough falls. It was thought necessary to keep the matter a secret, till the time should arrive when it was to be executed. The English had no suspicion of what was passing, and the march commenced under the most favorable auspices. But all at once a house which took fire on Mount Independence, roused by its glare of light the attention of the English, who immediately perceived all that had taken place. The Americans finding themselves discovered, marched hastily, and in some disorder, as far as Hubbardton, where they halted to refresh themselves and rally the dispersed. But the English were not idle. General Frazer, at the head of a strong detachment of grenadiers and light troops, commenced an eager pursuit by land, upon the right bank of Wood Creek. General Reidesel, behind him, rapidly advanced with his Brunswickers, either to support the English, or to act separately, as occasion might require. General Burgoyne determined to pursue the Americans by water. But it was first necessary to destroy the boom and bridge which had been constructed in front of Ticonderoga. The British seamen and artificers immediately engaged in the operation, and in a short time, those works, which had cost so much labor and so vast an outlay, were cut through and demolished. The passage thus cleared, the ships of Burgoyne immediately proceeded with extreme rapidity in search of the Americans; all was in movement at once upon land and water. By three in the afternoon, the van of the British squadron, composed of gun-boats, came up with and attacked the American galleys, near Skenesborough. In the mean time, three regiments, which had been landed at South Bay, ascended and passed a mountain with great expedition, in order to cut off a retreat to Fort Anne. But the Americans eluded this stroke by the rapidity of their flight. The British frigates having joined the van, the galleys, already hard pressed by the gun-boats, were completely overpowered. Two of them surrendered; three were blown up. The Americans now despaired; having set fire to their works, mills, and bateaux, and otherwise destroyed what they were unable to burn, they escaped as well as they could, without halting till they reached Fort Anne. Their loss was considerable, for the bateaux they burnt were loaded with baggage, provisions and munitions, as necessary to their sustenance as to military operations. The corps which had set out by land were in no better situation. The vanguard, conducted by St. Clair, had arrived at Castleton; the rear, commanded by Colonels Francis and Warner, had rested the night of the sixth, at Hubbardton, six miles below Castleton.

At Hubbardton, the advanced corps of the British army overtook the rear of the American troops, on the morning of the 7th of July. The American army, all but part of three regiments, were gone forward; these were part of Hale's, Francis' and Warner's regiments. The enemy attacked them with superior numbers, and the highest prospect of success. Francis and Warner opposed them with great spirit and vigor; and no officers or troops could have discovered more courage and firmness than they displayed through the whole action. Large reinforcements of the enemy arriving, it became impossible to make any effectual opposition. Francis fell in a most honorable discharge of his duty. Hale surrendered with his regiment. Surrounded on every side by the enemy, but calm and undaunted, Colonel Warner fought his way through all opposition, brought off the troops that refused to capitulate with Hale, checked the enemy in their pursuit, and contrary to all expectations, arrived safe with his troops at Manchester. To the northward of that town the whole country was deserted. The colonel determined to make a stand at that place; encouraged by his example and firmness, a body of the militia soon joined him; and he was once more in a situation to protect the inhabitants, harass the enemy, and break up their advanced parties.

The loss of the royal troops in dead and wounded amounted to about one hundred and eighty. General St. Clair, upon intelligence of this discomfiture, and that of the disaster at Skenesborough, which was brought him at the same time by an officer of one of the galleys, apprehending that he should be interrupted if he proceeded toward Fort Anne, struck into the woods on the left, uncertain whether he should repair to Massachusetts, or endeavor to reach the army at Fort Edward. But being joined two days after, at Manchester, by the remains of the corps of Colonel Warner, and having collected the fugitives, he proceeded to Fort Edward, in order to unite with General Schuyler.

While these events were passing on the left, the

English generals resolved to drive the Americans from Fort Anne, situated higher up toward the sources of Wood Creek. Colonel Hill was detached for this purpose from Skenesborough; and to facilitate his operations, the greatest exertions were made in carrying bateaux over the falls at that place, which enabled him to attack the fort by water. Upon intelligence that the Americans had a numerous garrison there, Brigadier Powell was sent with two regiments to the succor of Colonel Hill. The American Colonel Long, who, with a great part of his corps, had escaped the destruction of the boats at the falls, commanded the garrison of Fort Anne. Having heard that the enemy was approaching, he gallantly sallied out to receive him. The English defended themselves with courage, but the Americans had already nearly surrounded them. Colonel Hill, finding himself too hard pressed, endeavored to take a stronger position. This movement was executed with as much order as intrepidity, amidst the reiterated and furious charge of the Americans. The combat had lasted for more than two hours, and victory was still doubtful, when all at once the Americans heard the horrible yells of the savages, who approached, and being informed at the same instant that the corps of Powell was about to fall upon them, they retired to Fort Anne. Not thinking themselves in safety even there, they set it on fire, and withdrew to Fort Edward, on the river Hudson.

General Schuyler was already in this place, and St. Clair arrived there on the twelfth, with the remains of the garrison of Ticonderoga. It would be difficult to describe the hardships and misery which these troops

15*

had suffered, from the badness of the weather and the want of covering and provisions, in their circuitous march through the woods, from Castleton to Fort Edward. After the arrival of these troops, and of the fugitives, who came in by companies, all the American troops amounted to little over four thousand men, including the militia. They were in want of all necessaries, and even of courage, from the effect of their recent reverses. The Americans lost, in these different actions, no less than one hundred and twenty-eight pieces of artillery, with a prodigious quantity of warlike stores, baggage and provisions, particularly of flour, which they left in Ticonderoga and Mount Independence. To increase the calamity, the whole of the neighboring country was struck with terror by this torrent of disasters.

During the reverses of the American army, and the triumphant progress of Burgoyne, the consternation of the people in northern New York and on the New-Hampshire Grants, was greatly increased by the numerous murders and cruelties of Burgoyne's Indian allies — for the efforts of that general to dissuade them from the perpetration of their cruel enormities were ineffectual. Restrain them he could not; and it was admitted by the British writers of that day, that the friends of the royal cause, as well as its enemies, were equally victims to their indiscriminate rage. It was even ascertained that the British officers were deceived by their treacherous allies into the purchase of the scalps of their own comrades. Among other instances of cruelty, the well-known murder of Miss Jane M'Crea, which happened in the early part of the campaign, filled the public mind with horror. Every circumstance of this unnatural and bloody transaction, around which there lingers a melancholy interest to this day, served to heighten alike its interest and its enormity.* Many have been the versions of this bloody tale. General Gates, who had been most unjustly directed to supersede General Schuyler in the northern department, assailed General Burgoyne with great

* The tragic fate of Miss M'Crea forms a prominent feature in the brilliant tale, entitled, "The Rangers," by the novelist of the Green Mountains, Hon. Daniel P. Thompson. The facts in regard to her murder, stripped of their romance, are these :— She belonged to a family of tories, and had engaged herself in marriage to a young refugee, named Jones, a lieutenant in the British service, who was advancing with Burgoyne. When the people fled before the victorious Briton, she remained behind with some friends, in the expectation of meeting her lover. A party of Indians in advance of the army, seeking for plunder, took her a prisoner and retired toward the British camp. When they reached the army, Miss M'Crea was not with them, but they bore a scalp which was recognized to be hers. Whether they quarreled about the division of the reward they were accustomed to receive for their prisoner, or whether, as they averred, she was shot by a party of Americans in pursuit of them, cannot now be known. Her mutilated corpse was afterward found under a pine tree near a spring, and the tree and spring were afterward known by her name. It was known in the camp, that Lieutenant Jones was betrothed to Jenny, and the story got abroad that he had sent the Indians for her ; that they had quarreled with another party, which they met on their return, respecting the reward he had offered, and murdered her to settle the dispute. Receiving high touches of coloring, as it went from one narrator to another, the sad story produced a deep and wide-spread indignation. Jones, chilled with horror and broken in spirit by the event, tendered a resignation of his commission, but it was refused. He purchased the scalp of his Jenny, and with this cherished memento, deserted and retired to Canada. There he lived to be an old man, and died only a few years ago. The death of Jenny was a heavy blow, and he never recovered from it. In youth he was exceedingly gay and garrulous ; but after that melancholy event, he

violence upon the subject of these outrages — charging him with encouraging the murder of prisoners, and the massacre of women and children, by paying the Indians a stipulated price for scalps. Burgoyne indignantly denied the charge of encouraging the Indians, although he could not but admit the horrible extent of their barbarities among unarmed and inoffensive inhabitants. "I would not," he said in reply to General Gates, "be conscious of the acts you presume to impute to me, for the whole continent of America, though the wealth of worlds was in its bowels, and a paradise upon its surface."

The retreat of the American army from Ticonderoga, on the approach of Burgoyne, while it filled the public mind with dismay, as the surrender of a position on which the safety of the north depended, was regarded with gloomy apprehension, as the prelude to further reverses. The mind of Washington, however, by a happy forecast, perceived a gleam of hope, even in this hour of despondency; and with a sort of prophetic skill, seems to have foretold, with extraordinary precision, the auspicious change of affairs which was in store. In reply to a letter of General Schuyler, of the 17th of July, communicating the unfavorable state and prospects of the army, he says: "Though our affairs have, for some days past, worn a gloomy aspect, yet I look forward to a happy change. I trust General

was sad and taciturn. He never married, and shunned society as much as business would permit. Toward the close of July in every year, when the anniversary of the tragedy approached, he would shut himself in his room, and refuse to speak with any one. His friends avoided any reference to the Revolution in his presence.

Burgoyne's army will meet, sooner or later, an effectual check; and, as I suggested before, that the success he has had will precipitate his ruin. From your accounts, he appears to be pursuing that line of conduct, which, of all others, is most favorable to us, I mean acting in detachment. This conduct will certainly give room for enterprise on our part, and expose his parties to great hazard. Could we be so happy as to cut one of them off, though it should not exceed four, five, or six hundred men, it would inspire the people and do away much of their present anxiety. In such an event they would lose sight of past misfortune, and, urged at the same time by a regard for their own security, they would fly to arms and afford every aid in their power."

It must be confessed that it required no ordinary share of fortitude to find topics of consolation in the present state of affairs. The British were advancing with a well-appointed army into the heart of the country, under the conduct, as it was supposed, of the most skillful officers, confident of success, and selected to finish the war. The army consisted in part of German troops, veterans of the Seven Years' War, under the command of a general of experience, conduct, and valor. Nothing could have been more ample than the military supplies, the artillery, munitions, and stores, with which the army was provided. A considerable force of Canadians and American loyalists furnished the requisite spies, scouts, and rangers; and a numerous force of savages in their war-dresses, with their peculiar weapons and native ferocity, increased the terrors of its approach.

On the evacuation of Ticonderoga, and the further

advance of such an army, the New-England states, and particularly New Hampshire and Massachusetts, were filled with alarm. It was felt that their frontier was uncovered, and that strenuous and extraordinary efforts for the protection of the country were required. The committee of safety of what was then called the New-Hampshire Grants, (the present state of Vermont,) wrote in the most pressing terms to the New-Hampshire committee of safety at Exeter, apprising them, that, if assistance should not be sent to them, they should be forced to abandon the country, and take refuge east of the Connecticut river. When these tidings reached Exeter, the assembly had finished their spring session and had gone home. A summons from the committee brought them together again, and in three days they took the most effectual and decisive steps for the defense of the country. Among the patriotic members of the assembly, who signalized themselves on this occasion, none was more conspicuous than John Langdon. The members of that body were greatly inclined to despond; the public credit was exhausted; and there were no means of supporting troops, if they could be raised. Meantime the defenses of the frontier had fallen, and the enemy, with overwhelming forces, was penetrating into the country. At this gloomy juncture, John Langdon, a merchant of Portsmouth, and speaker of the assembly, thus addressed its members:—"I have three thousand dollars in hard money; I will pledge my plate for three thousand more; I have seventy hogsheads of Tobago rum, which shall be sold for the most it will bring. These are at the service of the state. If we succeed in defending our fire-sides and homes, I may be remunerated; if we do not, the property will be of no value to me. Our old friend Stark, who so nobly maintained the honor of our state at Bunker Hill, may be safely intrusted with the conduct of the enterprise, and we will check the progress of Burgoyne."

This proposal infused life into the measures of the assembly. They formed the whole militia of the state into two brigades. Of the first they gave the command to William Whipple, of the second to John Stark.*

* The exploits of Stark in the vicinity of Lake Champlain, in the last French war, have already been mentioned in these pages. At the close of the peace of 1763, he had returned to his farm in New Hampshire, where he resided until the opening of the Revolution. When the report of the battle of Lexington reached him, he was engaged at work in his saw-mill: fired with indignation and a martial spirit, he immediately seized his musket, and with a band of heroes proceeded to Cambridge. The morning after his arrival, he received a colonel's commission, and availing himself of his own popularity and the enthusiasm of the day, in two hours he enlisted eight hundred men. On the memorable 17th of June, at Breed's hill, Colonel Stark, at the head of his backwoodsmen of New Hampshire, poured on the enemy that deadly fire from a sure aim, which effected such remarkable destruction in their ranks, and compelled them twice to retreat. During the whole of this dreadful conflict, Colonel Stark evinced that consummate bravery and intrepid zeal, which entitle his name to perpetual remembrance. After the British evacuated Boston, Stark joined our northern army while retreating from Canada, and in 1776, he had command of the troops employed in fortifying the hill on the east side of Lake Champlain, opposite Ticonderoga. On the 8th of July, the Declaration of Independence was received and proclaimed to the army, who hailed it with shouts of applause. The hill upon which the regiment of Stark was stationed, was named Mount Independence in honor of the event which had just been proclaimed. Soon after, Stark joined General Washington, and was with him during that dark period when he fled before a haughty army through New Jersey. In the spring of 1777, he returned to New Hampshire on a recruiting expedition.

They ordered one fourth part of Stark's brigade and one fourth of three regiments of Whipple's to march immediately under the command of Stark, "to stop the progress of the enemy on our western frontiers."

Agreeably to his orders, Stark proceeded to Charleston; his men very readily followed; and as fast as they arrived, he sent them forward to join the troops under Colonel Warner, at Manchester. At that place he joined Warner with about eight hundred men. Schuyler repeatedly urged Stark to join the troops under his command; but he declined complying. He was led to this conduct not only by the reasons which have been mentioned, but by a difference of opinion as to the best method of opposing Burgoyne. Schuyler wished to collect all the American troops in the front, to prevent Burgoyne from marching on to Albany. Stark was of opinion that the surest way to check Burgoyne was to have a body of men on his rear, ready to fall upon him in that quarter, whenever a favorable opportunity should be presented. The New-England militia had not formed a high opinion of

---

Having filled his regiment, and while waiting orders, he learned that several junior officers had been promoted by congress, while he was left out of the list. Feeling greatly aggrieved, he resigned his commission and left the army, not, however, to desert his country in the hour of peril, for, like General Schuyler, he was active for good while divested of military authority. He was very popular, and the assembly of New Hampshire regarded him as a pillar of strength in upholding the confidence and courage of the militia of the state. When that body offered him the command of the new recruits, laying aside his private griefs, he once more hastened to the field, stipulating, however, that he should not be obliged to join the main army, but hang upon the wing of the enemy, strike when opportunity should offer, according to his own discretion, and be accountable to no one but the assembly of New Hampshire.

Schuyler as a general; and Stark meant to keep himself in a situation in which he might embrace any favorable opportunity for action, either in conjunction with him, or otherwise; Stark assured Schuyler that he would yield to any measure necessary to promote the public good, but wished to avoid a course that was not consistent with his own honor; and if it was thought necessary, he would march to his camp. He wrote particularly, that he would lay aside all private resentment, when it appeared in opposition to the public good. But in the midst of these protestations, he was watching for an opportunity to evince his courage and patriotism, by falling upon some part of Burgoyne's army.

While the American army was thus assuming a more respectable appearance, General Burgoyne was making very slow advances toward Albany. From the 28th of July, to the 15th of August, the British army was continually employed in bringing forward bateaux, provisions, and ammunition from Fort George to the nearest navigable part of Hudson river; a distance of not more than eighteen miles. The labor was excessive; the Europeans were but little acquainted with the methods of performing it to advantage, and the effect was in no degree equivalent to the expense of labor and time. With all the efforts that Burgoyne could make, encumbered with his artillery and baggage, his labors were inadequate to the purpose of supplying the army with provisions for its daily consumption, and the establishment of the necessary magazines. And after his utmost exertions for fifteen days, there were not above four days' provisions in store, nor above ten bateaux in the Hudson river. More effective measures to replenish his stores seemed necessary. Informed that the Americans had a large quantity of these, and of cattle and horses at Bennington and in the vicinity, he resolved to send a detachment of his army thither to capture them. Both Philips and Reidesel, the most experienced of his generals, were opposed to the measure; but Burgoyne, actuated by an overweening confidence in his strength, and deceived as to the extent of the royalist party in the colonies, dispatched Lieutenant-colonel Baum thither with five hundred Hessians, Canadians and tories, and one hundred Indians. Burgoyne's instructions to the commander of the expedition, dated August 9th, 1777, declared the objects to be to try the affections of the country, to disconcert the councils of the enemy, to mount Reidesel's dragoons, to complete Peters' corps [of leyalists,] and to obtain large supplies of cattle, horses and carriages. Baum was directed "to scour the country from Rockingham to Otter creek," to go down Connecticut river as far as Brattleborough, and to return by the great road to Albany, there to meet General Burgoyne, and to endeavor to make the country believe his corps was the advanced body of the general's army, who was to cross Connecticut river, and proceed to Boston. He ordered "that all officers, civil and military, acting under the congress, should be made prisoners." Baum was also instructed "to tax the towns where they halted with such articles as they wanted, and take hostages for the performance, &c.; to bring all horses fit to mount the dragoons to serve as battalion horses for the troops, with as many saddles and bridles as could be found." Burgoyne stipulated the number of horses to be brought at thirteen hundred at least, and more if they could be obtained, and directed them to be "tied in strings of ten each, in order that one man might lead ten horses."

On the 13th of August, information reached General Stark, that a party of Indians attached to Baum's force had been perceived at Cambridge, about twelve miles north-west from Bennington. He immediately detached Lieutenant-colonel Gregg with two hundred men, to stop their march. In the course of the night, he was advised by express, that a large body of the enemy, with a train of artillery, was in the rear of the Indians, in full march for Bennington. He immediately rallied his brigade, with all the militia which had collected at Bennington. Orders were at the same time dispatched to the officer in command of Colonel Warner's regiment at Manchester, to march that body of men down to Bennington, and an animated call was made upon all the neighboring militia. These various dispositions were carried promptly into effect.

On the morning of the 14th, Stark moved forward to the support of Colonel Gregg with the entire force under his command. At the distance of four or five miles, he met the colonel in full retreat, and the enemy within a mile of him. Stark instantly halted, and drew up his men in order of battle. The enemy, perceiving that he had taken a stand, immediately came to a halt on very advantageous ground, and there intrenched themselves. Unable to draw them from their position, he fell back for a mile, leaving only a small party to skirmish with the enemy. This was done with considerable effect. Thirty of their force, with two Indian chiefs, were killed or wounded, without any loss on the American side.

The following day, the 15th, was rainy, and nothing was attempted beyond skirmishing with the enemy. This was done with spirit, and the Indians began to desert the army of Colonel Baum, " because," as they said, "the woods were filled with Yankees." This respite enabled the enemy to complete their breastworks, to apprise General Burgoyne of their situation, and to ask for reinforcements. Colonel Breyman, with an additional body of German troops, was immediately detached to the assistance of Baum.

During the night, Colonel Symonds, with a body of Berkshire militia, arrived. Among them was the Rev. Mr. Allen, of Pittsfield, whose bellicose ardor was of the most glowing kind. Before daylight, and while the rain was yet falling, the impatient shepherd, who had many of his flock with him, went to Stark, and said, " General, the people of Berkshire have often been summoned to the field without being allowed to fight, and, if you do not now give them a chance, they have resolved never to come out again." " Well," said Stark, " do you wish to march now, while it is dark and raining?" "No, not just this moment," replied the minister of peace. "Then," said the general, " if the Lord shall once more give us sunshine, and I do not give you fighting enough, I'll never ask you to come out again." Sunshine did indeed come with the morrow, for at the opening of the dawn, the clouds broke away, and soon all nature lay smiling in the sunlight of a clear August morning; and "fighting enough" was also given to the parson and his men, for it was a day of fierce conflict. Mr. Allen was not the man to shrink from that bloody affray. He had ardently espoused the cause of freedom, and when, in anticipation of a battle at Bennington, the neighboring country was roused to arms, he used his influence to increase the band of patriots, and urged his congregation to hasten to the service of their country. But the company which was raised in his parish were, from some cause, retarded in their progress. Hearing of the delay, he proceeded immediately to join them, and accompanied them to Bennington. On the morning of the battle, his men would not prepare for the engagement until he had prayed to the God of armies "to teach their hands to war and their fingers to fight." When the opposing forces were about advancing toward each other, Mr. Allen, insensible to fear, proceeded so near to the British troops, that he could be distinctly seen and heard, and then called upon the enemy to prevent the effusion of blood by laying down their arms! He was answered by a discharge of musketry, and the log upon which he stood was pierced with bullets. Turning calmly to a friend who had followed him under cover of the breastwork formed by the log, he said, "Now give me a gun!" and he deliberately fired the first gun from the American ranks on that memorable occasion.

On the morning of the 16th, Stark made preparations for an attack. The German mercenaries, with their battery, were advantageously posted upon a rising ground at a bend in the Walloomscoick (a branch of the Hoosac) on its north bank. The ground fell off to the north and west, a circumstance of which Stark skillfully took advantage. Peters' corps of tories were intrenched on the other side of the stream, in lower ground, and nearly in front of the German battery. The little river that meanders through the scene of the action, is fordable in all places. Stark was encamped upon the same side of it as the Germans, but, owing to its serpentine course, it crossed his line of march twice on his way to their position. Their post was carefully reconnoitered at a mile's distance,* and the plan of attack was arranged in the following manner: Colonel Nichols, with two hundred men, was detached to attack the rear of the enemy's left, and Colonel Herrick, with three hundred men, to fall upon the rear of their right, with orders to form a junction before they made the assault. Colonels Hubbard and Stickney were also ordered to advance with two hundred men on their right and one hundred in front, to divert their attention from the real point of attack. The action commenced at three o'clock in the afternoon on the rear of the enemy's left, when Colonel Nichols, with great precision, carried into effect the dispositions of the commander. His example was followed by every other portion of the little army. General Stark himself moved forward slowly in front, till he heard the sound of the guns from Colonel Nichols' party, when he

---

* Before the commencement of the battle, Stark rode forward with Warner, to reconnoiter the enemy, and was fired at by a cannon. Stark exclaimed: "Those rascals know I am an officer; don't you see they honor me with a big gun as a salute?" His well known speech to his men was characteristic: "Boys, those are your enemies, the red-coats and tories! We must conquer them, or to-night Molly Stark will be a widow!"

rushed upon the tories, and in a few moments the action became general. "It lasted," says Stark, in his official report, "two hours, and was the hottest I ever saw. It was like one continued clap of thunder."*

* A soldier who was in the battle gave the following interesting account of it to the Rev. James Davie Butler: "We were marched round and round a circular hill till we were tired. Stark said it was to amuse the Germans. All the while a cannonade was kept up upon us from their breastwork. It hurt nobody, and it lessened our fear of the great guns. After a while I was sent, with twelve others, to lie in ambush on a knoll a little north, and watch for tories on their way to join Baum. Presently we saw six coming toward us, who, mistaking us for tories, came too near us to escape. We disarmed them and sent them, under a guard of three, to Stark. While I sat on the hillock, I espied one Indian whom I thought I could kill, and more than once cocked my gun, but the orders were not to fire. He was cooking his dinner, and now and then shot at some of our people.

"Between two and three o'clock the battle began. The Germans fired by platoons, and were soon hidden by smoke. Our men fired each on his own hook, aiming wherever they saw a flash. Few on our side had either bayonets or cartridges. At last I stole away from my post, and ran down to the battle. The first time I fired I put three balls into my gun. Before I had time to fire many rounds, our men rushed over the breastwork, but I and many others chased straggling Hessians in the woods. We pursued till we met Breyman with eight hundred fresh troops and larger cannon, which opened a fire of grape-shot. Some of the grape-shot riddled a Virginia fence near me: one struck a small white oak tree behind which I stood. Though it hit higher than my head, I fled from the tree, thinking it might be aimed at again. We skirmishers ran back till we met a large body of Stark's men, then faced about. I soon started for a brook I saw a few rods behind, for I had drank nothing all day, and should have died with thirst had I not *chewed a bullet* all the time. I had not gone a rod when I was stopped by an officer, sword in hand, and ready to cut me down as a runaway. On my complaining of thirst, he handed me his canteen, which was full of rum. I drank and forgot my thirst.

"But the enemy outflanked us, and I said to a comrade: 'We must run or they will have us.' He said: 'I will have one more fire first.' At

The Indians, alarmed at the prospect of being inclosed between the parties of Nichols and Herrick, fled at the commencement of the action, their main principle of battle array being to contrive or to escape an am-

that moment a major on a black horse rode along behind us, shouting: 'Fight on, boys; reinforcements close by.' While he was yet speaking, a grape-shot went through his horse's head and knocked out two teeth. It bled a good deal, but the major kept his seat and spurred on to encourage others. In five minutes we saw Warner's men hurrying to help us. They opened right and left of us, and half of them attacked each flank of the enemy, and beat back those who were just closing around us. Stark's men now took heart and stood their ground. My gun-barrel was by this time too hot to hold, so I seized the musket of a dead Hessian, in which my bullets went down easier than in my own. Right in front were the cannon, and seeing an officer on horseback waving his sword to the artillerymen, I fired at him twice. His horse fell. He cut the traces of an artillery horse, mounted him and rode off. I afterward heard that that officer was Major Skene.

"Soon the Germans ran and we followed. Many of them threw down their guns on the ground, or offered them to us, or kneeled, some in puddles of water. One said to me: *wir sind ein, bruder!* I pushed him behind me and rushed on. All those near me did so. The enemy beat a parley, minded to give up, but our men did not understand it. I came to one wounded man, flat on the ground, crying *water* or *quarter*. I snatched his sword out of his scabbard, and, while I ran on and fired, carried it in my mouth, thinking I might need it. The Germans fled by the road and in a wood each side of it. Many of their scabbards caught in the brush and held the fugitives till we seized them. We chased them till dark. Colonel Johnston, of Haverhill, wanted to chase them all night. Had we done so, we might have mastered them all, for they stopped within three miles of the battle-field. But Stark, saying he would run no risk of spoiling a good day's work, ordered a halt and return to quarters.

"I was coming back, when ordered by Stark himself, who knew me, as I had been one of his body-guard in Canada, to help draw off a field-piece. I told him I was worn out. His answer was: 'Don't seem to disobey; take hold, and if you can't hold out, slip away in the dark.' Before we had dragged the gun far, Warner rode near us. Some one, bush or an attack in the rear. The tories were soon driven over the river, and were thus thrown in confusion on the Germans, who were forced from their breastwork. Baum made a bold and resolute defense. The German dragoons, with the discipline of veterans, preserved their ranks unbroken, and, after their ammunition was expended, were led to the charge by their colonel with the sword; but they were overpowered and obliged to give way, leaving their artillery and baggage on the field.

They were well inclosed in two breastworks, which, owing to the rain on the 15th, they had constructed at leisure. But, notwithstanding this protection, with the advantage of two pieces of cannon, arms and ammu-

---

pointing to a dead man by the wayside, said to him: 'Your brother is killed.' 'Is it Jesse?' asked Warner; and when the answer was, yes, he jumped off his horse, stooped and gazed in the dead man's face, and then rode away without saying a word. On my way back I got the belt of the Hessian, whose sword I had taken in the pursuit. I also found a barber's pack, but was obliged to give up all my findings till the booty was divided. To the best of my remembrance, my share was four dollars and some odd cents. One tory with his left eye shot out, was led by me mounted on a horse who had also lost his left eye. It seems cruel now — it did not then.

"My company lay down and slept in a cornfield near where we had fought; each man having *a hill of corn for a pillow*. When I waked next morning I was so beaten out that I could not get up till I had rolled about a good while. After breakfast I went to see them bury the dead. I saw thirteen tories, mostly shot through the head, buried in one hole. Not more than a rod from where I fought, we found Captain McClary dead, and stripped naked. We scraped a hole with sticks and just covered him with earth. We saw many of the wounded who had lain out all night. Afterward we went to Bennington and saw the prisoners paraded. They were drawn up in one long line, the British foremost, then the Germans, next the Indians, and hindmost the tories."

nition in perfect order, and an auxiliary force of Indians, they were driven from their intrenchments by a band of militia just brought to the field, poorly armed, with few bayonets, without field-pieces, and with little discipline. The superiority of numbers, on the part of the Americans, will, when these things are considered, hardly be thought to abate any thing from the praise due to the conduct of the commander, or the spirit and courage of his men.

The enemy being driven from the field, the militia dispersed to collect the plunder. Scarcely had they done so, before intelligence was brought, that a large reinforcement from the British army was on the march, and within two miles' distance. This was the corps of Colonel Breyman, already mentioned, which had been dispatched by General Burgoyne, on receiving from Baum intelligence of his position. The rain of the preceding day and the badness of the roads had delayed his arrival; a circumstance which exercised an important influence on the fate of the battle. On the approach of Breyman's reinforcements, the flying party of Baum made a rally, and the fortune of the day was for a moment in suspense. Stark made an effort to rally the militia; but happily at this juncture Colonel Warner's regiment came up fresh and not yet engaged, and fell with vigor upon the enemy.

This regiment, since the battle fought at Hubbardton, had been stationed at Manchester. It had been reduced, by the loss sustained in that action, to less than two hundred men. Warner, their colonel, as we have seen, was at Bennington, and was with General Stark on the 14th. The regiment at Manchester was

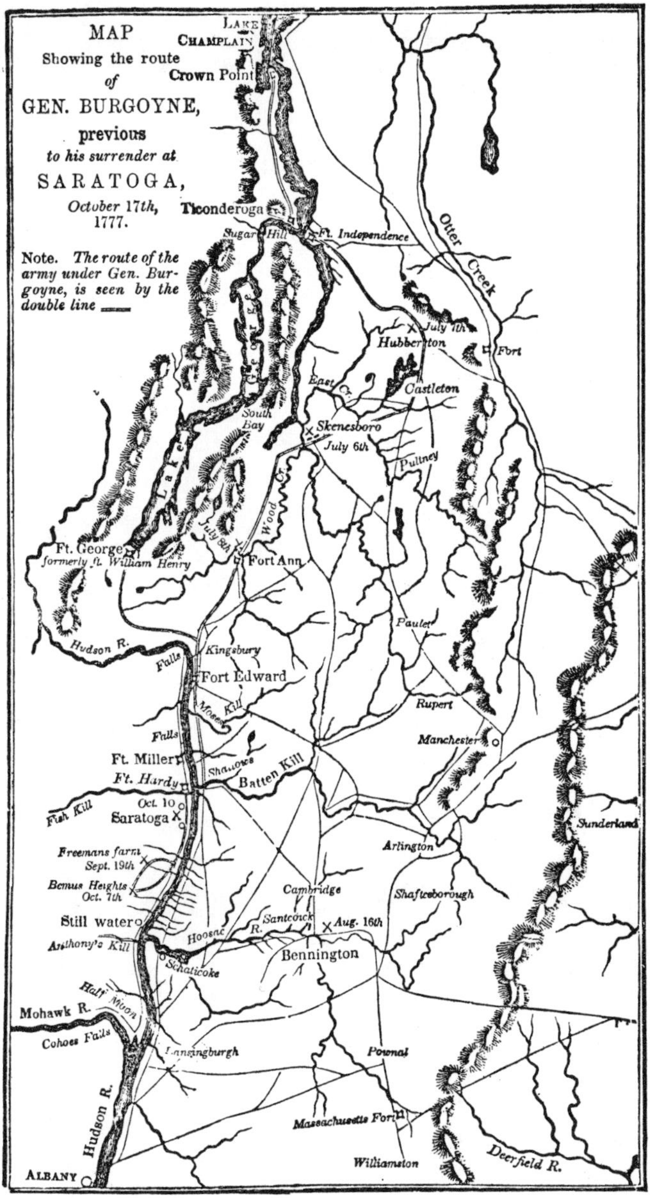
MAP
Showing the route
of
GEN. BURGOYNE,
previous
to his surrender at
SARATOGA,
October 17th,
1777.
Note. The route of the army under Gen. Burgoyne, is seen by the double line
LAKE CHAMPLAIN
Crown Point
Ticonderoga
Sugar Hill
Ft. Independence
Otter Creek
July 7th
Hubberton
Fort
East Cr.
Castleton
South Bay
Skenesboro
July 6th
Pultney
Lake
Wood Cr.
July 8th
Ft. George
formerly ft. William Henry
Fort Ann
Paulet
Hudson R.
Falls
Kingsbury
Fort Edward
Moses Kill
Rupert
Manchester
Falls
Ft. Miller
Shallows
Batten Kill
Ft. Hardy
Fish Kill
Oct. 10
Saratoga
Sunderland
Arlington
Freemans farm
Sept. 19th
Bemus Heights
Oct. 7th
Cambridge
Shaftesborough
Still water
Hoosac
Santcoick R.
Aug. 16th
Anthony's Kill
Bennington
Schaticoke
Half Moon
Mohawk R.
Cohoes Falls
Lansingburgh
Pownal
Hudson R.
Massachusetts Fort
Williamston
Deerfield R.
ALBANY

under the command of Major Samuel Safford. In consequence of the absence of a large number of the men on a scouting party, and other causes, it was not possible to put the regiment in motion on the 14th; on the 15th they marched for Bennington. Owing to the heavy rain of that day, it was near midnight when the troops arrived within a mile of Bennington. Fatigued with the march of the preceding day, their arms and equipments injured by the rain, and their ammunition scanty, a considerable portion of the ensuing day was exhausted, before the men could prepare themselves for battle. The first assault had been made in the manner described, and the enemy driven from the field, before this regiment came into action. At the most critical moment of the day, when the arrival of Breyman's reinforcement threatened a reverse of its good fortune, Warner's troops appeared in the field. Stark, with what men he had been able to rally, pushed forward to his assistance, and the battle was contested with great obstinacy on both sides till sunset, when the enemy were obliged to give way. General Stark pursued their flying forces till dark, and was obliged to draw off his men, to prevent them from firing upon each other under cover of night. "With one hour more of daylight," as he observes in his official report, "he would have captured the whole body." The fruits of the victory were four pieces of brass cannon, several hundred stand of arms, eight brass drums, a quantity of German broad-swords, and about seven hundred prisoners. Two hundred and seven were killed upon the spot; the number of the wounded was not ascertained. Colonel Baum was wounded and made a prisoner, but shortly after died of his wounds. The loss of the Americans was thirty killed and forty wounded. The general's horse was killed in the action.

Too much praise cannot be bestowed on the conduct of those who gained the battle of Bennington, officers and men. It is perhaps the most conspicuous example of the performance by militia of all that is expected of regular, veteran troops. The fortitude and resolution with which the lines at Bunker Hill were maintained, by recent recruits, against the assault of a powerful army of experienced soldiers, have always been regarded with admiration. But at Bennington, the hardy yeomen of New Hampshire, Vermont and Massachusetts, many of them fresh from the plough and unused to the camp, "advanced," as General Stark expressed it in his official letter, "through fire and smoke, and mounted breastworks that were well fortified, and defended with cannon."

Fortunately for the success of the battle, Stark was ably seconded by the officers under him; every previous disposition of his little force was most faithfully executed. He expresses his particular obligation to Colonels Warner and Herrick, "whose superior skill was of great service to him." Indeed, the battle was planned and fought with a degree of military talent and science which would have done no discredit to any service in Europe. A higher degree of discipline might have enabled the general to check the eagerness of his men to possess themselves of the spoils of victory; but his ability, even in that moment of dispersion, and under the flush of success, to meet and conquer a hostile reinforcement, evinces a judgment and resource not often equaled in partisan warfare.

In fact, it would be the height of injustice not to recognize, in this battle, the marks of the master mind of the leader, which makes good officers and good soldiers out of any materials, and infuses its own spirit into all that surround it. This brilliant exploit was the work of Stark, from its inception to its achievement. His popular name called the militia together. His resolute will obtained him a separate commission,— at the expense, it is true, of a wise political principle,— but on the present occasion, with the happiest effect. His firmness prevented him from being overruled by the influence of General Lincoln, which would have led him, with his troops, across the Hudson. How few are the men who, in such a crisis, would not merely not have sought, but actually have repudiated, a junction with the main army! How few, who would not only have desired, but actually insisted on taking the responsibility of separate action! Having chosen the burden of acting alone, he acquitted himself in the discharge of his duty, with the spirit and vigor of a man conscious of ability proportioned to the crisis. He advanced against the enemy with promptitude; sent forward a small force to reconnoiter and measure his strength; chose his ground deliberately and with skill; planned and fought the battle with gallantry and success.

The consequences of this battle were of great importance. It not only cost the army of Burgoyne more than one thousand of his best troops, but it wholly deranged the plan of his campaign, and materially contributed to the loss of his army. By advancing beyond Ticonderoga, his communication with the country in his rear was interrupted. He relied on these lateral excursions to keep the population in alarm, and to prevent their flocking to Gates. He also depended on procuring his supplies by such inroads into the country. The catastrophe of Baum's expedition, by which he hoped to furnish himself with an ample store of provisions collected at Bennington, disappointed that expectation, and compelled him to halt till he could procure them in detail from other quarters, and thus retarded his advance toward Albany for a month, during all which time the militia poured to the standard of General Gates, and placed him in a condition to compel the surrender of the British army.*

Five days after the battle of Bennington, congress being still ignorant of the transaction, a resolution was introduced to censure Stark for not submitting to the regulations of the continental army, and refusing obedience to its commander. Thereupon, a member from New Hampshire rose and expressed the belief that the first battle they should hear of at the north would be fought by Stark and the troops under his command, and that he was not afraid to stake his life or his honor on a wager that Stark's men would do as much as any equal number of troops in defense of their country. In a letter home, that gentleman said : "Judge of my feelings when the very next day I had a confirmation of all I had asserted, by an express from Schuyler, detailing the defeat of Baum and Breyman." The resolution of censure was immediately changed to one

* See Life of Stark by Edward Everett.

of thanks, accompanied with the appointment of Stark to be a brigadier-general in the army of the United States.

If Burgoyne was astonished when an antagonist he had never heard of thus unexpectedly defeated a body of his best troops, what would he have thought had he known that antagonist's history?—for, twenty-five years before, Stark had been a captive in Canada, and was ransomed for an Indian pony worth one hundred dollars! "The repulse on the banks of the Walloomscoik," says an eloquent Vermonter,[*] " plucked out the crowning keystone from that well-nigh finished arch, so that the whole structure cracked, crumbled by piecemeal, tottered and fell, a wreck of ruin, never to rise again." The result of the action was in exact accordance with the prophetic wish expressed by Washington in his letter to Schuyler, written only a few days previous. Washington, on hearing the joyful tidings of Stark's victory, said, " one more such stroke, and we shall have no great cause for anxiety as to the future designs of Britain."

The revolution wrought by this event, in Burgoyne's feelings, is betrayed by the contrast between his letters just before and just after the expedition. In the former he writes to the leader of the corps sent against Vermont : " Mount your dragoons, send me thirteen hundred horses, seize Bennington, cross the mountains to Rockingham and Brattleborough, try the affections of the country, take hostages, and meet me a fortnight hence in Albany." Four days *after* the battle he

---

[*] James Davie Butler, from whose Address on the Battle of Bennington, many of the facts in this narrative are derived.

writes to England: "The Hampshire Grants in particular, a country unpeopled and almost unknown in the last war, now abounds in the most active and rebellious race on the continent, and hangs like a gathering storm upon my left."* Burgoyne was far from overrating the influence of Stark's success. Within three days thereafter, Schuyler wrote to Stark: "The signal victory you have gained, and the severe loss the enemy have received, cannot fail of producing the most salutary result." Within a week, a hand-bill was issued at Boston, containing an exaggerated account of Stark's triumph; the news was there proclaimed by criers, and rung out from all the bells. Clinton wrote: "Since the affair at Bennington, not an Indian has been heard of · the scalping has ceased; indeed, I do not apprehend any great danger from the future operations of Mr. Burgoyne." Washington, writing to Putnam, was high in hope that New England, following the great stroke struck by Stark, would entirely crush Burgoyne; and a rumor that Burgoyne *was* crushed, raised the siege of Fort Stanwix, and broke his right wing. All this was within one week after Baum and Breyman

* An officer in Burgoyne's army, in allusion to the event, in a series of letters written to his friends in England, and afterward published, said: "The courage and obstinacy with which the Americans fought, were the astonishment of every one, and we now became fully convinced, they are not that contemptible enemy we had hitherto imagined them, incapable of standing a regular engagement, and that they would only fight behind strong and powerful works. If the other provinces enter as heartily into the cause of rebellion, I am afraid we shall find it a very difficult task to subdue them; for, exclusive of all the various modes of furnishing men and supplies, it is in these provinces, in some measure, become a religious cause, in which the people being enthusiasts, their clergy artfully increase a warlike spirit among their flocks."

were discomfited. In one day more a rumor was rife in New Hampshire that Burgoyne had been taken at Stillwater:

"As the sun,
Ere he be risen, sometimes paints his image
In the atmosphere, the shadows of great events
Precede the events, and in to-day already walks to-morrow."

The spoils taken by Stark, after his victory at Bennington, were equally distributed among his soldiers, and the prize-money given to each soldier was five dollars. Before thus dividing the spoils, Stark selected certain articles to be presented as trophies to the states of Vermont, New Hampshire, and Massachusetts, namely: for each state, one Hessian gun and bayonet, one broad-sword, one brass-barreled drum, and one grenadier's cap. These presents called forth from each of the states, a letter of thanks. The gift to Massachusetts is still suspended in the senate-chamber at Boston. Only a portion of Stark's present to his own state is preserved, while that given to Vermont, to commemorate his victory, has been lost. The cap of Colonel Baum was for many years worn to the legislature by the representative from Pownal, and his sword still hangs in the bar-room of a Bennington tavern. Baum's maps were long used by Stark as curtains in his log-cabin. The whole expense of Stark's brigade, in the achievement of a victory which secured the destruction of Burgoyne's army, was sixty-six thousand dollars; but, owing to the depreciation of continental money, only two thousand dollars were actually paid by congress.

The four pieces of cannon taken by Stark at Bennington were of Dutch manufacture. They were alternately in the hands of the British and Americans during the battle. Their history is somewhat singular. After the war, the following inscription was placed upon them: "Taken from the Germans at Bennington, August 16th, 1777." Thirty-five years afterward they were in the park of artillery which Hull surrendered with his army to the British at Detroit. The British fired their evening salute with them, and it was determined, and preparations were made, to have their history continued, by engraving upon them the inscription, "Retaken from the Americans, August 16th, 1812." But before this plan was executed, the cannon were again taken from the British at the capture of Fort George, and afterward removed to the arsenal at Washington, where they remained many years unclaimed and forgotten by the Vermonters, to whom they belonged. They were finally discovered by the Hon. Henry Stevens, the indefatigable Vermont antiquary, while at Washington in pursuit of documents connected with the early history of his native state, and upon his recommendation were claimed by Vermont, and cheerfully restored by congress. They now grace the principal hall of the Vermont statehouse, at Montpelier — a memento of the heroic patriotism of the Green-Mountain Boys of '76.

The German and British prisoners were conducted to Bennington, after the battle, and shut up in the meeting-house. As soon as the necessary arrangements could be made, they were removed to a place of greater security in Massachusetts. The tories being held in special abhorrence, were treated with considerable severity. They were bound two and two, like slaves in a coffle, and led by persons on horseback. The women of Bennington very cheerfully furnished all their bed-ropes to tie the prisoners with. The people gathered in crowds to see them as they passed. One of the British officers roughly addressed a very old lady, who was looking at them, "So, you old fool, you must come to see the lions." "Lions! lions!" replied the old lady, good-humoredly, "I declare, now, I think you look more like lambs."

The prisoners taken at Bennington were soon after joined by the whole of Burgoyne's army, who had fallen into the hands of Gates. They were taken to Cambridge, near Boston. A British officer, who was among the prisoners, tells the following anecdote of their journey thither. The spiteful manner in which he alludes to the New-England people, may be excused in consideration of his unfortunate position among them. "The lower class of the New-Englanders," says he, "are impertinently curious and inquisitive; at a house where Lord Napier was quartered, with other officers, a number of the inhabitants flocked to see a lord, imagining he must be something more than man; they were continually looking in at the window, and peeping at the room door, saying, 'I wonder which is the lord!' At last four women, intimate friends of the landlord, got into the room, when one of them, with a twang, peculiar to the New-Englanders, said: 'I hear you have got a lord among you; pray, now, which may he be?' His lordship, who, by the by, was all over mire, and scarcely dry from the heavy rain that had fallen during the day's march, whispered to an officer named Kemmis, whose turn for wit and jocularity was well known to the army. Kemmis accordingly got up, and pointing to his lordship, in a voice and manner as if he was herald-at-arms, informed them that 'that was the Right Honorable Francis Lord Napier, &c., &c., &c.,' going through all his lordship's titles, with a whole catalogue of additions; after he had finished, the women looked very attentively at his lordship, and while he and the other officers were laughing at the adroitness of Kemmis, the women got up, and one of them lifting up her hands and eyes to heaven, with great astonishment, exclaimed, 'Well, for my part, if that be a lord, I never desire to see any other lord but the Lord Jehovah,' and instantly left the room."

The same officer also relates the following affecting circumstance: "A few days since, walking out with some officers, we stopped at a house to purchase vegetables; while the other officers were bargaining with the woman of the house, I observed an elderly woman sitting by the fire, who was continually eyeing us, and every now and then shedding a tear. Just as we were leaving the house she got up, and bursting into tears, said, 'Gentlemen, will you let a poor, distracted woman speak a word to you before you go?' We, as you might naturally imagine, were all astonished, and upon inquiring what she wanted, with the most poignant grief and sobbing, as if her heart was on the point of breaking, asked if any of us knew her son, Colonel Francis, who was killed at the battle of Hubbardton? Several of us informed her, that we had seen him after he was dead. She then inquired about his pocket-book, and if any of his papers were safe, as some related to his estates, and if any of the soldiers had got his watch; if she could but obtain that in remembrance of her dear, dear son, she should be happy. Captain Ferguson, of our regiment, who was of the party, told her as to the colonel's papers and pocket-book, he was fearful they were either lost or destroyed ; but, pulling a watch from his fob, said, "There, good woman, if that can make you happy, take it, and God bless you." We were all much surprised, not knowing that he had made a purchase of it from a drum-boy. On seeing it, it is impossible to describe the joy and grief that was depicted in her countenance; I never, in all my life, beheld such a strength of passion ; she kissed it, looked unutterable gratitude at Captain Ferguson, then kissed it again ; her feelings were inexpressible ; she knew not how to express or shew them ; she would repay his kindness by kindness, but could only sob her thanks ; our feelings were lifted up to an inexpressible height ; we promised to search after the papers, and I believe, at that moment, could have hazarded life itself to have procured them."

The severe measures of General Burgoyne had roused the resentment and indignation of the New-England states; the prospect of success after the battle of Bennington, had increased their courage and animation; and the people were everywhere in motion. Finding that reinforcements were, and probably would be constantly arriving, General Lincoln determined to make a diversion in the rear of the enemy. He marched himself with the militia that had joined him, from Manchester to Pawlet. From thence, on September the thirteenth, he sent off Colonel Brown with five hundred men to the landing at Lake George, to destroy the British stores, and to release the American prisoners that had been collected at that place. Colonel Johnson was dispatched with the same number of men to Mount Independence. Johnson was to amuse and alarm the enemy at the north end of Lake George, while Brown was executing the business at the south end. If circumstances and opportunity favored, they were to join their troops, and the one was to attack Ticonderoga, and the other Mount Independence; but they were not to risk the loss of many men in these attempts. The same number of men were also sent on under Colonel Woodbridge, to Skenesborough; thence to Fort Anne, and so on to Fort Edward. The design was to alarm and divide the British forces and attention, by assaulting all their outposts and stations at the same time. With so much secrecy and address were these operations conducted, that by September the eighteenth, Brown had effectually surprised all the outposts between the landing-place at the north end of Lake George, and the body of the fortress at Ticonderoga. Mount Defiance, Mount Hope, the "French lines," and a block-house, with two hundred bateaux, an armed sloop, and several gun-boats, were almost instantly taken. Four companies of foot, with nearly an equal number of Canadians, and many of the officers and crews of the vessels, amounting in the whole to two hundred and ninety-three, were made prisoners; and at the same time they set at liberty one hundred Americans, who had been made prisoners, and were confined in some of those works. Encouraged by this success, they summoned General Powel, the British commander at Ticonderoga, to surrender that fortress; but after maneuvering four days, they found they were wholly unable to attempt the works either at Ticonderoga or Mount Independence; abandoning the design, they returned in safety to Lincoln's camp. By this well-conducted enterprise, the Americans had alarmed the enemy on the lakes, captured a considerable number of their men and vessels, recovered the continental standard which they had left when they abandoned Ticonderoga, and returned to their camp with scarcely any loss to themselves.

Meanwhile, General Burgoyne, having collected about thirty days' provisions, and thrown a bridge of boats over the Hudson, crossed that river on the 13th and 14th of September, and encamped on the heights and plains of Saratoga. General Gates, who had recently taken the chief command of the northern department of the American army, advanced toward the British, and encamped three miles above Stillwater. On the night of the 17th, Burgoyne encamped within four miles of the American army; and about noon on the 19th advanced in full force against it. The right wing was commanded by General Burgoyne, and covered by General Fraser and Colonel Breyman with the grenadiers and light infantry, who were posted along some high grounds on the right. The front and flanks were covered by Indians, provincials, and Canadians. The left wing and artillery were commanded by Major-generals Phillips and Reidesel, who proceeded along the great road. Colonel Morgan, who was detached to observe their motions, and to harass them as they advanced, soon fell in with their pickets in front of their right wing, attacked them sharply, and drove them in. A strong corps was brought up to support them, and, after a severe encounter, Morgan was compelled to give way; but a regiment was ordered to assist him, and the action became more general. The commanders on both sides supported and reinforced their respective parties; and about four o'clock, Arnold, with nine continental regiments and Morgan's corps, was completely engaged with the whole right wing of the British army. The engagement began at three o'clock in the afternoon, and continued till after sunset, when the Americans thought proper to retire, and leave the British masters of the field of battle. The loss on each side was nearly equal, six hundred being killed and wounded on the part of the British, and the same number on the side of the Americans. No advantages resulted to the British troops from this encounter; while the conduct of the Americans fully convinced every one that they were able to sustain an attack in open plains with the intrepidity, the spirit, and the coolness of veterans. For four hours they maintained a contest hand to hand; and when they retired, it was not because they were conquered, but because the approach of night made a retreat to their camp absolutely necessary.* Both armies lay some

* In a history of Burgoyne's campaign, written by an officer of his army, the following examples of the heroism and devoted patriotism of the Americans are given. A soldier who had been badly wounded was taken prisoner by the Indians, and carried before General Fraser, who made inquiries of him in regard to the condition of the American army. "But he would give no answer to any question," says the British officer, "and behaved in the most undaunted manner. The general, imagining that by shewing him attention he might gain some information from

time in sight of each other, each fortifying its camp in the strongest manner possible. Meanwhile, the difficulties of the British general were daily increasing; his auxiliary Indians deserted him soon after the battle of Stillwater; and his army, reduced to little more than five thousand men, was limited to half the usual allowance of provisions; the stock of forage was also entirely exhausted, and his horses were perishing in

him, ordered him some refreshment, and when the surgeon had examined his wound, told him he must immediately undergo an amputation, which being performed, he was requested to keep himself still and quiet, or a lock-jaw would inevitably ensue; to this he replied with great firmness, 'then I shall have the pleasure of dying in a good cause, that of gaining independence to the American colonies.' I mention this circumstance, to show how cheerfully some of them will sacrifice their lives in pursuit of this favorite idol. Such was the man's restless disposition, that he actually died the next morning."

Another prisoner was interrogated by General Fraser. The soldier would give no other answer than that the American army was commanded by General Gates. Fraser, exceedingly provoked because he could gain no intelligence, told him if he did not immediately inform him as to the exact situation of the American army, he would hang him up directly; the soldier, with the most undaunted firmness, replied, "Then you must hang me, for I will not betray my country." Fraser's threat was not executed.

While the British camp was on the north side of the Fish Creek, a number of the officers' horses were let loose in the meadows to feed. An expert swimmer among the Americans who swarmed upon the hills east of the Hudson, obtained permission to go across and capture one of the horses. He swam the river, seized and mounted a fine bay gelding, and in a few moments was recrossing the stream unharmed, amid a volley of bullets from a party of British soldiers. Shouts greeted him as he returned; and, when rested, he asked permission to go for another, telling the captain that *he* ought to have a horse to ride as well as a private. Again the adventurous soldier was among the herd, and, unscathed, returned with an exceedingly good match for the first, and presented it to his commander.

great numbers; the American army had become so augmented as to render him diffident of making good his retreat; and, to aggravate his distress, no intelligence had yet been received of the approach of General Clinton, or of any diversion in his favor from New York. In this exigency, General Burgoyne resolved to examine the possibility of dislodging the Americans from their posts on the left, by which means he would be enabled to retreat to the lakes. For this purpose he drew out fifteen hundred men, whom he headed himself, attended by Generals Phillips, Reidesel and Fraser. This detachment had scarcely formed, within less than half a mile of the American intrenchments, when they made a furious attack, which, though bravely resisted, was decidedly to the advantage of the assailants. General Burgoyne now became convinced that it was impossible to conduct any further offensive operations, and endeavored to make good his retreat to Fort George. Artificers were accordingly dispatched, under a strong escort, to repair the bridges, and open the roads, but they were compelled to make a precipitate retreat. The situation of his army becoming every hour more hazardous, he resolved to attempt a retreat by night to Fort Edward; but even this retrograde movement was rendered impracticable. While the army was preparing to march, intelligence was received that the Americans had already possessed themselves of the fort, and that they were well provided with artillery. No avenue to escape now appeared. Incessant toil and continual engagements had worn down the British army; its provisions were nearly exhausted, and there were no means of procuring a supply; while the American army, which was daily increasing, was already much greater than the British in point of numbers, and almost encircled them. In this extremity, the British general called a council of war; and it was unanimously resolved to enter into a convention with General Gates. Preliminaries were soon settled, and the royal army, to the number of five thousand seven hundred and fifty, surrendered prisoners of war.

The capture of an entire army was justly viewed as an event that must essentially affect the contest between Great Britain and America; and while it excited the highest joy among the Americans, it could not but have a most auspicious influence on their affairs in the cabinet and in the field. The thanks of congress were voted to General Gates and his army; and a medal of gold, in commemoration of this splendid achievement, was ordered to be struck, to be presented to him by the president, in the name of the United States.

After the surrender of Burgoyne, the garrison left by him at Ticonderoga retreated into Canada. They were pursued by fifty Green-Mountain Rangers, who captured forty-nine of their number, together with horses, cattle, and boats in great numbers. Previous to the retreat of the British from Ticonderoga, a Vermonter, named Richard Wallace, swam across the lake, through a hostile fleet, for the purpose of learning the strength of the forces there, as an attack was contemplated by Warner and Herrick. This act of daring was equal to a story of another Green-Mountain hero one Johnson, who, at the battle of Bennington, met a file of German soldiers in the woods, and, having no other weapon than a club, wrenched the file-leader's sword from his grasp, and compelled the whole party to surrender themselves prisoners of war. A grandson[*] of that hero still keeps the Hessian blade thus bravely won.

The brave and hardy inhabitants of the Green Mountains, who thus nobly stood forth in defense of their country, had other difficulties than those inseparable from the war with the mother country to encounter. Not having been recognized as an independent state, they were deprived of a regular government, under which they could act with system and effect. They had, at first, no rallying point, and no bond of union, save a common interest to resist the claims of New York, as they had subsequently no other tie than that of a common determination to resist the invasion of the British forces. However, the necessity which drove them to resistance, gave the effect of law to the recommendations of their conventions and committees; while a few bold and daring spirits, as if formed for the occasion, gave energy and system to their movements. But a better organization was obviously needed, to sustain a protracted conflict. The change produced by the Declaration of Independence in the relations between Great Britain and her colonies, rendered the importance of this course still more imperative. The people had, as we have seen, originally purchased their lands under royal grants from the governor of New Hampshire. But New York claimed the jurisdiction and right of soil, and insisted that the occupants of the lands should repurchase them, and at exorbitant rates.

[*] Rev. Charles Johnson, of Locke, Cayuga County, New York

The settlers had petitioned the crown for redress, and while they were encouraged with indications favorable to their rights, the connection between the crown and contending parties was suddenly dissolved. There no longer remained, therefore, any earthly power, recognized by the parties as a *superior*, possessing the right of settling the controversy. This state of things could not fail to suggest to the settlers the expediency of declaring themselves independent. Having never submitted to the authority of New York, and finding no safety for their dearest rights in doing so, they considered the time had arrived, as they no longer acknowledged allegiance to the British crown, when a regard for their own safety required, and justice sanctioned, their formal assumption of the powers of self-government. Accordingly, toward the close of the year 1775, a number of individuals repaired to Philadelphia, where the continental congress was then in session, desiring the advice of that body as to the course they should pursue. No formal action was taken by congress, although several of its prominent members recommended a separate state organization. A convention of delegates from thirty-five towns accordingly assembled at Dorset, July 24th, 1776; but for the purpose of more thoroughly obtaining the views of the people, adjourned to the 25th of the following September. By the adjourned meeting, it was unanimously resolved "to take suitable measures, as soon as may be, to declare the New-Hampshire Grants a free and separate district."

In January, 1777, another convention was held at Westminster, which finally adopted the following

DECLARATION OF INDEPENDENCE.

"In convention of the Representatives from the several counties and towns of the New Hampshire Grants, holden at Westminster, January 15, 1777, by adjournment.

Whereas, the Honorable the Continental Congress did, on the 4th day of July last, declare the United Colonies in America to be free and independent of the crown of Great Britain; which declaration we most cordially acquiesce in. And whereas by the said declaration, the arbitrary acts of the crown are null and void, in America. Consequently, the jurisdiction by said crown granted to New York government over the people of the New Hampshire Grants is totally dissolved.

We therefore, the inhabitants, on said tract of land, are at present without law or government, and may be truly said to be in a state of nature; consequently a right remains to the people on said Grants, to form a Government best suited to secure their property well being and happiness. We the delegates from the several counties and towns on said tract of land, bounded as follows: South on the north line of Massachusetts Bay; East on Connecticut River; North on Canada line; West as far as the New Hampshire Grants extend: After several adjournments for the purpose of forming ourselves into a distinct separate State, being assembled at Westminster, do make and publish the following DECLARATION, viz:

"That we will at all times hereafter, consider ourselves as a free and independent State, capable of regulating our internal police, in all and every respect whatsoever. And that the people of said Grants have the sole and exclusive, and inherent right of ruling and governing themselves, in such manner and form as in their own wisdom shall think proper, not inconsistent to any resolve of the Honorable Continental Congress.

Furthermore, we declare by all the ties which are held sacred among men, that we will firmly stand by and support one another in this our declaration of a State, and endeavoring as much as in us lies to suppress unlawful routs and disturbances whatever. Also we will endeavor to secure to every individual his life, peace and property, against all invaders of the same.

Lastly, we hereby declare, that we are at all times ready, in conjunction with our brethren in the United States of America, to do our full proportion in maintaining and supporting the just war, against the tyrannical invasions of the ministerial fleets and armies, as well as any other foreign enemies, sent with express purpose to murder our fellow brethren, and with fire and sword to ravage our defenceless country.

The said State hereafter to be called by the name of New Connecticut."

At another convention, held in June, 1777, the name of New Connecticut was changed to VERMONT. Information of this important step was transmitted to congress, with the assurance that the people of Vermont "were at all times ready, in conjunction with their brethren in the United States, to contribute their full proportion towards maintaining the present just war, against the fleets and armies of Great Britain." They also sent a deputation to Philadelphia to solicit congress to recognize their existence as an independent state, and admit their delegates to seats in the national legislature. New Hampshire readily consented to the separate independence of Vermont; Connecticut and Massachusetts gave it their approval; but New York remonstrated against the measure, and even insisted that congress should recall the commission granted to the noble Warner, who was denounced as an outlaw and insurgent. This remonstrance had its effect upon congress, and the application for the recognition of the independence of Vermont, was peremptorily dismissed.

While this subject was before congress, the people of Vermont were engaged in forming a constitution. A convention, chosen for this purpose, met at Windsor the second of July. The draft of a constitution was prepared, and the convention were deliberating upon its provisions when the intelligence of the evacuation of Ticonderoga was received. "The frontiers," says Ira Allen in his History of Vermont, "were exposed to the inroads of the enemy. The family of the president of the convention, as well as those of many other members, were exposed to the foe. In this awful crisis, some were for leaving precipitately; but a severe thunder-storm came on, and during the rain, they had time to reflect; while other members, less alarmed at the news, called the attention of the whole to finish the constitution, which was then reading for the last time. The constitution was read through; the convention proceeded to appoint a council of safety to conduct the business of the state, and adjourned without day.

"The members of the council of safety, appointed as aforesaid, agreed to meet and form at Manchester, where they repaired without loss of time. Colonel Thomas Chittenden was elected president, and Mr. Ira Allen (then twenty-seven years old) secretary to said convention. The council of safety had no public money, nor had they any authority to lay taxes, or credit, as a public body, to make or borrow money to answer the necessities of government. The government was in its infancy, and all expenses were supported at private expense. The council were generally men of small property, yet in this situation, it became necessary to raise men for the defense of the frontiers, with bounties and wages. Ways and means were to be found out; and the day was spent in debating on the subject. Nathan Clark, Esq., not convinced of the practicability of raising a regiment, moved in council, that Mr. Ira Allen, (the youngest member of the council, who insisted on raising a regiment, while a large majority of the council were for only two companies of sixty men each) might be appointed a committee, to discover ways and means to raise, arm and support a regiment, and to make his report at sunrise, on the morrow. The council acquiesced, and Mr. Allen took the matter into consideration, and spent the night alone in concerting plans; and he reported the ways and means, viz: that the council should appoint commissioners of sequestration, with authority to seize the goods and chattels of all persons who had, or should join the common enemy; that all movable property so seized should be sold at public vendue, and the proceeds paid to a treasurer, to be appointed by the council, for the purpose of paying a bounty of ten dollars, and one month's pay in advance."

This is said to have been the first instance of the seizure of the property of the tories for the defense of the country, although the practice was afterward adopted by all the states. This energetic measure enabled the council of safety to bring a regiment of hardy mountaineers into the field. They appealed to New Hampshire for aid. Stark was promptly sent to their assistance—the battle of Bennington was fought—Burgoyne's expected supplies were thereby cut off, and the surrender of his army to Gates became inevitable.

Previous to the adjournment of the convention which framed the state constitution, the first election of officers was directed to be held in December, 1777; but the military movements in that vicinity rendered its postponement necessary. In March, 1778, Thomas Chittenden was elected governor, and Ira Allen secretary.

THOMAS CHITTENDEN was born January 6, 1730, at Guilford, Conn. His father being a farmer, in moderate circumstances, the subject of this memoir received no other education than that afforded by the common school in Guilford. Until the eighteenth year of his age he was employed on his father's farm; but being of an active and adventurous temperament, he engaged in a mercantile enterprise, and made a voyage to the West Indies. But England being then at war with France, the vessel in which he had embarked was captured by a cruiser of the latter country, and he was landed on a West-India island, without friends or resources. He finally reached home, after undergoing much suffering and fatigue. At the age of twenty he married Elizabeth Meigs, removed to Salisbury, and by his industry and energy, soon acquired a considerable fortune. He was then appointed a justice of the peace, a colonel of the militia, and represented the town of Salisbury in the Connecticut legislature from 1765 to 1772. Having purchased a large tract of land on the Winooski river, he removed to the New-Hampshire Grants in the spring of 1774, and in a short period was surrounded with all the comforts that wealth could bestow. At this time the war of the Revolution commenced, and Mr. Chittenden, with several other persons, repaired to Philadelphia to learn the views of the members of the continental congress, in regard to the momentous crisis then impending, and to receive advice as to the manner in which the people occupying the New-Hampshire Grants, could, in their peculiar position, most effectually serve the cause of freedom.

Upon the retreat of the American army from Canada, in the spring of 1776, the frontier settlements were exposed to the enemy, and Mr. Chittenden found it necessary to abandon his pleasant home, and remove his family to Massachusetts. After doing this, he entered with much zeal into the measures adopted to impede the progress of the enemy, and was appointed the first president of the committee of safety at Bennington. Entering with deep interest into the controversy with New York respecting the titles of the lands in the New-Hampshire Grants, and being more acquainted with public business than any of the settlers, in consequence of the offices which he had held in his native state, he was universally regarded as the man most suitable to be placed at the head of their operations. Mr. Chittenden perceived that the general struggle for independence, in which the colonies were now engaged, presented a favorable opportunity for terminating the controversy with New York, by erecting the disputed territory into a new state, and establishing a separate government; and having adopted this decisive plan of sound policy, he steadily pursued it, till he saw the independence of Vermont acknowledged by the neighboring states and by the general government.

He was a member of the first convention of delegates from the several townships, which met at Dorset, September 25, 1776, for the purpose of taking into consideration the expediency of declaring Vermont an independent state; and at the subsequent meeting of the convention at Westminster, January 25, 1777, he was one of the committee who draughted the declaration of independence, which was there adopted; and also a member of another committee, which, at that time, petitioned congress, praying that body to acknowledge

Vermont a free and independent state. He assisted in forming the first constitution of Vermont, which was adopted by the convention, July 2d, 1777, and in 1778 he was elected the first governor of Vermont, which office he held, with the exception of one year, till his death.*

Governor Chittenden possessed in an eminent degree, precisely those qualifications which fitted him for the sphere in which he was called upon to act. He had not, indeed, enjoyed many of the advantages of education, but his want of education was amply compensated by the possession of a strong and active mind, which, at the time he emigrated to Vermont, was matured by age, practiced in business, and enriched by a careful observance of men and things. His knowledge was practical rather than theoretic. He was regular in his habits — plain and simple in his manners — averse to ostentation in equipage or dress, and he cared little for the luxuries, the blandishments or the etiquette of refined society. In short, though he was destitute of many of the qualifications now deemed essential in a statesman, he possessed all that were necessary, and none that were superfluous, in the times in which he lived, and was probably far better fitted to be the leader and governor of the independent, dauntless and hardy, but uncultivated settlers of Vermont, than would have been a man of more theoretic knowledge, or polite accomplishments.

Ira Allen, who was chosen the first secretary of state, had also been the secretary of the committee of

---

* History of Vermont, by Rev. Zadock Thompson — a most able and elaborate work.

safety, and as such, performed services of incalculable benefit to the country. Many of the inhabitants of the Green Mountains sanctioned the policy of the British crown, in opposition to the interests of the colonies, and on the approach of Burgoyne; hundreds of them fled to his camp. The whole country was in the utmost consternation. Successful resistance to the triumphant march of the haughty Briton was scarcely hoped for. The committee of safety at Bennington were about to give up in despair. The committee were destitute of means, and yet Allen insisted that they should enlist a regiment to aid the army of freedom. But how were the men to be paid? how armed? Ira Allen shrunk not from the question. "We must use the means of those who have gone over to the enemy, to defend ourselves against them," said he. The measure was adopted, the regiment was raised, arms and ammunition were procured, and at Bennington, "that cluster of poor cottages," as Burgoyne denominated it, was fought the battle which rendered the ultimate surrender of the British army inevitable. "Let us turn," says a distinguished Vermont author,[*] in describing the members of the committee of safety, "Let us turn to the youthful secretary of the council, Ira Allen. So much the junior of his colleagues was he, that a spectator might well wonder why he was selected as one of such a sage body. But those who procured his appointment knew full well why they had done so; and his history thenceforward was destined to prove a continued justification of their opinion. Both in form

[*] Daniel P. Thompson, Esq., in his popular historical novel, entitled "The Rangers."

and feature, he was one of the handsomest men of his day; while a mind, at once versatile, clear and penetrating, with perceptions as quick as light, was stamped on his Grecian brow, or found a livelier expression in his flashing black eyes, and other lineaments of his intellectual countenance. Such, as he appeared for the first time on the stage of public action, was the afterward noted Ira Allen, whose true history, when written, will show him to have been either secretly or openly the originator or successful prosecutor of more important political measures, affecting the interests and independence of the state, and the issue of the war in the northern department, than any other individual in Vermont; making him, with the many peculiar traits he possessed, one of the most remarkable men of the times in which he so conspicuously figured."

Many difficulties attended the establishment of the new government. Congress had disapproved of the Vermont declaration of independence, and New York vigorously resisted the movement. The Vermonters, in the expectation of increasing their strength, incautiously admitted another occasion of embarrassment to the adjustment of the serious controversy in which they were involved. The original charter under which New Hampshire was settled, was limited to a margin of sixty miles in width along the sea-coast. But the jurisdiction of the colony was afterward extended westward to the Connecticut river, and Governor Wentworth even claimed jurisdiction to Lake Champlain. Sixteen townships, situated on the east side of the Connecticut, but within the limits of the original charter, applied to the Vermont legislature for admission into their new state. The application was made in March, 1778. The people on the east side of the Green Mountains were ardently in favor of the measure, and as it was represented to the legislature that the persons inhabiting the sixteen townships almost unanimously approved of the proposed union, the subject was referred to the people. In June the legislature again met, and as a majority of the towns composing the state of Vermont had declared in favor of the union, the legislature gave its formal consent to the measure. New Hampshire at once protested against the dismemberment of its territory, and appealed to congress for protection.

In the mean time, Ethan Allen had been exchanged for an officer taken at the capture of Burgoyne, and, after having visited Washington at Valley Forge, had returned to his beloved Green-Mountain companions, and was welcomed home amid universal rejoicings. Congress, not unmindful of his services, granted him a brevet commission of colonel in the continental army, "in reward of his fortitude, firmness and zeal in the cause of his country, manifested in the course of his long and cruel captivity, as well as on former occasions." Allen, on his return to Vermont, was appointed general and commander-in-chief of the militia of the state. The people of Vermont having seen their error in becoming a party to the dismemberment of New Hampshire, General Allen was appointed a special agent to visit Philadelphia and counteract the unfavorable feeling in congress respecting the independence of Vermont, occasioned by its course toward a sister state. The delicate duties of this mission Allen performed with consummate tact, and on his return to his constituents, urged them to recede from the union with a portion of New Hampshire, expressing the assurance that should they do so, congress would recognize their independence. The legislature met at Windsor, in October, and in compliance with Allen's recommendation, receded from the union with the towns east of the Connecticut river. The members from these towns withdrew from the legislature, and were followed by a number of others representing the east side of the Green Mountains, and these afterward occasioned the administration much trouble.

During the occurrence of these events, Governor Clinton, of New York, issued a proclamation claiming jurisdiction over Vermont, but confirming the title of the settlers to the lands which had been granted by the governor of New Hampshire. Many persons were eager to acquiesce in the jurisdiction of New York upon these conditions. But Allen prepared an answer to the proclamation of Clinton, stating the grounds of the claims of Vermont to the right of self-government, and exhorting the people not to relax for a moment their efforts to attain the end for which they had struggled so long and so hard. This address had a powerful effect upon the Vermonters, and doubtless prevented the dissolution of the state government.

It should be said to the praise of Allen, considering the scenes he had passed through, that on no occasion did he encourage or countenance laxness in government, or disobedience to the laws and magistrates, recognized as such by the people themselves. "Any one," he remarks, "who is acquainted with mankind and things, must know, that it is impossible to manage the political matters of this country without the assistance of civil government. A large body of people destitute of it, is like a ship at sea, without a helm or mariner, tossed by the impetuous waves. We could not enjoy domestic peace and security, set aside the consequences of a British war and the New-York strife, without civil regulations. The two last considerations do, in the most striking manner, excite us to strengthen and confirm the government already set up by the authority of the people, which is the fountain of all temporal power, and from which the subjects of the state of Vermont have already received such signal advantages." These sentiments he avowed repeatedly, and even when he was stirring up and leading out the mobs of Bennington, he always declared it was in self-defense, the result of a necessity forced upon them by their enemies; and he never ceased to recommend order, good faith, and submission to the laws, as essential to the prosperity and happiness of the community.

This desire on the part of Allen to maintain good order in society by adherence to the law, is happily illustrated by an occurrence which took place soon after his return from captivity. One David Redding had been accused of supplying the enemy on the lakes with provisions, and was charged with several other acts unfriendly to the country. He was at first tried by a jury of *six* persons and convicted, and was sentenced to be executed on the sixth day of June, 1778. In the mean time, John Burnam, an attorney at law, who had recently arrived from Connecticut, with Blackstone' Commentaries in his saddle-bags, appeared before the council of safety and showed them that Redding's conviction had been irregular, inasmuch as no man could be legally convicted of a capital crime, but by the verdict of twelve jurymen. The council, perceiving their error, granted a new trial. But the curiosity which, not much to the honor of human nature, has ever been manifested on such occasions, was on this, greatly heightened by the fact that no execution had ever taken place in Vermont. To this curiosity was added the strong feeling of indignation which such a crime as that of Redding was calculated to excite at that period. The intelligence that a new trial had been granted was received at the moment when the excited throng were collecting to witness the execution. With such a multitude and on such an occasion, it was useless to talk of law. They had pronounced the culprit guilty, and were not in a mood to reflect upon the motive for setting aside the verdict of the whole community with so little ceremony. The excited populace were preparing to seize the prisoner, regardless of the reprieve which had been granted, and unceremoniously hang him. Upon this, Ethan Allen pressed through the crowd, mounted a stump, and waving his hat, exclaimed in thundering tones, "Attention the whole!" Silence was at once restored, for all were eager to hear what he would say. He then proceeded to announce the reasons which had produced the reprieve — advised the multitude to depart peaceably to their habitations, and return on the day fixed for the execution by the council of safety, adding with a tremendous oath, "You shall see somebody hung, at all events; for if Redding is not then hung, I will be hung myself." The crowd quietly dispersed, and after having been a second time convicted, Redding was finally executed.*

Levi, one of Ethan Allen's brothers, joined the tories and fled with them to Canada. This greatly incensed Ethan, and he applied to the proper authorities for the confiscation of his brother's property for the benefit of the state.† Levi heard of this, and challenged his brother to fight a duel! This Ethan refused to do, on the ground that it would "be disgraceful to fight a tory!" Levi afterward abandoned the royal cause, and became a staunch patriot.

* Another anecdote, illustrative of Allen's character, may be appropriately narrated here, and, like the above, is undoubtedly authentic. Allen was for a short time a resident of Tinmouth, Vt. On one occasion while at the house of the village physician, a lady entered to have a tooth extracted; but as often as the physician attempted to apply his instrument to the offending tooth, the lady's courage failed. Allen, who was an uneasy spectator, at length said to the physician, "Here, Doctor, take out one of my teeth." "But your teeth are all sound," said the physician, after carefully examining his molars and incisors. "Never mind — do as I direct you," said Allen; and there was suddenly a gap in his array of ivory. "Now take courage, madam, from the example I have given you," said Allen to the trembling lady. Pride overcame her fears, and she was soon relieved of her apprehensions of pain, and of her tooth also.

† The following is a literal copy of Ethan Allen's complaint concerning his brother:

BENNINGTON COUNTY, ss.—*Arlington, 9th of January,* 1779.

To the Honorable the Court of Confiscation, comes Col. Ethan Allen, in the name of the freemen of this State, and complaint makes that Levi Allen, late of Salisbury, in Connecticut, is of tory principles, and holds in fee, sundry tracts and parcels of land in this State. The said Levi has been detected in endeavoring to supply the enemy on Long Island, and in attempting to circulate counterfeit continental currency, and is guilty of holding treasonable correspondence with the enemy, under cover of doing favours to me, when a prisoner at New-York, and Long Island; and in talking, and useing influence in favour of the enemy, associating

After the surrender of Burgoyne, the southern states became the theater of the important operations of the British, leaving no opportunity for the American troops to distinguish themselves in the north. Warner, with the Green-Mountain Rangers, was in constant service on the Hudson river and elsewhere, as the exigencies of the country required, and always met the expectations of the great Washington. The indefatigable exertions of Warner in the cause of freedom, and the constant exposure and fatigue to which he was subjected, undermined his constitution, and he returned to his family at Bennington, toward the close of the war, a dying man. Disease in an aggravated form had struck its fangs into his system. But he bore the distressing maladies of his last days with unbounded fortitude. His agonies were solaced by the reflection that he had discharged his duty to his country, and had successfully struggled to obtain her freedom. He was saddened, however, by the reflection that his wife and three children would be left in destitute circumstances. The lands which he once owned, had, while he was engaged in active service at the head of his regiment, been

with inimical persons to this country, and with them monopolizing the necessaries of life, in endeavoring to lessen the credit of the continental currency, and in particular, hath exerted himself in the most falacious manner, to injure the property and character of some of the most zealous friends to the independency of the United States, and of this State likewise ; all which inimical conduct is against the peace and dignity of the freemen of this State : I therefore pray the Honorable Court to take the matter under their consideration, and make confiscation of the estate of said Levi before mentioned, according to the laws and customs of this State in such case made and provided.

ETHAN ALLEN.

sold for taxes. So much had he been engrossed by his duties as a patriot, that he thought not of saving his own property while the freedom of his beloved country was endangered. He was not permitted to die in his senses. Prior to his decease, he was the victim of a raging delirium; and, in his wild imaginings, fancied himself at the head of his regiment of Rangers, and, on his dying couch, restrained by a constant guard of able-bodied men, he would fight his battles over again. The preternatural strength with which he was endowed, decreased, at last, with the progress of his insidious malady; and the skillful botanist, whose prescriptions had prolonged the lives of others, could not restore his own reason or save his own life. The practiced huntsman, the sinews of whose gigantic frame were hardened in the hunting-grounds of Vermont, and who had never feared the face of any man, paled and trembled before the grim visage of that huntsman whose name is Death.— His earthly doom was finally sealed! His earthly sands had run out! He obeyed the mandate to join the majority — *abiit ad plures* — and was gathered to his fathers in the prime of life — " ere his eye was dim or his natural force abated." The gold was refined and the crucible was broken! The toil-worn body was laid in the "narrow house appointed for all living," that the soul might escape into life. A short time before his death, he had removed to Roxbury, Conn., and there his ashes were consigned to the earth, with all the honors of war, in a grave remote from the hills he loved so well, and for whose sake he had yielded up his life in the bloom of manhood. On a white marble memorial-stone in

Roxbury, over which the moss has been suffered to grow, may now be deciphered with much pains-taking, the following inscription:

<blockquote>
In memory of
COL. SETH WARNER, ESQ.,
Who departed this life, December 26, A. D. 1784,
In the 42d year of his age.

Triumphant leader at our armies' head,
Whose martial glory struck a panic dread,
Thy warlike deeds engraven on this stone,
Tell future ages what a hero's done.
Full sixteen battles he did fight,
For to procure his country's right.
Oh! this brave hero, he did fall
By death, who ever conquers all.

When this you see, remember me.
</blockquote>

The proprietors of several townships had given him tracts of land, of considerable value, as a reward for his services in defense of the New-Hampshire Grants; but the greater part, if not all of them, were sold for taxes, and his heirs never received any considerable benefit from them. In 1777, the legislature of Vermont generously granted to his heirs 2,000 acres of land, in the north-west part of the county of Essex. It was then supposed that this land would become valuable by a settlement of that part of the county; but when that section of the state was explored, this tract of land was found to be of little or no value, and it yet remains unsettled.*

* In 1786, Mrs. Warner petitioned congress for remuneration for the services of her husband, but the amount of relief afforded her was small. The following are the closing sentences of her memorial: "The circumstances of your disconsolate petitioner as to her interest and circumstances in life, will appear by certificate of DANIEL SHERMAN, judge of probate, herewith transmitted, by which your honors will see that your unhappy petitioner hath nothing to support herself and three children, only her own industry — having two sons and a daughter, two of which

Although the current of the war swept southward after the capture of Burgoyne, the people of Vermont, while agitated by their political contest with the neighboring states, were frequently harassed by parties of Indians in the interest of the British crown, led on by tories even more fiendish than the Indians themselves. Nevertheless, the greater portion of the inhabitants who had fled from their homes on the approach of Burgoyne, returned again after the storm

are unable to earn anything by their labor. Your petitioner would further represent to your honors, that the colonel was so taken up in the defense of the country in the late war, that he wholly neglected his own interest, by means of which he lost much of his estate, as it lay chiefly in lands of the state of Vermont, for want of taking seasonable care thereof, and although your petitioner had a hard task in looking after the colonel in his last sickness, as the colonel lay long confined, unable to help himself, and your petitioner had the unhappiness to see her dear companion, as it were, die by inches, (as a mortification began in his feet and by a slow progress proceeded up to his body, which continued for months before it put an end to his valuable life.) Notwithstanding your petitioner had the chief care of looking after her dear companion, it yielded her some consolation that she had the opportunity of looking after the colonel in his last sickness. Had it been the colonel's fate to have fallen in battle, as many did that were engaged with him, your petitioner is informed that she should be entitled to receive some gratuity from your honors. Your petitioner, therefore, can but hope inasmuch as the death of her dear husband was in consequence of the wounds and hardship he received in his country's service in the late war, your honors will be graciously pleased to take her distressed circumstances into your wise consideration and grant her such a bounty as that she may be able to support herself and children, and give them such education as that they might not be contemptible among the human race. The which your petitioner is the more embolden to ask your honors, as she hath been informed your honors have, in some instances, been liberal to the posterity of those who have distinguished themselves in their country's service in the late war — for which, as in duty bound, your unhappy petitioner shall ever pray."

had passed. Those on the frontiers were in constant peril, and many were the midnight assaults upon their feeble settlements, and many were the occasions upon which their fortitude and heroism were called into action. The memory of most of these has been lost in the lapse of years. Among the most remarkable of these early settlers, who are yet remembered, was Mrs. Storey, of Salisbury. Her husband had emigrated to the Grants at an early day, but was killed by the fall of a tree, leaving Mrs. Storey with half a score of children. Thus left a widow, she endured almost every hardship, laboring in the field, chopping down timber and clearing and cultivating the soil. She retreated several times to Pittsford during the Revolution, on account of the danger apprehended from the enemy, but at length she and a Mr. Stevens prepared themselves a safe retreat. This was effected by digging a hole horizontally into the bank, just above the water of Otter creek, barely sufficient to admit one person at a time. This passage led to a spacious lodging-room, the bottom of which was covered with straw, and upon this their beds were laid for the accommodation of the families. The entrance was concealed by bushes which hung over it from the bank above. They usually retired to their lodgings in the dusk of evening, and left them before light in the morning, and this was effected by means of a canoe, so that no path or footsteps were to be seen leading to their subterraneous abode.* This afforded her perfect security during the continuance of the war.

*Mrs. Storey and her underground room occupy a prominent place in the thrilling novel of "The Green-Mountain Boys," by D. P. Thompson, Esq

ATTACK ON ROYALTON.

The most disastrous incursion of the Indians against the people of Vermont, resulted in the destruction of the town of Royalton. In the beginning of October, 1780, an expedition was planned against Newbury, on Connecticut river, the principal object of which was to capture a Lieutenant Whitcomb, who, the Canadians asserted, had mortally wounded and robbed a British General Gordon, during Montgomery's disastrous campaign several years before. Against this man the British and Indians had conceived a violent aversion, and planned the present expedition in order to get him in their power. The expedition consisted of two hundred and ten men, nearly all of whom were Indians, under the command of a British officer named Horton. In proceeding up Winooski river, they fell in with two hunters, who informed them that the people of Newbury were expecting an attack, and had prepared themselves for it; and they therefore decided to direct their course toward Royalton. They found the inhabitants wholly unprepared for an attack, and an easy prey to their rapacity. After destroying twenty houses at Royalton and several in the neighboring towns, killing some persons who attempted to escape, and taking many prisoners and much plunder, they commenced a hasty retreat. The news quickly spread, and a party of the resolute inhabitants of neighboring towns soon assembled, chose a leader and commenced pursuit. So great was their dispatch that they soon came up with the trail of the savages, in the night, who, having posted their sentries, and partaking excessively of the intoxicating portion of their spoils, had lain down to rest, not dreaming of an attack.

Great was their consternation on finding that their sentries were fired upon; but with savage cunning they sent word to their pursuers that if attacked, they would put all the prisoners to death; and while the subject matter of this threat was debating among their enemies, they picked up their prisoners and camp-equipage, and made a hasty retreat under the cover of the darkness. In the morning it was thought useless to pursue them, and the party returned. Most of the prisoners eventually returned from captivity.

Several authentic anecdotes are related of this expedition, which go to show the Indian character in a less ferocious light than it has generally been held, under similar circumstances. They did not evince any desire to molest the women or female children. In some of the cases, where the women who had left their burning houses stood motionless and stupefied, not knowing what to do, the Indians brought them their clothes, with the assurance that "Indian would'nt hurt 'em." One woman had firmness enough to reproach them for their conduct in burning down houses, and taunted them for not daring to cross the river and attack the men at the fort. They bore her gibes with the utmost patience, and only replied that "squaw should'nt talk too much." Another woman, named Hannah Handy, whose young son they were carrying off, followed them with another child in her arms, and besought them to return her little boy. They complied; and following up her success, she prevailed upon them to give up ten or fifteen of the children of her neighbors. One of the Indians offered to carry her on his back across the stream; she accepted his politeness, and though the water was up to his waist, he conveyed her over in safety, and she returned with her little band of boys, to the surprise and joy of their parents.

As the Indians usually sought only for plunder, and seldom molested women or children, it was customary for the men, when their settlements were attacked by a superior force, to flee into the woods till the Indians had performed their work of plunder. At one time a party of them entered the house of Mr. Stone, of Bridgeport, giving him but just time to escape, and after stripping it of every thing of value to them, the principal, Sanhoop, put on the finest shirt it afforded, and swaggering away to the hogsty, selected the best hog, and officiated as chief butcher, flourishing his fine bloody sleeves, while his comrades, whooping and dancing, carried it away to their canoes. At another time, a party of Indians, coming up the bank, were discovered by Mrs. Stone in season to throw some things out of a back window into the weeds, put a few in her bosom, and sit down to her carding. The Indians, after taking what they could find elsewhere, came around Mrs. Stone and the children. One of them seeming to suspect that she had some valuable articles concealed about her person, attempted to pull them from her bosom; whereupon she struck him on the face with her card so violently that he withdrew his hand, while a tall young savage was flourishing his tomahawk over her head. Upon this an old Indian cried out, "*Good squaw, good squaw,*" and burst into a laugh of derision at his companions for being beaten. On another occasion, previous to the evacuation of Ticonderoga by the British, a party of Americans plundered the house of a tory, by the name of Prindle, who was a neighbor to Mr. Stone. Prindle, not owning the house, set it on fire, and, retreating on board a British armed vessel on the lake, implicated Mr. Stone in the robbery and burning. He, anticipating mischief, kept in the bushes near the bank to observe their movements, where the British discovered him, and let off a volley of grape-shot, which struck among the trees above him, and also fired upon his house, some of the shot entering the room where the family was. They then sent a boat on shore, took Mr. Stone and carried him a prisoner to Ticonderoga, where he remained three weeks. Mrs. Stone expecting he would be sent to Quebec, went to him in a canoe, a distance of twelve miles, with no other company than her brother, a lad only ten years old, to carry him clothes, leaving her two children, the oldest but four years old, alone at home. She had to tarry all night before she could gain admittance. On her return she found her children safe, the oldest having understood enough of her directions to feed and take care of the younger.*

In 1777, the town of Brandon was visited by a party of Indians, who killed two men, George and Aaron Robins, made prisoners of most of the other inhabitants, and set fire to their dwellings and to a saw-mill which they had erected. Joseph Barker, his wife, and a child eighteen months old, were among the prisoners. Mrs. Barker, not being in a condition to traverse the

---

* See Thompson's Gazetteer of Vermont—one of the most complete and interesting works of the kind, which should be in the hands of every one proud of the name of Vermonter.

wilderness, was set at liberty with her child. The next night, with no other shelter than the trees of the forest and the canopy of heaven, and with no other company than the infant above named, she had another child. She was found the following day and removed with her children to Pittsford. Mr. Barker was carried to Middlebury, where, feigning to be sick, he succeeded in the night in making his escape, and arrived safely at Pittsford.

The rival claims of New York and New Hampshire to the territory of Vermont, came near proving fatal to the separate identity of the infant state. A proposition was made that they should authorize congress to arbitrate between them, in which court the matter would doubtless have been compromised by giving New York the west and New Hampshire the east slope of the Green Mountains. To such a division of Vermont, both states were willing to accede. But in this emergency Massachusetts interfered, and brought forward a third claim to the territory in dispute, founded on the fact that the original grant to Mason, of the colony of New Hampshire, extended only sixty miles from the ocean, and that all west of Mason's line belonged to Massachusetts—that its right had not only been conceded by New Hampshire, but by the crown, because, while the former had distinctly declined to support Fort Dummer on the ground that it was beyond its jurisdiction, the crown had decided that it belonged to Massachusetts to maintain that important frontier post, which was done at a great expense. This claim was certainly more plausible than either of the others, because Massachusetts had been the first actual occupant of the territory, and had defended it against the common enemy. The original charters from the crown were ambiguous and even contradictory, and were quite as favorable to the claims of Massachusetts as to those of either of the other states. That Massachusetts really wished to enforce this claim is not supposed, for the statesmen from that glorious colony were favorable to the independence of Vermont, and their movement had the effect, which was undoubtedly its object, of saving Vermont from dismemberment by congress. Massachusetts declining to submit its claims to the arbitrament of congress, relieved the young state from the impending peril. The question was one of great delicacy for congress. Every exertion was required to defend the country against the British arms, and the imminent danger that would occur from arousing the enmity of either New York or New Hampshire must be its apology for pursuing a vacillating and indecisive course in regard to the difficult question urged upon it by the conflicting parties. Under the pressure of these circumstances, congress, in 1780, passed a resolution declaring the course of Vermont to be "subversive of the peace and welfare of the United States." Although its representatives had been excluded from any participation in the councils of the nation, the fidelity of Vermont to the cause of freedom and the country was unquestioned, for its heroes had given the most signal and important proofs of this. It is not surprising, however, that when the above-named resolution was adopted by congress, Governor Chittenden should have replied, that if Vermont was not included in the United States, it was at liberty to offer or accept terms for the cessation of hostilities with Great Britain. But, he added, the people of Vermont were so strongly attached to liberty that they would again ask to be admitted to the colonial union. Ira Allen and Stephen R. Bradley were deputed as agents to renew this proposition to congress. The consideration of the representations of these agents was indefinitely postponed, and the question was left undetermined.

Vermont was fortunate in having statesmen who possessed the courage and the ability requisite to the defense of its just rights. Despite the arms of New York and New Hampshire, and the frowns of congress, they found the means to successfully maintain the independence of the little community for which they acted. They now resorted to a course of policy which placed them in a more powerful attitude, and determined to enforce a compliance with their demands. The towns in New Hampshire, which had once been accepted as a portion of Vermont and afterward excluded by a resolution of the legislature, again solicited to have its jurisdiction extended over them. This was done. The government of Vermont then turned westward with a view to a further extension of its limits.* After consultation with the people in that portion of New

---

* The following spirited lines, the author of which is unknown, very happily express the sentiments of the Vermonters during that trying period:

   Ho — all to the borders! Vermonters, come down,
   With your breeches of deer skin, and jackets of brown;
   With your red woolen caps, and your moccasins, come
   To the gathering summons of trumpet and drum!

   Come down with your rifles! — let gray wolf and fox
   Howl on in the shade of their primitive rocks;

York, Vermont boldly claimed that its boundary line extended from the point where the Massachusetts line would touch the Hudson, thence up that river to its

> Let the bear feed securely from pig-pen and stall;
> Here's a two-legged game for your powder and ball!
>
> On our south come the Dutchmen, enveloped in grease;
> And, arming for battle, while canting of peace;
> On our east, crafty Meshech has gathered his band,
> To hang up our leaders, and eat out our land.
>
> Ho — all to the rescue! For Satan shall work
> No gain for his legions of Hampshire and York!
> They claim our possessions — the pitiful knaves —
> The tribute *we* pay, shall be prisons and graves!
>
> Let Clinton and Ten Broek, with bribes in their hands,
> Still seek to divide us, and parcel our lands; —
> We've coats for our traitors, whoever they are;
> The warp is of *feathers* — the filling of *tar!*
>
> Does the "Old Bay State" threaten? Does Congress complain?
> Swarms Hampshire in arms on our borders again?
> Bark the war-dogs of Britain aloud on the lake?
> Let 'em come! — what they *can*, they are welcome to take.
>
> What seek they among us? The pride of our wealth
> Is comfort, contentment, and labor and health;
> And lands which, as Freemen, we only have trod,
> Independent of all, save the mercies of God.
>
> Yet we owe no allegiance; we bow to no throne;
> Our ruler is law, and the law is our own;
> Our leaders themselves are our own fellow-men,
> Who can handle the sword, or the sythe, or the pen.
>
> Our wives are all true, and our daughters are fair,
> With their blue eyes of smiles, and their light flowing hair;
> All brisk at their wheels till the dark even-fall,
> Then blithe at the sleigh-ride, the husking, and ball!

source, and from its source due north to the Canada line, comprising all the land east of the Hudson, and for thirty miles west of Lake Champlain, thus doubling

> We've sheep on the hill-sides: we've cows on the plain;
> And gay-tasseled corn-fields, and rank-growing grain;
> There are deer on the mountains; and wood-pigeons fly
> From the crack of our muskets, like clouds in the sky.
>
> And there's fish in our streamlets and rivers, which take
> Their course from the hills to our broad-bosomed lake;
> Through rock-arched Winooski the salmon leaps free,
> And the portly shad follows all fresh from the sea.
>
> Like a sunbeam the pickerel glides through his pool
> And the spotted trout sleeps where the water is cool,
> Or darts from his shelter of rock and of root
> At the beaver's quick plunge, or the angler's pursuit.
>
> And ours are the mountains, which awfully rise
> Till they rest their green heads on the blue of the skies;
> And ours are the forests, unwasted, unshorn,
> Save where the wild path of the tempest is torn.
>
> And though savage and wild be this climate of ours,
> And brief be our season of fruits and of flowers,
> Far dearer the blast round our mountains which raves,
> Than the sweet summer zephyr, which breathes over slaves.
>
> Hurra for VERMONT! for the land which we till
> Must have sons to defend her from valley and hill;
> Leave the harvest to rot on the field where it grows,
> And the reaping of wheat for the reaping of foes.
>
> Far from Michiscoui's valley, to where
> Poosoomsuck steals down from his wood-circled lair,
> From Shocticook river to Lutterlock town,—
> Ho — all to the rescue! Vermonters, come down!
>
> Come York or come Hampshire,— come traitors and knaves;
> If ye rule o'er our *land,* ye shall rule o'er our *graves;*
> Our vow is recorded — our banner unfurled;
> In the name of Vermont we defy *all the world!*

the former limits of the state. Notwithstanding the difficulties which surrounded the people of Vermont, the New-Hampshire towns on its east border, and the New-York towns on its western limits, which were thus summarily annexed, were eager for their union. What arguments could have been urged to induce them to join their fortunes with those of Vermont, it is not easy to imagine. The fact gives, at all events, a striking proof of the skill of the trusted leaders of the Green-Mountain Boys.

The British, ready to avail themselves of every advantage which the Vermont difficulties might yield them, were gradually increasing their force in Canada, and another campaign against the northern frontier was unquestionably determined on. The indications of this were alarming. Knowing the effect that the apprehension of this would have upon the people, the British generals entertained the hope that they might detach Vermont from the United States and make it a British possession. In the expectation of accomplishing this, Colonel Beverly Johnson wrote a letter to Ethan Allen, dated March 30, 1780. He began his letter by expressing a wish that his proposals might be received with the same good intention with which they were made. He then proceeds:—"I have often been informed that you and most of the inhabitants of Vermont, are opposed to the wild and chimerical scheme of the Americans in attempting to separate from Great Britain and establish an independent government of their own; and that you would willingly assist in uniting America to Great Britain, and in restoring that happy constitution so wantonly and unadvisedly destroyed. If I have been rightly informed, and these should be your sentiments and inclination, I beg that you will communicate to me without reserve, whatever proposals you would wish to make to the commander-in-chief; and I hereby promise that I will faithfully lay them before him according to your directions, and flatter myself I can do it with as good effect as any person whatever. I can make no proposals to you until I know your sentiments; but think, upon your taking an active part, and embodying the inhabitants of Vermont under the crown of England, you may obtain a separate government under the king. If you should think proper to send a friend here with proposals to the general, he shall be protected, and allowed to return whenever he pleases."

Allen communicated the contents of this letter to Governor Chittenden, and it was decided that no answer should be returned. In February, 1781, Johnson again wrote to Allen, renewing his former proposal. Allen communicated these letters to congress, with a powerful letter vindicating the policy of Vermont. He closed it with the following striking sentences: "I am confident that congress will not dispute my sincere attachment to the cause of my country, though I do not hesitate to say, I am fully grounded in opinion, that Vermont has an indubitable right to agree on terms of a cessation of hostilities with Great Britain, provided the United States persist in rejecting her application for a union with them. For Vermont would be, of all people, most miserable, were she obliged to defend the independence of the United claiming States, and they be, at the same time, at full liberty to overturn and ruin the independence of Vermont. When congress consider the circumstances of this state, they will, I am persuaded, be more surprised that I have transmitted them the inclosed letters, than that I have kept them in custody so long; for I am as resolutely determined to defend the independence of Vermont, as congress is that of the United States; and rather than fail, I will retire with the hardy Green-Mountain Boys into the desolate caverns of the mountains, and wage war with human nature at large."

Soon after, the British, under the command of General Haldimand, appeared in great force at the north end of Lake Champlain. Governor Chittenden sent a flag of truce, proposing an exchange of prisoners. General Haldimand returned a favorable reply, and Colonel Ira Allen and Major Joseph Fay were appointed commissioners on the part of Vermont, to negotiate the exchange. During the interview with the British agents, the latter renewed the proposal for Vermont to place itself under the royal authority. Allen and Fay, without committing themselves, left the impression upon the minds of the British generals that the proposed arrangement might be perfected. This was done because Vermont had no other way of protecting itself against an army of ten thousand royal troops, which had been poured into Canada. Accordingly, a formal attempt at negotiation was made — Allen and Fay being secretly appointed commissioners by Governor Chittenden, and General Haldimand acting for the British. Their negotiations were continued for a long period, and their existence has been adduced by historians as evidence of a disposition on the part of the Vermont leaders to join the enemy. The full history of these events, when properly written, will show that the odium thus cast upon the names of these men is grossly unjust; that they were not only inspired by the purest devotion to the cause of liberty, but that their policy actually kept at bay a large hostile army, which otherwise would have been able to march through the northern portion of the union, (Washington being employed at the south,) and to crush the hopes of freedom. The following papers, never before published, which have been politely furnished for these pages by the Hon. Henry Stevens, the distinguished and indefatigable Vermont antiquary, from his very large and rich collection of documents in reference to the early history of Vermont, will not only prove this assertion, but serve to show, when the history of Chittenden, the Allens, and other Vermont leaders of that day is properly viewed, that they performed services in behalf of their country, which entitle them to the lasting admiration and gratitude of those who enjoy the blessings of the freedom which their services so greatly aided in establishing. Numbers I. and II. are the commissions furnished to Allen and Fay; number III. is General Haldimand's commission to the British agent; and number IV. is the report of interviews with Allen and Fay, as given to General Haldimand by his agent.

I.

State of Vermont, June, 1781.

Whereas Col. Ira Allen has been with a Flag to the Province of Quebeck for the Purpose of settling a

Cartel or Exchange o Prisoners and has used his best Policy by Feigning or Endeavouring to make them believe that the State of Vermont had a Desire to Negociate a Treaty of Peace with Brittain — thereby to Prevent their Immediate Invasion or Incursion upon the Frontiers of this State as appears by the Letter he sent to General Haldimand Dated May 8th, 1781 Inclosing a copy of Col. Beverly Robinson's Letter to Gen'l Allen and General Allen's Letter to Congress as also a Letter of Col. Allen sent to Congress and the resolutions of the Assembly of Vermont approbating the same, as also the circular Letter to the several States Delivered to Dundas according to his Verbal Report made us this Day — we are of the opinion that the critical circumstances this State is in being out of union with the United States and thereby unable to make that Vigorous Defence we could wish for—think it to be a Necessary Political manœuver to save the Frontiers of this State.

Jonas Fay	Tho's Chittenden
Sam'l Safford	Moses Robinson
Sam'l Robinson	Tim'y Brownson
Joseph Fay	John Fasset.

II.

State of Vermont, 10 *July*, 1781.

Whereas this State is not in union with the United States altho' often Requested &c.

This the British Power are acquainted with and are endeavouring to take the advantage of these disputes Thereby to court a connection with this State on the Principle of Establishing it a British Province — from various accounts we are well assured that the British have a force in Canada larger than this State can at present raise and support in the field and this State having no assurance of any assistance from any or either of the United States however hard the British forces may crowd on this State from the Province of Quebeck by the advantage of the waters of Lake Champlain &c. Altho' several Expresses have been sent by the Gov'r of this State to several of the respective Gov'rs of the United States with the most urgent requests to know whether any assistance would be afforded in such case and no official answer has been made by either of them.

Wherefore we the subscribers do fully approbate Col. Ira Allen sending a Letter dated Sunderland July 10th 1781 and directed to General Haldimand and another Letter to Captain Justice Sherwood, Purporting an Intention of this State's becoming a British Province &c. This we consider as a Political proceedure to prevent the British forces invading this State and being a necessary step to Preserve this State from Ruin when we have too much reason to apprehend that this has been the wishes of some of our assuming neighbours in the mean time to strengthen the State against any Insult until this State receive better treatment from the United States or obtain a seat in Congress.

Tho's Chittenden   J. Fay
John Fasset   Sam'l Robinson
Tim'y Brownson   Joseph Fay.

III.

" Having given you full power in my name to negotiate in conjunction with M—— with the people of Vermont for the exchange of prisoners by my Letter of the 29th October. I now instruct you in what you may assure and promise to them as the means of accommodation, and their return to their allegiance. Sensible of the Injustice which Individuals in the New York Government attempted against them in soliciting and obtaining Grants of Lands which had in consequence of Grants from New Hampshire been cultivated by the labour and industry of the Inhabitants of the Green Mountains, I always regretted the measures which were taken by the Government of New York and felt compassion for the unhappy people who were the objects of them—I have always been of opinion that a people who during the last war were so ready on every occasion to oppose the Enemies of Great Britain and never have been prevailed upon to seperate themselves from a Country with which they were intimately connected by religion laws and language had their properties been secured to them. It is therefore with great cheerfulness that I authorise you to give these people the most positive assurances that their country will be erected into a seperate province, independant and unconnected with every Government in America, and will be entitled to every prerogative and Immunity which is promised to other Provinces in your Proclamation of the King's Commissioners. This I hope will be sufficient to remove every jealousy of Great Britain wishing to deprive them of their Liberties or of my ever becoming an Instrument to oppress them. I sincerely wish to bring back to their allegiance brave and unhappy people, so that they may enjoy the Blessings of peace Liberty and an honest Industry. From the report you made me, I consider these people as sincere and candid in their propositions. I will therefore act towards them with the sincerity of a Soldier unpractised in deceits and chicane, and you may assure them that I would be sorry to engage them in any enterprise which might prove ruinous to them. I am sensible that their situation is delicate that the utmost caution is necessary not only with regard to the powerful Enemies which surround them, but with regard to their own people, whose prejudices are great and many, and who cannot at first view, see the advantages which will accrue to America in general as well as to themselves in particular from a reconciliation with the mother Country. I am so much convinced of the present infatuation of these people, and so far removed from expecting that the people with whom you negotiate will betray any trust reposed in them that I agree that this negotiation should cease and any step that leads to it be forgotten, provided the Congress shall grant the State of Vermont a Seat in their Assembly, and acknowledge its independency. I trust that time, and other methods, will bring about a reconciliation, and a return to their allegiances, and hope, and expect, they will act towards me with the same frankness and sincerity, and apprise me by your means of their intentions, prospects and measures, so that I may be more able to assist them.

"In order to entitle the Inhabitants of the State of Vermont to the provisions of Half Pay which His Majesty has been pleased to make to the officers of Provincial Corps who take arms in support of his Government, I propose to raise two Battallions consisting of Ten Companies each to be commanded by Messrs Allen and Chittenden or any other whom the Governor and Council of Vermont shall appoint with the rank and pay of Lieutenant Colonels Commandants of which I shall myself be Colonel, but to which the Lieutenant Colonels Commandants shall, subject to my approbation, have the Appointment of the Officers and if the defence of the state should require it more will hereafter be raised on the same footing.

"For the further encouragement of the persons who shall exert themselves in promoting the happy re-union I promise besides the above appointments, that they shall have Gratuities suitable to their merits.

F. HALDIMAND.

QUEBEC, 20th December, 1780."

IV.

Substance of what passed in Conference with Col. Ira Allen, between the 8th and 25th of May, 1781.[*]

"8th. Colonel Allen says, he is not authorised to treat of a Union, but is verbally instructed by Governor Chittenden and General Allen to lay their present situation before General Haldimand, and to inform him that matters are not yet ripe for any permanent proposals, that they with some part of the Council, are anxious to bring about a neutrality, being fully convinced that Congress never intended to admit them as a State, but they dare not make any agreement with Britain until the populace are better modelled for the purpose; wish, however, to settle a Cartel for the Exchange of Prisoners, and thereby keep open a door for

---

[*] Want of room compels the omission of a portion of this document; the most important portion, and the spirit of the whole are given.

further negociation. * * 10th. Walked and discoursed fully with Colonel Allen. He is very cautious and intricate. I urged him to make some proposals, telling him it is now in the power of Vermont to become a Glorious Government under Great Britain — to be the Seat of peace and plenty, with every degree of Liberty that a free people can wish to enjoy. That he must see General Haldimand had in his instructions to me, conceded every thing he could in reason ask or expect. He replied General Haldimand did not allow them to choose their own Governor, a privilege they never could relinquish with propriety: that when they were ripe for proposals they could not go farther than Neutrality during the War, at the end of which they must as a seperate Government be subject to the then ruling power if that power would give them a free Charter in every sense of the word; but if not, they would return to the Mountains, turn Savages, and fight the Devil, Hell and Human Nature at large. I told him Vermont could not accomplish those extravagant flights: * * I did not pretend to know how far these Chimeras might intimidate Congress, but I could assure him General Haldimand had too much experience and good sense to take any further notice of them than by that Contempt they meritted. Colonel Allen now began to reason with more coolness, and made up a long chain of arguments advanced by General Allen to me at Castletown. I told him those arguments had already been exhibited to General Haldimand, and were then satisfactory to him, but I was certain the General would now expect some further advances; would therefore advise him, if he could not make any propositions in behalf of Vermont to give his Excellency some reasons why he did not. The conversation again became warm and spirited.

   * * * * * *

"11th. Colonel Allen observed he did not think the parliament had passed any Act in favor of Vermont. I answered I did not think the Parliament of Great Britain has yet considered Vermont of consequence enough to engross the attention of that Assembly. He replied in his opinion Vermont must be considered of consequence enough to engross the attention of Parliament before any permanent Union can take place between Great Britain and that people. 12th. This day had a long and very friendly conference with Colonel Allen. He seems anxious to convince me that a respectable number of the leading-Men of Vermont are endeavouring to bring about a Union by way of Neutrality. He appears less reserved, and again repeated the Arguments advanced by General Allen respecting the impossibility of an Union with Great Britain until Vermont had fortified herself against the neighbouring States by a firm internal Union and observed they must firmly unite the extra Territories lately taken in and form the population into a proper system for such a revolution. * * * Allen thinks when the Western Union is complete they can raise Ten Thousand fighting Men. He says this great and sudden revolution has been brought about upon the principles of an Union with Great Britain, or at least of Vermont being a neutral power during the War. Allen does not aggree with Mr. Johnson that the Majority wish to compromise with Britain, but says their prejudices are yet so great that it would not be safe to propose it but to a few of the population and they have not yet dared to mention it to half of the ruling Men.

13th. Colonel Allen still appears desirous to convince me that the principal Men in Vermont are striving to prepare the people for a change in favour of Government. He wishes me to represent every thing in the most favourable manner to the General and hopes he will not be impatient. He says it is as requisite the people should be prepossessed against the proceedings of Congress before they are invited to a Union with Britain as it is for a Christian New light to be perfectly willing to be ——— before he can become a true Convert. This Evening Mr. Allen observed the ——— bustles among the powers of Europe would, within six Months change the face of American Affairs but did not know nor care, whether for the better or worse. I replied he must have a predominant wish as Neutrality was, in principle, in my opinion inadmissable. He said he should not deny but principle inclined him and Vermont in general for the success of America but interest and self-preservation if Congress continued to oppress them, more strongly inclined them to wish for the success of Great Britain, and fight like Devils against their oppressors, be they who they might.

* * * * * * * *

"15th. Colonel Allen seems exceedingly anxious to return and often says his presence will be very necessary at the next Assembly, as they will not know how to proceed until they hear what he has to report from General Haldimand.

"18th. I endeavoured to persuade Colonel Allen to make some overtures to General Haldimand but he still says he is not authorised and cannot do any thing of the kind. He thinks the General will be convinced by the reason he has given in writing that the leaders in Vermont are doing all that is possible to effect an Union or Neutrality, and that General Allen was obliged for his own safety, to send Colonel Robinson's Letters to Congress, as it was previously known in public that such Letters had been sent to him.* · * *

"23rd. Colonel Allen expatiates on the dangers and difficulties attending the bringing about a Re-union as a number of the Council, and the major part of the Legislature have not as yet the least idea of anything farther than neutrality, and many of them are ignorant of that. He expresses fears that it will not be accomplished though he sincerely wishes it may. He still thinks the principles on which America first took arms were just, but he sees, with regret, that Congress has learned to play the Tyrant, and is convinced that it is for the interest and safety of Vermont to accept of General Haldimand's terms. I told him he talked well, but I wished he had said as much when he first arrived, for however convinced I may be of his candour the change gave some room for suspicion that he now acts from design. He replied that General Haldimand's candour demands the same from him, and that he has not altered his sentiments, but only throws them out more freely than he at first intended till he had farther instructions from his Employers, but the candid open manner in which the General had written forbid his acting with any disguise.

"24th. Colonel Allen much the same in conversation as yesterday, but observes that he knows the General will very soon hear what reports he makes, and how he conducts himself after he gets home, he wishes me clearly to inform the General with the method he must take to comply with his demand of undeceiving the other States respecting the Truce, &c. He says he must, as far as he dares possess the minds of the people with the idea of a re-union. He shall therefore tell their own Officers Commanding at Castletown that he cannot tell what may take place, but they must keep themselves in readiness for all events. But to the other States he shall positively declare that no Truce nor probability of one subsists between General Haldimand and Vermont, and this he should have done for their own safety. But in compliance with the General's desire he shall be very particular in this declaration.

'25th. I communicated C't. Matthews' letter to Colonel Allen respecting News. He says the News gives him no further anxiety than to excite in him a desire to know how this war will terminate for under the present uncertainty of Vermont, he does not know whether this News is favorable or otherwise. But he well knows that he and his Family have large Fortunes which they do not intend to lose, if there is a possibility of saving them. At all risks he is determined that Congress shall not have the parcelling of his Lands to their avaricious Minions. I then shewed him C't. Matthews' Letter of the General's sentiments. He appeared very much pleased with it, and engaged his honor that the General should hear from their Assembly by the 20th of next July and as much sooner as possible, but did not think he should be able to send any certain account of the result until that time, as they are not to assemble till about the middle of June and must sit sometime before the Business could be fairly opened to the whole House, after which it would necessarily occasion long and warm Debates let it turn out as it might in the end. Mr. Allen and myself have agreed on a signal for his Messenger, which we put in writing and both signed. Should General Haldimand find it absolutely necessary to send a private Express to Vermont, Colonel Allen desires it may be by a man of trust who may be directed to make himself known, either to Governor Chittenden Colonel Allen or General Allen or one of the following Gentlemen Colonel Brownson Dr. Fay Judge Faut or C't. Lyon. The Contents of the message should be a secret to the Messenger written on a small piece of paper, which he should be directed to swallow, or otherwise destroy if in danger of being taken by a scout from New York and he should be very careful to shun the Vermont Scouts. On these conditions Col. Allen engaged that the Messenger shall be immediately sent back. Colonel Allen after expressing much satisfaction with the polite treatment he had received embarked about 12 o'clock.

These negotiations were maintained until the close of the war; Ira Allen,* the principal agent in the affair, always finding a plausible reason for postponing final and decisive action. But while he, and a few others, were thus successful in preventing any hostile movement against the northern frontier of the United

---

* Ira Allen was born in 1752. He went to Vermont at a very early age. After the establishment of the government, he was the first secretary of state. Subsequently he was treasurer, member of the council and surveyor-general. He rose to the rank of major-general of militia, and in 1795 went to Europe to purchase arms for the supply of his state. Returning with several thousand muskets, and some cannon, he was captured by an English vessel and carried to England, where he was accused of supplying the Irish, then in open rebellion, with arms. A litigation of eight years, in the court of admiralty, was the consequence; but a final decision was made in his favor. He died at Philadelphia, January 7, 1814, aged 62 years.

States, the people at large were in entire ignorance concerning the negotiations which were carried on, although agents were, during the whole progress of the affair, passing and repassing the borders.

Vermont, after completing its eastern and western armies, sent delegates to congress to again undertake to have the state admitted into the union. In 1781 congress appointed a committee to confer with them, but adopted a resolution, declaring that the negotiation of the independence of Vermont could not take place, unless the state should recede to its former limits, and relinquish its claim to the territory which it had acquired from New Hampshire on the east, and New York on the west. Vermont at first refused to do so, but at this juncture, General Washington opened a correspondence with Governor Chittenden on the subject, and the candor, good sense, and conciliatory style of the Father of his Country, effected what congress could not have done, and Vermont finally consented to comply with the requirement in regard to its boundaries. But after this had been done, congress found occasion to defer its final action in regard to the admission of Vermont into the union.

Notwithstanding the unsettled and embarrassing state of her relations to congress and the neighboring states, the internal tranquillity of Vermont had been, for some time, but little disturbed. Her political institutions had been gradually maturing, and the organization of her government had assumed a regularity and efficiency which commanded the obedience and respect of the great body of the citizens. New York had not relinpuished her claim to jurisdiction over the territory, but she had not, of late, made any serious effort to exercise it; and had contented herself with opposing the admission of Vermont into the union, and by endeavoring, in the manner we have just related, to bring over the people to her own interest. But while a vast majority of the people of Vermont yielded a willing obedience to her authority, and were ready to make almost any sacrifice to sustain her independence and government, there were some among her citizens whose submission was reluctant, and who were ready to embrace any favorable opportunity to renounce their allegiance and support the claims of New York.

This opposition was principally confined to the town of Guilford — at that period the most populous village in the state. The two parties in this town, (the friends of Vermont and those of New York,) had each an organization of their town; and, in some cases, there were two sets of town-officers. Between these, skirmishes often occurred, which not unfrequently ended in bloodshed. The enmity of these parties was carried to an alarming extent during the years 1783 and 1784. Social order was entirely at an end; and even physicians were not allowed to pursue their avocations, without procuring a pass from the several committees. In this unpleasant state of affairs, General Ethan Allen was directed to call out the militia, for the purpose of enforcing the laws, and of suppressing the symptoms of civil war exhibited among the people of Windham county. In accordance with these directions, he marched from Bennington with a force of about one hundred Green-Mountain Boys; and, upon his arrival at Guilford, he issued the following unique proclamation:

"I, Ethan Allen, declare, that unless the people of Guilford peaceably submit to the authority of Vermont, I will make the town as desolate as were the cities of Sodom and Gomorrah!" After some resistance, from the adherents of New York, Allen was enabled to enforce their subjection to the laws of Vermont.

Affairs continued in this condition until 1789, when liberal councils prevailed in New York, and the legislature consented to the independence of Vermont There was no further obstacle to the admission of Vermont into the union, and on the 4th of March, 1791, the auspicious end to all the difficulties which had attended the organization of the new state, was formally announced.

Previous to the admission of Vermont into the union, Ethan Allen was actively engaged in the maintenance of the rights of the people he loved so well, and of the state which his exertions had been so greatly instrumental in founding. After that event, he retired to private life, and in the intervals of relaxation from business, wrote a work entitled, "Reason the only Oracle of Man," the aim of which, we regret to say, was to controvert the truths of revealed religion. He gave great attention to its composition, and was very proud of it. He had been for many years in the habit of making memoranda of his thoughts on the subject, and evidently believed his work would subvert Christianity. Its style was the same which characterized his political pamphlets — bold, artful, egotistical and unpolished, but evincing remarkably strong mental powers. Only one edition was ever published, and the greater portion of that was destroyed by the burning of the office in which it was printed. It is now rarely to be met with, and the existence of the work upon which Ethan Allen confidently relied for enduring fame, is scarcely known to one in a thousand of those who remember with patriotic pride, the sturdy Hero of Ticonderoga.

A very affecting story has long been current in connection with Ethan Allen's peculiar views concerning religion. It is that one of his daughters who had been instructed in the principles of Christianity by a pious mother, when about to die, expressed a desire to see her father. When he appeared at her bedside, she said to him, "I am about to die — shall I go to my grave with the principles you have taught me, or shall I believe what my mother has taught me?" His reply, it is said, was, "Believe what your mother has taught you!" The anecdote, although often quoted, as a striking illustration of the inefficiency of infidelity on the death-bed, and the consolation that is afforded by a strong religious faith at such a time, has not, it is asserted by Allen's family, any foundation in truth.

Notwithstanding his views on religion, Allen was a thoroughly honest man, and detested any thing like falsehood or meanness. On one occasion, an individual to whom he was indebted had commenced a suit against him. Allen being unable to pay the debt, employed a lawyer to have the execution of legal process against him postponed for a short period. As an easy measure to effect this, and throw the case over to the next session of the court, the lawyer denied the genuineness of the signature; Allen, who was present, stepped angrily forward, and exclaimed to his astonished counsel, "Sir, I did not employ you to come here and lie; I wish you to tell the truth. The note is a good one — the signature is mine; all I want is for the court to grant me sufficient time to make the payment!" It is almost needless to add that the plaintiff acceded to his wish.

General Allen, who had at various times resided at Bennington, Arlington and Tinmouth, at last took up his residence on the Winooski. His first wife had never removed from Connecticut, but died there during the war. His courtship of his second wife was characteristic. During a session of the court at Westminster, Allen appeared with a magnificent pair of horses and a black driver. Chief Justice Robinson and Stephen R. Bradley, an eminent lawyer, were there, and as their breakfast was on the table, they asked Allen to join them. He replied that he had breakfasted, and while they were at the table, he would go in and see Mrs. Buchanan, a handsome widow who was at the house. He entered the sitting-room, and at once said to Mrs. Buchanan, "Well, Fanny, if we are to be married, let us be about it." "Very well," she promptly replied, "give me time to fix up." In a few minutes she was ready, and Judge Robinson was at once called upon by them to perform the customary ceremony. Said Allen, "Judge, Mrs. Buchanan and I have concluded to be married; I don't care much about the ceremony, and as near as I can find out, Fanny cares as little for it as I do; but as a decent respect for the customs of society require it of us, we are willing to have the ceremony performed." The gentlemen present were much surprised, and Judge Robinson replied, "General Allen, this is an important matter; have you thought seriously of it?" "Yes, yes," exclaimed Allen, looking at Mrs. Buchanan, "but it don't require much thought." Judge Robinson then rose from his seat and said, "Join your hands together. Ethan Allen, you take this woman to be your lawful and wedded wife : you promise to love and protect her according to the law of God and ———" "Stop, stop, Judge. The law of God," said Allen, looking forth upon the fields, "all nature is full of it. Yes, go on. My team is at the door." As soon as the ceremony was ended, General Allen and his bride entered his carriage and drove off.*

Allen conversed much on the subject of religion, and expressed his skeptical views on all convenient occasions. At one time, while he was in Westminster, Judge Sessions and Stephen R. Bradley, who were zealous Christians, were discussing the affairs of the church. Allen, who entered the room at the time, interrupted them by an argument against the divine origin of the Bible. Judge Sessions, not liking to hear his reasons, said, "Mr. Bradley, I think we had better retire, and not hear this man talk." Allen exclaimed, "Deacon Sessions, you belong to the church militant— I belong to the church military; and without that," he continued with an oath, "you can never belong to the church triumphant!"

General Allen's kindness of heart was proverbial,

---

* This anecdote is given on the authority of Hon. William C. Bradley, (son of Stephen R. Bradley,) formerly a member of congress from Vermont, who was present with his father on the occasion.

and he was always ready to afford relief to the suffering. At one time, two little girls, daughters of one of the pioneers of Vermont, wandered into the woods The distressed parents, with a few neighbors, commenced a search, which was continued through the night without success. The next day a large number of persons from the neighboring towns joined them, and the search was continued till the afternoon of the third day, when it was relinquished, and the people who had been out were about to return to their homes Among them, however, was *one* who thought the search should not be abandoned; and this was Ethan Allen. He mounted a stump, and soon all eyes were fixed upon him. In his laconic manner, he pointed to the father and mother of the lost children — now petrified with grief and despair — bade each individual present, and especially those who were parents, make the case of these parents his own, and then say whether they could go contentedly to their homes without one further effort to save those dear little ones, who were, probably, now alive, but perishing with hunger, and spending their last strength in crying to father and mother to give them something to eat. As he spoke, his giant frame was agitated — the tears rolled down his cheeks, and in the assembly of several hundred men, but few eyes were dry. "I'll go! I'll go!" — was at length heard from every part of the crowd. They betook themselves to the woods, and before night the lost children were restored in safety to the arms of the distracted parents.

In all the trying scenes of Allen's life — in all the vicissitudes of a protracted and cruel captivity — he was never forgetful of the rights of his fellow-men, or of the cause of his country's liberty. He nobly spurned, as unworthy of the principles which governed him, the honors which were offered him to join the royal standard. He stood firmly by his country, even while it frowned upon the course of his adopted state — and his memory will ever be cherished by a free and grateful people. He died at Burlington, Vt., Feb. 12th, 1789, of apoplexy, while yet in the full vigor and maturity of manhood, and his remains rest in a beautiful valley near the Winooskie, where his grave is surrounded by those of many of his kindred. A plain marble tablet marks the spot, upon which is the following inscription:

> The
> Corporeal Part
> of
> Gen. Ethan Allen,
> rests beneath this stone.
> he died
> the 12th day of February, 1789,
> aged 50 years.
> His spirit tried the mercies of his God,
> In whom he believed and strongly trusted.

FINIS.